Love Doesn't Have to Hurt

Nastassia Johnson

Printed in the United States of America

Published: by Legacy Voice Productions

Copyright © 2022 by Nastassia Johnson

All rights reserved. This book or parts thereof may not be reproduced in any form, stored in a retrieval system, or transmitted in any form by anymeans- electronic, mechanical, photocopy, recording, or otherwise-without prior written permission of the author, except as provided by United States of America copyright law.

Cover Design by: Chris Kitt Jr.

ISBN: 978-1-7351253-9-8

To contact author for ordering additional copies,go to: nastassiaj26@gmail.com

Special Dedications

First and foremost, I would like to thank God.

For never giving up on me, even when I tried to give up on myself.

For blessing me with this gift and showing me how to fulfill the purpose He has placed on my life.

Secondly, I would like to thank my mother for always praying for me when I couldn't pray for myself. For always lifting me up and never tearingme down. I will always love her for that.

Special Thanks to:

My dad, for showing me that hard work pays off.

My little sister, Krista for being the one who readsmy works and letting me know if she liked them ornot.

My cousin Tamiko, who always let me know howmuch she believes in me.

My cousin Malik, who helped me come up with titles over and over again.

My pastor/aunt who always shows me her love and guidance. And for showing me that it's okayto believe in myself.

There are so many others, but I will leave those for future books.

Thank you all for your never-ending support.

I Love You All! This is the first of many!

Chapter 1:

Trina

I carried my tray around the club, stopping to get drink orders in the process. The loud music paired with the bass had the entire club vibrating. The ache in my side was getting harder to ignore, but I knew I still had four hours left on my shift, so I was going to have to tough it out. I stopped at the bar and gave my order to the bartender P.J. "P.J., I need a Bob Marley, 2 shots of Patron, 2 amaretto sours, and 2 Fuzzy Navels." P.J. grabbed cups and immediately started making the drinks. I rested my hand on my side, trying to ease the discomfort that was settled there. I felt someone touch me, and I nearly jumped out of my clothes. I turned to see who it was, my eyes landing on a gorgeous chocolate colored man staring at me with nervousness in his eyes.

"I'm sorry, I didn't mean to scare you. I stumbled when someone bumped me, and I didn't want to knock you over." I calmed my breathing down, smiling at him as I looked at P.J. "Thanks P.J." I looked back at the guy in front of me and balanced the tray on my hand. "It's okay. You just stunned me. Have a nice night." I walked away from him with my drink orders and carried them to the patrons.

At the end of my shift, I helped with clean up and left the club. I hoped and prayed that I could get right in the bed and go to sleep. With class until noon, my day job starting at one and ending at seven. Followed by being back at the club from nine until four. I was determined to get through college. My scholarship paid for my books and tuition, but I still had rent to pay, groceries to buy, as well as utility bills. My three older brothers would help, but none of them knew I was doing it all alone. I would do everything in my power to make something of myself, even if I got very little sleep.

I started the short walk to my apartment, my side and back throbbing in pain. A pain that I had gotten used to a long time ago. My music blasted in my ears as I walked down the sidewalk, the dark sky soothing me, keeping me focused until I reached my destination.

I walked quietly into my dark apartment, my heart in my throat as I made my way to my bedroom. When I walked inside, it was empty. There was no sign of the person I prayed wouldn't be there. I turned on the light and pulled out my iPhone, the only thing my boyfriend of three years had ever bought me. I pressed the buttons needed to dial my best friends' number and waited for her to pick up.

"What's up Trina? You ready for me to come get you?" I stepped out of my black combat boots and placed them in the closet. "No. I'm already home. I just wanted to let you know." I braced myself for the anger. The fussing that was sure to come, but I would just have to deal with it. The last thing I needed was Cheyenne noticing my pained expressions. So, until the pain was gone, I would find my own way home in the evenings while my car was in the shop.

"Trina, how did you get home? I hope you didn't walk." I rolled my eyes and sat on the edge of my bed with my fingers on the bridge of my nose. "I did. It was late and I was too tired to wait for you, so I put one foot in front of the other. I'm fine. I'm safe. I'm about to take a shower and go to bed. I have an 8 a.m. class that I need to sleep for." I could hear Cheyenne sigh, but she didn't comment on it any further. "Okay Lil Bit. I love you girl. Sleep well." I stood once again and walked to my dresser to pull out some pajamas. "Love you too Chey. I will. You do the same." My body froze when I heard the door open as I ended the call. I continued digging through the drawers, hoping that he was in a good mood.

"Hey baby. How was your day?" He smiled at me, something I rarely saw anymore. "It was good. I went out to party with the boys after work. I'm going to regret it in the morning." "That's good. Stephan, let me know what you want for dinner, and I'll make it before work so it will be ready when you get home." Stephan nodded so I grabbed my things, walked in the bathroom, and locked the door behind me.

My pounding heart slammed against my chest, the fear I was faced with whenever he was around causing my body to shake uncontrollably. I walked to the sink slowly, turning the water on so I could brush my teeth. I took my time, trying to delay whatever would be waiting for me when I got finished with my shower.

I looked at the fresh bruises on my back and side, trying to determine whether or not I should go to the doctor. I'd had worse so I decided against it. Doctor's asked questions got the police involved. And after what happened the last time, I would avoid that all costs.

I exited the bathroom, waiting for him to step into my line of sight. I scanned the room and thanked God when I saw him under the covers sleeping. I knew he was a light sleeper and the last thing I wanted to do was wake him. So, I grabbed my pillow and walked into the living room. I plugged my phone up and laid on the sofa, pulling the throw that hung on the back of it down over my body. I closed my eyes and within minutes, sleep had encompassed me.

A sharp pain sliced into my once uninjured side. My eyes flew open, and I saw Stephan's angry face staring down at me. "I thought I told you not to sleep on the sofa!" Another blow from his balled-up fist hit my side again. How I was going to walk normally with both sides in pain, I had no idea. "You were sleeping. You told me not to wake you when you were sleeping, so I came out here so I wouldn't wake you getting in the bed." Dark eyes stared at me, tight fists at his sides. "Next time just sleep on the floor. I better not catch you asleep on this sofa again. I don't want to have to hurt you next time. Understood?" I suppressed the urge to roll my eyes, knowing that would only make matters worse. "Understood. Can I ask you a question?" Stephan nodded, so I got off the sofa and folded the cover. "Did you decide what you wanted for dinner? I'll drop it off at your place before work." Stephan shook his head and then answered my question. "Don't worry about it. I'm going to pick up my brother tomorrow so I'm leaving after work. I won't be back in Seattle until sometime Sunday. Q will officially be out of prison." That was the best thing he could have told me right then. Him being gone for two days, maybe I could finally sleep without being beaten up out of it. "Okay. Well, be safe. Let me know if you change your mind." Stephan nodded and leaned forward to kiss my cheek. "Love you Trina. I'm going to work." I forced a smile onto my face and answered automatically. "I love you too. Have a good day." Stephan walked away from me and once he had exited the apartment, I rushed to get ready for school. The school he told me to drop out of two years prior.

    I couldn't wait until my car was fixed. Walking to school in the rain was definitely something I could do without. I looked down at my jeans, the bottom of them covered in water. With a shake of my head, I continued my trek to school.

    I walked into class and found a seat in the back. I took off my jacket that was damp with water. The only thing my umbrella seemed to protect was my hair. "Hey. Is anyone sitting here?" I saw a hand coming toward my arm and slid back in my chair. Fear consumed me and I looked up at the person standing in front of me. When I saw the guy, I shook my head at him. "No." He stared at me, but I looked down at my desk. "I don't want to be in your business but are you okay? I'm Jamere by the way." I kept my head down, not wanting him to see the fear, that for some reason I couldn't hide from him. "Trina. I'm fine." The professor walked in, so Jamere sat in the seat beside mine and said nothing else.

    I walked back towards home to change into my work clothes. The rain wasn't coming down as hard as it had been earlier that morning, but it was still raining steadily. I decided I was going to have to ignore the pain and run the rest of the way home. It was just after noon, and I wanted to take a shower before work. The last thing I needed was my boss complaining about my appearance. So, I started to run, my sides aching, but I managed to push past the pain. I thought I would never see my apartment, but when it came into view, I slowed to a jog.

    I walked into my apartment and rushed into my room. I pulled out my work clothes and went to the bathroom to take a quick shower. When I came out, I fixed my hair, put on lotion, and then went to get dressed.

    I rushed out of the apartment in black slacks, gray button down, and black flats. Walking in heels in this rain was out of the question, so I abandoned the thought of that. I walked as fast as I could, thanking God when I walked into the hotel with ten minutes to spare. I clocked in and went to my seat behind the front desk, relieving the person who was on the shift before mine. I greeted the guests with bright smiles, helping them all in whatever way I could until my lunch break.

"Hey Trina." I tried not to jump as I searched for the person the voice had come from. I put a smile on my face and watched Cheyenne walk toward me. "Hey Chey. What time do you get off again?" Chey stopped in front of me, her eyes scanning my face. "7. Same as you." I turned away from her gaze and picked up my phone. "Ready for lunch?" She nodded and the two of us walked toward the door to go get something to eat.

I eased into the passenger's seat, the pain that covered my entire torso throbbing with each movement. I exhaled slowly, trying not to let the pain I felt show. I pulled my door closed and slowly pulled the seatbelt across my body. "When will your car be fixed?" I kept my attention straight ahead and answered Cheyenne's question. "Monday. I have to pick it up after school and before my shift at the hotel." Cheyenne reached for the radio controls, and I had to stop myself from flinching. "Do you ever sleep? It seems like you're always on the move." I turned my head to look at her and adjusted myself in my seat. "I'll sleep when I'm dead." I turned my head away from her, and we went through the rest of the drive listening to music.

I changed into some black jeans and a black baby tee. The bruises on my arms from one of Stephan's bad days had disappeared days before and I was thankful to be able to show my arms again. But with his recent mood, it would be at least a month before I could expose my stomach. I pulled my hair up into a ponytail and curled the part that hung loose. My phone rang on my dresser, so I picked it up to answer.

"Hello?" I stepped into a pair of black combat boots, leaving the laces untied. "Hey Lil Bit. I'm outside. Are you ready?" I slid my jacket on my arms, grabbed my license, phone, and some loose cash from my purse, and turned the light off in my bedroom. "I'm heading out now." After Chey replied, I hung up and stuffed my phone into my back right pocket. I locked up my apartment, walking slowly to where Chey was parked.

"Call me when you get off. I don't want you walking home again, especially in this rain." I rolled my eyes but didn't say anything to her. "Lil Bit. I'm not joking." She maneuvered her car to a stop, and I opened my door. "Thanks, Chey. I'll see you later." I pushed the door closed and rushed into the building to start my night.

The bass thumped and drunken adults stumbled all around the packed club. I kept myself busy, not allowing any of my physical problems to keep me from doing my job. I leaned against the bar, waiting for the new bartender to give me my drink orders. "Hey. I didn't know you worked here. Well how would I? I didn't know you before today." I turned my head slowly, locking eyes with the guy from my morning class. "Hey." My heart thudded in my chest, something it did whenever I was around men. "Trina. Here you go." I jumped when I heard my name and picked up the tray with shaky hands. "Thank you." I nodded at the guy from class and walked away from him as quickly as I could.

When we closed at four, my manager made me clock out and leave. Usually, I would stay behind and help clean, but he told me not to. So, I did as he told me to and headed home for the night.

A car pulled up beside me sending a rush of fear through my body. I continued to walk, glancing in the direction of the car. "Trina, it's me Jamere." I stopped hesitantly and turned to look at him through the open window. "D-Do you need something?" Jamere put his car in park and walked around to where I stood. I backed away from him slowly, trying to keep a safe distance between the two of us. "Do you need a ride? If I had known you didn't have a car, I would have asked before I left the club." I looked at the ground and stuffed my hands in my pockets nervously. "I have a car, it's just in the shop. No thanks on the ride though. I don't live too far away. I'll be alright." I could feel my phone vibrating in my back pocket, but I chose to ignore it. "Let me give you a ride. I'd feel more comfortable. It's not safe for you walking this late by yourself." I looked at him again and let a sigh escape my mouth.

"Okay." Jamere smiled in victory and pulled open the passenger side door. I slipped into the seat, and he pushed the door closed. I watched as he walked around the car, pulling his door open and then sliding into his seat. "Thank you. You sound like my best friend fussing at me. She tells me to call when I get off, but I don't." Jamere started the car and looked at me. "Straight?" I nodded and he pulled away from the curb. "Why don't you listen to her?" I shrugged my shoulders, shaking my legs nervously. "Don't you have a boyfriend or someone else who could pick you up?" My heart pounded against my chest, but it wasn't surprising. Most times it was doing it anyway.

"My boyfriend is out of town until Sunday. Make a left here." Jamere did as I told him to and thankfully didn't ask anything else about rides home. It was quiet for a minute or two before Jamere spoke again. "So, what's your major?" I rubbed my hands on my jeans, thankful that my heart was no longer pounding in my chest. "Linguistics. You?" Jamere stopped at a light and looked at me. "Journalism. I want to work in publications. What about you? What do you want to do?" I didn't turn to face him; I just answered his question as he drove under the now green light. "I want to be a speech pathologist." I directed him into my complex and told him how to get to my building.

"Thanks for the ride. I'll see you in class." Jamere looked at me and opened his door. "Let me walk you up." Without thinking I grabbed his arm, fear overtaking my senses. "No! I'm good. I'll wave from the window. I'm on the ground level and my apartment is right there." I pointed to my window and let go of his arm. "Are you sure? I don't mind walking you." I opened my door and shook my head. "I'm sure, but thanks anyway. Be careful going home." I waved, pulling my ringing phone from my pocket as I closed the door.

"Hello?" I walked through the parking lot, hoping the pain shooting through my torso wasn't showing in my walk. "Are you off work?" I stopped at my door and stuck the key in to unlock it. "Yes." I walked into my dark apartment, and let my legs carry me to the window. I waved and Jamere flashed his lights before pulling away. "Why didn't you call me? I'm on the way." I stopped Cheyenne, letting her know that I had just walked in the apartment. "I know you didn't walk again! Damn it Trina! I told you not to walk home again." I cut her off, trying to get a word in. "I didn't walk. A classmate gave me a ride." I stood in front of my mirror and lifted my shirt, the bruises a deep purple. I let my fingers trail over them gently, trying to figure out what I had done to let myself get abused for two and a half years. "Oh okay. Well, I'm going to call it a night. Sleep well. See you at work." My fingers left my stomach and I spoke into the phone. "Okay Chey. Good night. You do the same." I ended the call and started pulling out the things I would need for my shower.

I opened my eyes and stared at the ceiling, the first time in weeks I had been able to wake up without being hit. I attempted to stretch, but the pain in my sides let me know that it wasn't a good idea. I slid from under the covers and onto the floor carefully. I made up my bed neatly, making sure there were no wrinkles on the covers. Once it was perfect, I proceeded to get ready for my day.

I put one foot in front of the other, thankful that it wasn't raining as it had been the day before. I was able to make it to class in less time, so I was the first one there. I walked to the back of the class and sat down. I put my earphones in my ears and let the music blast.

Students started to file in, sitting in seats and talking amongst themselves while waiting for our professor. I kept to myself as always, listening to song after song play while reading over my notes. No one bothered me, and in a way I liked that. With no one close, no one would know the abuse I had to deal with. But loneliness made me wish I had someone other than Chey and my brothers. Brothers I rarely saw so they wouldn't see the bruises. So, they couldn't see the pain. I lifted my head and pulled my earphones out when my professor entered the classroom.

"Good morning. Sorry I'm late but let's try to get through this lecture. It's been a trying day already." I took out my tape recorder and started it. I opened my notebook and started writing notes as she lectured on the scientific study of language.

I answered my ringing phone as I walked to my next class. I watched my feet, avoiding eye contact with anyone who was walking near me. "Hello?" The walk to my next class was short, and in about two minutes I was walking into the building. "Hey Lil Bit. What are you doing?" I walked into the classroom and went to a seat in the back. "Hey Ryan. Just got to class. What about you?" I rested my hand on my side, thankful that the pain was diminishing little by little. "Going to work early. Class got cancelled so I figured I'd get some extra hours in." I tapped my desk absently, the soft sound calming me. "Cool. What are your plans for the weekend?" RJ was quiet for a few seconds, but he responded using the same tone he had been using. "Working some overtime. You?" "Same." "Hey Lil Bit, DJ, Tay, and I wanted to get together with you next week. Go to lunch or something. Are you up for that?" My heart stopped in my chest, and I tried to come up with a believable lie. I only had to work at the hotel Monday, Thursday, Friday, and Saturday. So, I had plenty of time to have lunch, even with school. But I couldn't let them see me in the state that I was in. Their disappointment would have been evident and that I just couldn't live with. "Next week is swamped for me. I have school and work at both jobs every day." I could hear Ryan sigh and I knew he was more than a little hurt. "What's your schedule? Maybe we can work around it." It hurt to lie to my big brother, but it had to be done. He would forgive me, even if I couldn't forgive myself. "I have school from 8 a.m. until noon. My shift at the hotel is from 1 p.m. until 7 p.m. And I have to be at the club from 9 p.m. until 4 a.m. I do homework in the little time I have between school and both jobs." That was my schedule, just not my schedule for Wednesday, Thursday, or Sunday. The less he knew though, the better. "What about Sunday?" After church?" I sat on my bed and looked up at the ceiling. "Study group at noon. Hotel from 3 until 10." The study group didn't exist yet, but I'm sure I could ask Jamere if he wanted to get one together. He was the only one I had ever talked to in that class, so hopefully he could get a few other people into it.

"Lil Bit, you are overworking yourself. We never get to see you anymore. You are our baby sister, the only one we have, and we're worried about you." Guilt crept in and I felt like the worst person on the planet for lying to my brother. But I knew it was for the best. I loved Stephan and although he did things I didn't like, I knew no one else would have my back like he did. "I'm alright RJ. I know yall are worried but, I have it all under control. If I didn't, I'd readjust my work schedule." The sigh that exited his mouth was meant to make me feel bad, but I chose to ignore it. I didn't need anything to make me feel worse, so I acted as if I didn't hear it. "RJ, my class is about to start so I have to go. I'll talk to you later. Tell DJ and Tay I said hey." Ryan responded quickly in an effort to let me listen to my professor. "Okay. Have a good class. I'll tell them. I love you." That warmed my heart, and I knew he would get over our conversation. "Love you too. Bye." I ended the call and started my tape recorder. I wrote notes as my professor spoke and did the assignment we were given for homework before class was over.

After my last class, I started my walk home to get ready for my shift at the hotel. I jumped when I heard a horn honk and turned quickly to see where it had come from. "Need a ride?" I looked around and figured it was better than walking. "Sure. Thanks." I opened the door and slid into the passenger's seat of Jamere's car. Once the door was closed, he eased back into the correct lane and headed to my apartment.

"What do you have planned for the rest of your afternoon?" I sat my books on the floor and focused my attention on anything other than Jamere. "I'm about to go to work." I could hear the confusion that hung in the air, so I waited for him to ask. "You have to be at the club this early?" A smile graced my lips, but it was gone in less than a second. "No, I have two jobs. I work at a hotel not too far from my apartment." I saw his head move up and down from the corner of my eye. "What time? I can drop you off before I go to work." I turned to look at him for the first time since I had gotten in the car. "No Jamere. I can't ask you to do that. You've already used too much of your time to help me." "It's no problem. I insist. What time?" I shook my head, picking up my books as he stopped in a parking spot. "1. Just let me change and I'll be right back." Jamere nodded so I got out of the car and rushed to my apartment.

    I got back in the car wearing a gray skirt and a white button-down long-sleeved shirt. I told Jamere what hotel I worked at as I pinned my nametag to my shirt. "You look nice." I slowly turned my head to look at him, astonished that he even spared me a glance long enough to determine how I looked. No male had ever told me I looked nice, other than my brothers anyway. "Thank you." Jamere looked at me briefly, a smile lighting up his face. "You're welcome. How long have you worked for the hotel?" Jamere drove at a steady speed, making casual conversation the entire time. "3 years." I played with my phone, not sure how to continue the conversation. I was never one for small talk, even before Stephan, so I just waited for him to continue.

"Nice. Look, I was thinking about getting a study group together on Sunday's. I would love to have you be a part of it." Jamere pulled into a parking spot, and I smiled internally. "That would be good. I was thinking about doing the same, but as you probably noticed I don't really interact with people." Jamere nodded at me but didn't go into it. "Cool. Well let me get your number and I'll let you know the times. I'll adjust it in whatever way I need to for your schedule." I hesitantly called out my number and opened my door. "Hey Lil Bit. Who is this?" I looked at Chey as she looked into the car I was preparing to get out of. "Chey, this is my classmate Jamere. Jamere, this is my best friend Cheyenne." I flinched when Jamere stretched his arm out in front of me to shake Cheyenne's hand. "Nice to meet you. Yall have a good day. Trina, I'll see you in class on Monday." He smiled at me again, and I watched the way it lit up his eyes. It almost made me smile, but I pushed it back. "Okay. Thanks again for the ride." "Anytime. I'll see you later. I have to get to work." I nodded and eased myself out of the car. Once the door was closed, Chey and I waved and started to walk away. "He's cute." I glanced at her and shrugged my shoulders. "Is he?" Chey raised her eyebrows but didn't comment on my statement. For once in her life, she kept her thoughts to herself.

Chapter 2:

Jamere

I sat in class, waiting for Trina to arrive so that we could discuss hours for the study group. She usually came in before me, so maybe she wasn't feeling well and wasn't going to make it. Just as the thought left my mind, she walked into class. She was limping and holding her side, so I stood up and walked to her. I reached for her arm to help her, but she jumped as much as she could, cringing in pain as she did.

"Please don't touch me. I'm okay." I stepped away from her and let her walk past me. "What happened?" She didn't hesitate before she replied. She answered too quickly which made me think she wasn't telling me the entire truth. "I was running late so I was running here. A rock caught under my shoe, and I fell and rolled down a small hill. I'm alright. Just twisted my ankle and when I fell, I landed on my side." She eased slowly into her chair, and I sat in the one next to hers. Her story didn't add up. Her clothes were neat, no dirt or ripped areas anywhere. I had only known her for a week, and I was beyond worried about her. I didn't know what was going on, but I was determined to figure it out.

At the end of class, we stood, and I turned to face Trina. "I think you need to go to the E.R. Do you want me to take you?" Trina looked at me, squinting as she picked up her bookbag. "I was trying to avoid it, but I think I should. I have to go pick up my car though. I'll go after." We started to walk out of the classroom side by side. "I'll take you to the E.R. and then to go get your car. I'm on the night shift so I have until seven." I heard her sigh, but she finally gave in and agreed to let me take her to the Emergency Room. I took her bag from her and the two of us exited the building.

I sat in the waiting room, waiting for Trina to emerge. It had been nearly two hours but as soon as I knew that she was okay, I would breathe easier. She was being hurt. I could see the signs of it all over her. Why anyone thought it was okay to hurt her, I had no idea. But I wanted to be her help in whatever why I could. Even if it was by just being a friend.

"Mr. Hayes?" I stood up when I heard my name and watched a doctor walk toward me. "Hi Mr. Hayes. I'm Dr. Fuller. I'm the one that is examining your friend Trina Hart." I nodded and shook his hand firmly. "How is she?" The doctor looked at me suspiciously which put me in defense mode. "I shouldn't be saying this to you, but I'm concerned. Her story doesn't coincide with her injuries. I'm only going to say this once. Watch her. Something isn't right. She assured me that no one hurt her and begged me not to get the police involved so I'm going to respect her wishes. Just watch for any changes in her behavior. She won't talk to me so maybe she'll talk to you." I shrugged and looked the doctor in his eyes. "Maybe. I've only known her for a week so I'm not sure. She's really quiet and keeps to herself. I only see her in the one class we have together." The doctor watched me, a sigh escaping his mouth as he reached for my hand again. "I understand. Just try is all I can suggest. She seems lonely and needs a friend." I nodded and put my hand in his. He moved his hand up and down, so I mimicked the action. "I should get back. She should be out in the next thirty minutes or so." We let each other's hands go and I nodded once again. "Thank you, Dr. Fuller. I appreciate you talking to me." Dr. Fuller tipped his head at me and checked his buzzing pager. "You're welcome." I plopped back in my chair as Dr. Fuller turned and walked away from me.

    I tried to figure out what could have possibly been happening with Trina. I knew what it most likely was, but I just didn't, couldn't fathom anyone hurting Trina. But I was going to watch her. I refused to sit by and do nothing. I could be a friend to her and make sure she knew she could depend on me.

Trina emerged; a set of metal crutches tucked securely under her arms. She stopped at the nurse's station and dug through her purse that rested on her hip. I made my way to her and stopped as she handed her insurance card to the nurse. I didn't say anything to her, just let her handle the business at hand. When she finished, the two of us walked away from the nurse's station.

"So, what's the damage?" I drove the streets, listening to Trina as she gave directions ever so often. "Sprained ankle. A few bruised ribs. Nothing major." I didn't agree with that logic, but I kept that thought to myself. "Oh okay. Do you think you'll be able to drive?" Trina didn't look at me, but she muttered a few words. "I've done it before, so yeah." I studied her face briefly, noticing the loneliness that encompassed her. She said she had a boyfriend, and if she had a boyfriend and still looked that lonely, he obviously wasn't the one for her.

"Excuse me." Trina put her phone to her ear and seconds later spoke into it. "Mr. Jefferies, this is Trina Hart. I had to go to the emergency room and my doctor told me I couldn't return to work until Wednesday. So, can I switch my off days to today and tomorrow and come in Wednesday and Thursday instead?" I stared straight ahead, turning as Trina pointed with her finger in the direction I needed to go. "Okay. Thank you sir. I'll be there Thursday at one. Bye." Trina hung up her phone and slid it into her purse. I pulled into the parking lot of her mechanic's shop and turned the car off.

    I got out of my seat and grabbed Trina's crutches and bag before making my way to the passenger's side of my car. I opened the door and gave her crutches to her, looking at her with a small smile as she put her feet outside of the car. She pulled herself up and moved away from the car carefully. "Thank you Jamere. I really appreciate your help, but I think I'm good now. You can leave." I smiled at her again as she reached for her bag that I was still holding. "I will once I know you're all set." I put the bag on one shoulder and let her lead the way.

    While the two of us waited for her car to be brought around, I stole a few quick glances at her, admiring the strength that she exuded. "Thank you again Jamere, for all your help. I really appreciate it." Her eyes never met mine. She didn't even look up from the ground she was staring at. But I could hear the sincerity in every word she spoke. "You're welcome. I'm here whenever you need me. You have a friend in me, and friends look out for each other." Her gaze stayed focused on the ground, but a small smile graced her lips. But just as quickly as it had appeared, it was gone.

Trina stepped closer to me when her car was stopped in front of us. The guy driving got out and walked to Trina with her key in hand. She held her hand out and I noticed the slight shaking of her hand. "Thank you." She told him in a nervous tone. "No problem. Have a nice day." Trina went to the driver's side, her brief change in behavior gone. I opened the passenger's side door and put her bag on the seat. "Be careful going home. I'll see you in class Thursday." She looked at me for a second or two and then looked straight ahead. "I will and you do the same. See you then. Thanks again." I nodded and closed the door before making my way to my blue 2012 Chevy Impala.

I waited for Trina to pull off and I pulled off behind her. I still had a few hours before I had to be at work, so I decided to go to the gym. Maybe an hour or so worth of working out would take my mind off of the words Dr. Fuller had said to me. Something was going on in Trina's home life. Something that I had been aware of since the day I met her. I knew it wasn't my business, but I was concerned. More than concerned, I was worried. Afraid that she was being hurt, but for whatever reason, she refused to tell anyone. I had a feeling Cheyenne didn't even know and Cheyenne was her best friend. I exhaled soundlessly and drove to my destination with my thoughts running rampant in my mind.

 I walked into my apartment after spending two hours in the gym. I had to be at work in a little more than an hour, so I headed to the bathroom to shower. Working in a warehouse was not the best place for me, but it paid well so I learned to deal with it. When I had to work the evening shift, it threw my schedule off and I was always tired in class. But that was the cost of being an adult. So, I stepped under the steady stream of water and washed away the dirt of the day.

 I got dressed and sprayed my body with some cologne. Dark jeans, black t-shirt, and a black hoodie was enough to wear. I was going to have to change when I got to work anyway. I put my feet into some black Timberland boots and checked my phone for the time. I still had an hour, but I hadn't eaten so I picked up my keys and headed for the door.

I walked through the door of Jimmy John's and walked to the counter to order. By the time I was finished, my sandwich was waiting for me. I paid the cashier and grabbed my sandwich, letting my legs carry me to a nearby table. I sat down and prayed over my food and took bite after bite until it was gone.

I got rid of my trash and exited the restaurant. Once in my car, I started the engine and drove to work. My thoughts strayed to Trina once again. How she managed to stay in my mind, I didn't understand. I knew nothing about her other than her name and what she was in school for. Yet she occupied my thoughts as if I had known her my entire life. She invaded my thoughts and an instinctive need to protect her kicked in. There was just something about her that drew me to her, but I couldn't figure out exactly what it was.

I walked into the locker room to change into my work uniform after I had entered the building. "What's up Jamere?" I pulled my pants up my legs, my shirt still sitting in my locker. "What's up Lloyd? You heading home?" I pulled my work shirt over my wife beater and started buttoning it up. "Nope. I'm working a double. I'm here until three." I closed my locker and the two of us headed to the floor. "Are you working at 11 a.m. in the morning?" "Yeah. Need all the hours I can get. Moving L.J. down here is not going to be cheap. And I want my son being raised by me and no one else." That, I could respect. Lloyd, my best friend since middle school, loved his four-year old son to death. He would do anything to keep that little boy, my nephew happy. So, when little Lloyd's mom passed away in a car accident a few weeks ago, he was determined to get full custody of his son. But his grandparents were okay with it. They agreed to keep L.J. for a few weeks, and then they would bring him to Seattle from Dallas. Next week, little man would be here. I hadn't seen him since the funeral, and I couldn't wait. I probably was just as excited as Lloyd was. I didn't have any children of my own, but I felt like if I did, I would share Lloyd's sentiments.

"I understand that. I can't wait to see my nephew. I miss him." Lloyd smiled as the two of us walked onto the floor. "He misses you too. He tells me every night. I'm going to list you as his emergency contact when he starts daycare. There aren't too many people I would trust with my son, but you are definitely one of the ones that I do." I put my hand on his shoulder and the two of us stopped. "Thanks man. You know I would do anything to make sure he was good." Lloyd nodded, so

I moved my hand and the two of us walked in the appropriate directions.

I started loading trucks so that they could head out for their destinations. The sounds of the trucks and workers clouded my ears, so I focused on whatever I could to drown out the unwanted sounds. I loaded boxes into the appropriate trucks automatically, a task that I was so accustomed to, it was more of a habit.

The hours dragged by as if time knew I really wasn't feeling work today. After what seemed like the longest work night in history, three a.m. finally came. I headed back to the locker room to change and clock out so that I could head home.

"Jamere, want to go get something to eat?" I pulled my hoodie over my head and closed my locker. "No, I'll get something before class. I'm going to try to get a few hours of sleep before I have to get ready for school." "Okay cool. See you later then." I threw my hand up and dropped my work uniform in the dirty clothes bin. Once it was inside, I walked quickly out of the locker room, practically running to my car.

I stared at the wall, wishing I could stay asleep, but school called. I rolled out of the bed and made it up and went about the process of getting ready for school. After my teeth were brushed and my face was washed, I went back to my room to get dressed.

    I stepped into a pair of dark wash Levi's with my belt fitted to my waist. I pulled a red plaid button down Polo shirt over my head to avoid having to button the buttons. A navy-blue vest covered my button down and a pair of wheat colored Tim's were on my feet. I picked up my bookbag, my keys, and my phone and left the apartment.

    I decided against breakfast and went directly to school. I walked into class and sat at a desk in front. I decided to check on Trina, so I pulled my phone out and started a text to her. **Good morning Trina. I just wanted to check on you and see how you were doing. I hope you aren't in too much residual pain. Jamere.** I placed my phone on my desk and watched as students started to file into the classroom. I spoke to a few people I knew until my phone vibrated from its place on my desk. So, I picked it up and read the message that was on the screen. **Good morning Jamere. Thanks for thinking about me. I'm doing okay thanks. Have a good class. See you Thursday.** I smiled at the words, but when I realized how stiff they seemed, the worry creeped back in. I didn't have time to dwell on it though, because my professor walked in and started her lecture.

  I went to each of my classes, regretting not getting anything to eat earlier in the day. My stomach was letting me know just how long it had been since I'd last eaten. I hurried to my car, desperate to get some food in my stomach before I went to work.

  My phone rang as I drove, so I put it on speaker and answered it. "Hello?" The small voice of my six-year-old sister rang in my ear, bringing a smile to my face. "Hey Jam. What are you doing?" I kept my eyes on traffic, maneuvering my car around the other cars on the road with me. "Hey Amelia. I'm going to get something to eat before work. What about you? Why aren't you at school?" I stopped at a Jack-In-The-Box and cut the engine off. "I have a doctor's appointment. My asthma has been flaring up a lot. Daddy just got me from school." I stepped out of my car and locked the doors as I walked into the restaurant. "Oh okay. I remember you telling me that. Are you feeling okay now?" I stared at the menu, trying to decide on what I wanted to eat. "Yeah, I'm fine. When are you going to come see me? I miss you." A smile spread across my face, and I knew I would always be there for her. "I'll come this weekend. I'll even see if Lloyd can come too." The excitement in her voice let me know that she really wanted to see her big brother, and that I would always be happy about. "Yay! I can't wait. I gotta go Jam. I'll see you this weekend. I love you." My heart swelled and I spoke kindly to my baby sister. "Okay Amy. See you then. I love you too." I ended the call and moved to the cashier to place my order.

    I got to work at 2:45 p.m. and headed to clock in. Once I had, I changed clothes and went to the floor to load trucks once again. Thankfully, I remembered my Bluetooth, so I could listen to music and not the annoying talking that surrounded me.

    After my ten-hour shift, I made it home and to my waiting bed. I made myself a grilled cheese sandwich, not wanting to put anything too heavy on my stomach before bed. Once I had eaten it, I went to get in my waiting bed. I stared at the ceiling, images of Trina's defeated, broken, lonely face swimming in my otherwise empty mind. I closed my eyes and let the images send me into a restless sleep. My concern filtering into my dreams as if Trina were meant to be a constant part of my life.

    I tossed and turned all night, mind racing with all kinds of reasons that Trina acted the way she did. Pain was coming at her from somewhere and it hurt me that she was going through it seemingly all alone. This girl occupied my thoughts, but that wasn't the problem. The problem was, I wanted her in my thoughts. As crazy as it seemed, I wanted to be the one to protect her. It was more than obvious that her so called boyfriend wasn't doing so.

  I eventually gave up on sleep and got out of bed. Ever since meeting Trina, my sleep schedule had been off. For whatever reason, my schedule was so much different than it had been. Being awake in the middle of the night had never, ever happened to me. But since that was exactly what was now happening. I had to figure out what to do to pass the time.

  Playstation 4 was what I chose to do with my time. Hopefully after playing GTAV for a little while, my mind would have slowed down enough for me to sleep. It was right at three a.m., and I needed to be up at 7 to get ready for school. The more I thought about it, the more I realized, sleep was pointless for the night.

  I walked into the living room and turned on the console and the T.V. before picking up the controller. I waited for the game to load, tapping the corresponding buttons to get me to the start of the game. The longer I played, the more awake I seemed to become. I had no clue that that would happen but stopping in the middle of my game was not an option. So, I played for an hour or two before saving my place in the game. I started doing push-ups and then sit ups, alternating between the two until the sun started to rise high in the early morning sky.

 I went to take another shower, letting the warm water beat down on my body. The steady pitter patter of water slowed my racing thoughts down and the focus of them was no longer on Trina Hart.

 I exited the shower and dried my body off, securing the towel around my waist while I brushed my teeth and washed my face. My hair needed to be brushed, so I did that before walking out of the bathroom. I needed a line up in the worst way, so that needed to be done before I went to work.

 Once back in my room, I pulled on some black Calvin Klein boxer briefs. I hung my towel on my closet door and walked into the closet to search for an outfit to wear. A pair of black True Religion jeans stood out, so I grabbed the hanger they were on and looked for a matching shirt. I grabbed a white True Religion logo shirt and a black True Religion beanie and exited the closet. I dressed and put on some socks and my Concord Jordan's. I looked over myself in the mirror and once I was satisfied, I put on my black G-Shock. My black bomber jacket hung at the front of the closet, so I took it out and put it on. With my phone on hand and bookbag on, I made my way out of my apartment.

    I was smart enough this morning to stop and get breakfast. I really needed to go get groceries so I could stop wasting money on fast food. But after school and work, the last thing on my mind was going to the grocery store. I drove through the drive thru at Chick Fil A. I ordered some chicken minis and an orange juice and drove around to pay and get my food. The drive thru was wrapped around the building when I left, and I was happy that I managed to beat the breakfast rush.

    I pulled into a parking spot and finished my chicken minis before getting out of my car. I put the bag in the trash and walked into the building my class was held in with my orange juice in my hand and my bookbag hanging from one shoulder. I took my time, knowing I was at least twenty minutes early for class. But I had to get out of my apartment. I needed some fresh air, because my mind kept straying to the one person I knew I couldn't have.

"What's up Jamere?" My head turned in the direction of the voice and a smile formed on my face. "What's up Dani?" I waited as she walked toward me, putting my arm around her shoulders, and pulling her to me before letting go. The two of us walked into class, speaking to our professor as we passed his desk. "Not much. What about you? You're earlier than you usually are." My shoulders moved up and down as the two of us found desks next to each other. "Wanted Chick Fil A. Its way out of the way so I left home in enough time to get there and then here on time." Dani nodded her head and started pressing buttons on her phone. My eyes went to my phone, and I had to suppress the urge to check on Trina again. How long I would be able to suppress that urge, I had no idea. I opened my orange juice so that I would have something to do with my hands. I drank from the bottle and waited patiently for class to start.

At the end of my school day, I decided not to put off grocery shopping any longer. I didn't have to be at work until five, so I figured it was as good a time as any. I drove through the busy streets until I had made it to my destination. I stayed in my car, trying to build up the strength to go inside. If there was one thing I hated, it was definitely grocery shopping. I reached in my pocket for my phone, doing the one thing I had been trying to avoid all day. **Hey Trina. I don't want to bother you, I just wanted to know how you were feeling. I hope the pain is nearly gone. You don't have to reply if you don't want to, I was just concerned. See you in class.** I let out a sigh and opened my door to step out. Just as I was locking the doors, my phone rang in my hand. I read the words on the screen, relief washing over me. **Hey Jamere. You are not a bother so don't think that. I'm fine. The pain is pain, but I'm pushing through. Thank you for the concern. See you tomorrow.** The text still seemed guarded, but I was glad she was doing okay. Thankfully, I would get to see just how well she was doing the following morning in class. I put my phone in my pocket and walked through the parking lot and through the automatic doors of the store.

    I drove home with my car full of groceries, hopefully keeping me from having to go to the grocery store for at least a month. That I was grateful for. Cooking for one let food last a while. No girlfriend in the picture anymore, so the only person I had to cook for was myself. I let my head bob to the music that played from the speakers my mind focusing on what I wanted to make for dinner.

I stood at the stove, stirring a small pot of chicken alfredo. I moved the pot away from the heat and checked on my garlic bread that was in the oven. My mouth watered as I pulled open the door to the oven. I sprinkled some shredded sharp cheddar on the bread and pushed the door closed and waited for the cheese to melt.

I sat in front of my T.V. in the living room with my food, staring at the movie that was playing on the screen. I forked some of the alfredo and stuck it in my mouth and began to chew. There was nothing like a home cooked meal. Fast food got old really quick and since being on my own, I had a newfound respect for mothers who made dinner for their families every night. How I would love to have my mother still cooking my dinner every night. But that wasn't going to happen. Thankfully, she started teaching me to cook at a young age. Even though I didn't want to learn, she made me. She always said, 'Baby one day, you are going to grow up and become a man. You're going to have to take care of yourself and you can't live on fast food and cereal. One day you'll understand why I made you do this.' I found out, fairly quickly, just how true her words were. She always cooked for me when I visited, even when I told her it wasn't necessary. But I let her know as often as I could how thankful I was to have her and every time I did, she cried like a baby. A chuckle left my mouth thinking about my sensitive mother. I put the last piece of bread in my mouth and stood to get everything cleaned up.

With my phone and keys in hand, I left my apartment to head to work. My homework was finished, so I knew that when I got off, I could shower and go right to bed. That sleep was going to be heaven. One a.m. couldn't get here fast enough. My bed was already calling my name and I hadn't even made it to work it yet. I got in the car and listened to it turn over before driving toward the entrance of my apartment complex.

"Hey Lloyd. You should come by my mom's house Saturday after L.J. gets here. Amy wants to see you." Lloyd grinned at me and the two of us walked to the floor. "Cool. I think I can make that happen. I'll see you later man." I nodded my head and the two of us walked away from one another. I started loading trucks, counting the minutes until it was time for me to clock out and go home to my bed.

Chapter 3:

Trina

I crutched into class and ignored the stares that I could feel on me. I sat at my usual seat in the back and leaned my crutches against the wall. I had to return to work at one, and I knew Cheyenne was going to badger me about what happened. I told her I just switched my off days, but when she saw the crutches, I knew that wasn't going to sit well. It was going to have to be dealt with though, so I had to get my mind mentally prepared.

My body froze when I saw a shadow cast over me. "Hey Trina. How are you doing?" My head lifted and I saw Jamere sitting in his desk next to mine. "Hey Jamere. I'm alright. How are you?" He smiled at me, so I looked back down at my desk. "I'm good. How's your pain? Any better?" I tapped my desk with my fingers, responding to his question honestly. "It's okay. Not gone, but manageable." I didn't avert my gaze, but I wanted to. I wanted to see his eyes, his expression, but fear of what I may have seen stopped me. "Good. I hope it continues to get better. Question." I cut my eyes in his direction, but never lifted my head. "Thank you. I hope so too. And that would be?" I put my tape recorder on my desk along with my binder and textbook. I still didn't make eye contact with him, as much as I may have wanted to. "The study group is set for Sunday, but I need to give the others a time. What's your schedule for Sunday?" I held an ink pen in my hand, writing a date on my paper for my notes. "I go to church at 9 and its usually over by 11. My schedule is clear from then until about 8. I have work at the club from 9 until 4." "Cool. So how long should it last?" I thought about his question and answered with my opinion. "I would say between two and four hours." I lifted my head when I heard our professor's hello sound out. "That's perfect. So how about from 1 until 5." I nodded at him, trying to come up with a reason not to go home right after church. Stephan was sure to question me, so I needed to have my reason ready. "At your place?" "Yes, that cool with you?" I nodded again and looked at what our professor had written on the board. "You mind if I change there? I'm going to stop and get my brows done after church, that way I won't have to go home before going to your place." I wrote on my paper, listening to Jamere's whispered response. "That's fine. I'll text you the address." I told him okay and the two of us focused on the lecture that was being delivered.

"See you tomorrow Trina." I waved at Jamere as the two of us exited the building. "See ya." I turned in the direction of my next class and started to walk toward it.

I walked to the back of the class and sat in my usual seat and read over my notes that went with the exam we had to take. I drowned out the sounds of my classmates entering the room and focused on the words on the paper in front of me. I knew everything was engrained in my brain, but you could never be sure when it came to an exam in this particular class. So, I studied until my instructor came in and administered the exam.

When I completed my exam, I turned it in and left the classroom. I still had a little while before my next class, so I headed to the library. I could study in silence while waiting for my 10:15 class to begin. I didn't have anything else to do, so I could pass the time the best way I knew how. At the end of my last class, I wrote down my assignment and left the classroom. I watched the ground as I walked, looking up only when absolutely necessary. By the time I reached my car, I realized just how different I had become since I started dating Stephan. I knew in my heart that things needed to change, but I loved him. I didn't know if I could make it without him. I knew I deserved better, but I wasn't sure I would find anyone else if I left him. I had gotten to the point where I was tired of fighting. In the beginning, when the hitting started, I would fight back. But as the years passed, I slowly started to stop fighting as hard as I once had. I was tired, so I let myself succumb to it, until I felt like it was too much. But as each day passed, I knew I would have to do something. I knew I would have to get out of the situation I was in.

    I drove to my apartment to change for work, going over ways in my mind to get my old self back. My apartment complex came into view and that's when I realized, that to get away from Stephan, I would have to move out. It would be a while before I could save up enough to move, but I had to start somewhere. I pulled into a parking spot and let myself out of the car. When I saw Stephan's car, I knew to leave my bookbag in the back. My heart thudded fearfully in my chest as I watched the driver's side door open.

    When Quincy stepped out, I managed to breathe a little easier. "Hey Q. What are you doing here?" Quincy looked me up and down before replying. "Stephan asked me to come get some stuff. He said you would be here to let me in." I tensed up but headed toward my apartment. "Yeah. How long have you been here? I had to go pay the electric bill." Quincy followed, stopping beside me as I unlocked the door. "About twenty minutes. I was about to call Stephan and leave when you pulled up." I nodded, trying not to show my nervousness as we walked inside. "Oh okay. Well get what you need. I'm going to change into my work clothes." Quincy followed me into my room, stopping just inside the door as I grabbed my clothes. "I'll go in the bathroom." I crutched away from him and into the bathroom slowly. I closed and locked the door and leaned against the sink. I exhaled quietly, thoughts of Stephan looking into my lie that I had told Quincy flooding my brain.

Once I was back in my room, I looked around for Quincy. When I didn't see him, I slid my feet into a pair of black flats. With my gray skirt suit and white blouse, it didn't look right but I couldn't wear heels, so it was going to have to work. I could hear movement in the living room, so I made my way out of my bedroom and towards that area.

"All set?" Quincy turned from looking at pictures on the wall and looked at me. "Yep." He picked up a bag and followed me to the front door. "Trina, what happened?" I didn't look at him, but I answered his question while locking the door. "I fell Monday on my way to pick up my car." The two of us headed toward our vehicles side by side. "Oh. Well thanks for letting me in. See you later." I waved my hand and slipped into my car, backing out of my parking spot as Quincy started Stephan's car.

"Trina, what in the world happened to you?" I rolled my eyes as Cheyenne walked toward me. I knew it was coming, but no amount of mental preparation could have made me comfortable with lying to my best friend. But here I was, about to do that very thing. "I sprained my ankle Monday. It's not a big deal." Well, I hadn't lied yet, but with a friend like Chey, I knew it was coming. "How? What were you doing? Is this why you haven't been at work?" Here it was. The lies. I hated lying, but that was all I had been doing for nearly three years. "I fell. I was walking. Yes, the doctor told me I couldn't come back until yesterday, but Mr. Jefferies gave me until today. I just switched my off days." The two of us walked side by side to go clock in. "Are you okay?" I flinched when she touched me but nodded my head as if I hadn't done so. "I'm fine. Between you and Jamere, I don't know who is going to be more worried." Cheyenne grinned, holding my crutches as I eased into my chair. "Let me get to work. See you at lunch?" I nodded at her, and she sat my crutches on the floor before walking away.

Lunch rolled around quicker than it usually seemed to. I pressed the appropriate buttons on the computer so that my lunch break would show up. I picked up my crutches from the floor and got up on my good foot. Just as I was about to walk through the door, Cheyenne said my name, causing me to stumble with my crutches. "Sorry Lil Bit. Didn't mean to scare you. You ready?" I pulled the door open and watched Cheyenne walk past me. "Yeah." She pressed buttons on the computer and then followed me out the door.

"Have you talked to your brothers lately?" The two of us sat at a table, eating our salads while waiting for our entrees. "I talked to R.J. the other day, but I haven't talked to D.J. or Tay in a few weeks." Cheyenne stared at me, and I knew she had something to say, but she didn't speak. She had been filtering herself for the past couple of weeks and I was curious as to why. 20 years we had been friends and she chose now to want to hold her tongue. It was unreal, but I would just see how long it was going to last. With Chey, probably not long. She was so used to saying the first thing that popped in her mind, it would be torture for her not to do so. "Tell them I said hey next time you talk to them." I pushed my remaining salad away and told her that I would. "Are you working this weekend?" We waited for the waiter to put our food in front of us and walk away. Once he was gone, I answered her question. "At the hotel, only on Friday and Saturday. At the club, yes." I prayed over my food and the two of us made small talk while we ate our meals.

The two of us clocked back in when we got back to work, and Cheyenne went back to her area. "See you tomorrow Lil Bit." I waved at her as she walked away, smiling at the patron who had walked up to the counter. "Good afternoon sir. How may I help you?" I glanced at him but looked at the computer before we made eye contact with each other. "Hi, I need a room until Sunday." I nodded and started typing in information, asking questions when I needed to.

At eight o'clock I left the hotel, rushing to get home. I hadn't eaten since lunch, but I wasn't hungry, so I searched for something to wear. No one would see me since I couldn't work the floor, so I didn't have to dress for tips. I picked a pair of gray jeans and a purple Polo sweater. I wore a gray cami under the sweater and a pair of purple and gray Roma Pumas were on my feet. A pair of purple studs were in my ears and my iPhone 6 plus was in my hand. I checked myself in the mirror and exited my apartment once again.

I sat in the manager's office, organizing files, and making sure everything was where it could be found. I couldn't serve drinks, so I had to find another way to get the money I definitely needed. Missing work was out of the question. Every penny I earned, I needed desperately. I jumped in my chair when the door opened, holding my hand to my chest as my manager walked in.

"Sebastian, knock or call my name next time." My heart pounded in fear, and I tried to calm myself down. "Sorry, I didn't realize I had to announce myself before entering my own office." I shook my head and looked down at his once cluttered desk. "You're right. I'm sorry. You just scared me." The music from the club filtered through the open door, causing the walls to vibrate. "It's cool. I shouldn't have snapped. You are back here alone." I lifted my eyes from the desk and looked at him briefly before looking down again. "How long will you be on the crutches?" I sighed internally, once again reminded of the abuse I had to endure on a practically everyday basis. "A few weeks." Sebastian picked up a file, holding it down at his side. "I'm going to have to figure out something else for you to do. You already tackled my office, and I just knew that was going to take at least a week." I shrugged, keeping my eyes on the last of the files I was organizing. "It's not like I had anything else to do." "Yeah I guess you're right." You can do our inventory check list when you finish. By then it should be time to close up." I gave Sebastian the thumbs up sign, lowering my hand when I heard the door close. I looked up and stared at the closed door, exhaling loudly before finishing the task at hand.

    I unlocked the door to my apartment and pushed it open so that I could walk in. When I turned around after locking the door, a fist connected with my right cheek. I immediately swung back, the first time I had defended myself against Stephan in months. I felt my fist connect with what I assumed was his eye, but in the dark, I couldn't be sure. "Where the hell have you been?" Another blow landed this time to my chest. The wind exited my lungs and I keeled over, kicking at Stephan's leg but missing. "I called the hotel; they said your shift was over at eight. Its 4:30 a.m." I stood up straight, ignoring the old aches mingling with the new ones." I had to organize my boss's office. I was off the clock so no one could know I was still there." My right cheek throbbed, but I refused to let him know that. "I think you're lying. I think you were out with another man. And if I find out that I'm right, you will have hell to pay. Understand?" I nodded slowly, breathing in and out just as slowly. "Go get in the shower and go to bed. By the time I get back from getting something to eat, you better be asleep." I could make out his body by the streetlights that filtered through the room. I nodded again, my head jerking to the right after he slapped me. "I don't understand nods. Use your words." I ground my teeth together and spoke slowly. "I understand." "Good. I love you. Good night." I contained my anger, answering the way he expected me to. "I love you too." Stephan kissed my lips and walked through the door. I guess I would have to go to bed hungry. I shook my head and walked through the dark apartment to my room.

    I laid under the covers; my sprained ankle propped up on a pillow. I stared into the darkness, listening to the silence that hovered around me. These days I was terrified to sleep when Stephan was around because I didn't know what he would do. So those nights when he stayed with me, I was usually awake all night. My heartbeat quickened when I heard the front door open, and I closed my eyes tightly and kept my breathing steady. I heard his keys drop on the dresser, followed by the sound of him closing the bedroom door. Silence filled the room again, but seconds later I could smell the scent of his cologne. A smell that I once loved, now only made me sick to my stomach.

    His hot breath fanned over my face, and I prayed he wouldn't try to kiss me. That act now disgusted me as much as the smell of his cologne did. Any form of affection I avoided as much as I could. Kissing, sex, touching, I refused to give him. Sometimes it worked, most times it didn't. But there was no doubt in my mind that he was getting it from somewhere else. I didn't care, but I was worried about my health. He always used protection, but that wasn't enough to ease my worries. Especially not knowing if he was or wasn't using protection with some other girl. I casually moved, turning my body away from him in my pretend sleep. I felt his lips touch the back of my head before the bathroom door opened and then closed.

    I listened to Stephan's annoying breathing until his alarm went off at six thirty. I thought the sound would never come and when I felt him move to turn it off, I closed my eyes and moved around. I stayed where I was until he woke me up. "I'm going to work baby. I'll see you later. I'm staying at home tonight, so I won't see you until tomorrow or Sunday." I covered my mouth while I faked a yawn and sat up. "Okay. See you later." I stretched, ignoring my still sore sides. "Have a good day at work. Remember what I said." "Okay. Bye." Stephan turned and opened my bedroom door, looking back at me for a few seconds and winking before walking away.

When I knew that Stephan was really gone, I got out of bed and made it up. I looked for something to wear to school, thankful that it was Friday. I put my outfit on the bed and walked to the bathroom to brush my teeth, comb my hair, and wash my face.

The bruise on cheek made me shake my head and turn away. There was no way I could cover it up with makeup without drawing attention to the fact that I was wearing makeup. So, I brushed my teeth, avoiding the mirror as much as I could. I washed my face, wincing when I would rub the washcloth over my sore cheek. I put a few braids on the left side of my head and combed the rest over the right side. I put some curls in the loose hair and exited the bathroom so that I could get dressed. I glanced at the time on my alarm clock, speeding up the process when I realized I was running a few minutes behind schedule.

I walked into class and followed my normal path to the back of classroom. I sat in my chair and leaned my crutches against the wall. I waited for Jamere, shocking myself when I realized that I was doing it. Most men I didn't pay attention to, but Jamere was different for some reason. I looked forward to seeing him in class during the week. Surprisingly, I wasn't even afraid of him as I was with most men. That was a big thing for me.

    "Trina, good morning." I looked up and watched the smile, the gorgeous smile I loved to see fading from Jamere's face. "What happened to your face?" He asked in an irritated whisper. He started to touch my face but pulled his hand back as if he were afraid to touch me. "Good morning. I just got in a fight. I'm fine. It's just a bruise." Jamere stared at me, looking me up and down a few times. "You look nice. Yellow suits you." I looked at my white Polo sweater, yellow jeans, and white Keds that graced my feet. The shoes were lightweight, which would prevent any additional pain to my ankle. All in all, I looked basic, regular at best. But he told me that I looked nice. "Thanks. That's nice to hear." His smile returned which made me look down once again. "You're very welcome. You should hear it every day." I smiled, keeping my attention on my desk. I pulled out my materials, placing them on the desk and waiting for my professor to start lecturing.

"See you Sunday Trina. If you have any questions about directions, just call and ask me." I nodded my head and waved at Jamere, glancing back at him every few seconds as we walked away from one another.

I sat behind the computer at the hotel, counting down the minutes until I could leave. I was lost in my thoughts, so when I heard my name, I nearly fell out of my chair. "Lil Bit, are you okay? I called your name 2 times, and you didn't reply so I yelled it. I wasn't trying to scare you." I stared at Cheyenne, trying to slow my rapidly beating heart. "I wasn't paying attention. What do you need?" Chey stared at me, confusion written across her face. "D.J. just called me. He said he called you, but you didn't answer. He wanted to see if they could stop by the club and see you tonight. I told him I would relay the message and you would get back to them." I put my thumb up and picked up my cell phone from the table. "Thank you. I'll call him now." Chey stayed where she was and stared at me, her eyebrows furrowed on her forehead.

"Hey Dylan. What's up?" My big brother's voice filtered on the line, easing a smile onto my face. "Hey Lil Bit. Chey must have told you I called?" I glanced up at Cheyenne and responded to his question. "Yeah. She told me you, R.J., and Tay wanted to stop by the club tonight." I could hear the excitement in his voice, but it was going to be short lived. "Yeah. Is tonight good? We miss our little sister. We haven't seen you in months." I looked away from Chey, knowing the look she was going to give me when I said what I was about to say. "No. I sprained my ankle the other day and I'm on crutches. I'm not allowed on the floor so I'm doing office work until I can stop using them. You wouldn't even get to see me."

Silence. Pure silence. I looked at my screen, thinking that the call might have dropped or that he had hung up, but that wasn't the case. I said his name to make sure he was still on the line. "Dylan. Are you still there?" I heard him exhale and then he spoke. "Yeah, I'm here. It just sucks. Let us know when you're free and we can get together. I have to get back to work though. I love you Lil Bit." I pinched the bridge of my nose, the hurt I felt tearing at me internally. "I know it does. But I have to get back to work as well. I love you too. Talk to you later." The call ended and I placed my phone back on the table. I waited for the onslaught from Cheyenne, but when I looked up, she only looked hurt. "Why did you lie? You know Sebastian would have let you talk to your brothers." She shook her head, staring at me with hurt in her eyes. "I'll see you later." Cheyenne walked away from me, shaking her head slowly as she did.

I had never been more ready to be away from anywhere Cheyenne was than I was at that moment. Cheyenne had a way of making you feel bad without saying anything to you. And that was exactly what had just happened. I felt horrible and being away from her would be the best thing for me.

My phone rang in the cup holder as I made my way home, so I picked it up and answered it with no emotion in my tone. **Hello? Trina? Are you okay? You sound upset.** My mood lightened when I heard Jamere's soothing voice on the other end of the phone. I continued my drive, enjoying hearing his voice in my ear. **I'm alright. Just a rough day at work. Thanks for the concern. You doing okay?**

I feel you. I'm good. I just wanted to tell you something about the study group Sunday.

Okay? I promised my little sister that I would spend the weekend with her, so I'm moving the study group to my mom and stepdad's house. Is that okay with you? I smiled at the thought of him wanting to be a good big brother. It touched my heart in a place that only my brothers had ever touched before. **That's fine. How old is your sister? Is she your only sibling?**

She's six. No, I have an older brother too. And my best friend I consider my brother.

 What about you? Any siblings?

Yes, three brothers. All older.

Wow. How you have a boyfriend I will never understand. Three older brothers! I only have one little sister and I'll kill any boy who tries to touch her.

I cringed at the word boyfriend, trying not to let my disgust filter through my voice. **Yeah well, they don't know he exists yet. And he is my first real boyfriend, so it hasn't really been a problem.**

Three years and they haven't met him? How old are they? If you don't mind me asking.

Yeah, we don't get to see each other often. Trust me, if they knew about him, they'd be just as bad as you. I don't mind. Tay is 30, D.J., is 26, and R.J. is 22.

Okay and you're what, 20?

Yeah. You? How old is your brother?

The same. Juss is 24. My little sister's name is Amelia by the way. It was cute the way he talked about his sister. To me it was a peek into the love he would have for his daughter. **That's cute. I hate to go, but I have to change for work. I'll see you on Sunday okay?**

Thanks. That's okay. Have a good night at work. I'll see you then. I'll text you the address.

Okay. Later.

Be careful. Later.

    I changed into my work clothes for the club and stuffed my phone into my back pocket. With keys in hand, I grabbed my brown motorcycle jacket and my purse, turning my light off before walking through my apartment.

    I checked the inventory in the cooler, checking off the things that we needed to order for the upcoming week. This was really just busy work, but I couldn't really do too much of anything else, so I had to deal with it. After double checking the list, I walked out of the cooler and headed to Sebastian's office. I put my jacket and beanie on, cursing the fact that I didn't have any gloves. I picked up the freezer list from the desk and walked out of the office once again.

"Trina did you finish the inventory for the cooler and the freezer?" My eyes looked to the floor and then on the light blue Levi's I was wearing. "Yeah, and my ankle is letting me know." The throbbing felt like I had a heartbeat in my ankle and with each individual throb, the pain intensified immensely. "Good. I need that list in the morning. Thank you. This helped me out so much." I leaned against the wall with my crutches tucked under my arms. "You're welcome. What else do you need me to do?" I ignored the throbbing and pulled at the sleeve of my green long-sleeved shirt. "You're done for the night. Head on home and elevate that ankle." I raised my eyebrows at him and looked over his right shoulder so that I wasn't looking him in the eyes. "My shift isn't over yet. I can do something else." Sebastian shook his head at me and walked a few steps closer. My heart started to pound because I didn't have an escape route. "It's okay. I don't have anything else for you to do tonight. Go home. Get some rest and I'll have more for you to do tomorrow." I clutched the handles of my crutches in my hands tightly but avoided looking at him. "Are you sure?" I could hear the smile in his voice as he answered my question. "I'm positive. Go home. Be careful. See you tomorrow night." I stood up straight and turned in the direction of Sebastian's office. "Okay. Thanks. See you tomorrow." I moved away from him, retrieving my things from his office, and then headed to my car.

Once I was home, I took something for the pain that was pounding in my ankle. I changed into some pajamas and climbed into bed, letting myself fall into a much-needed sleep.

Chapter 4:

Jamere

I stood on the porch of my mom's house, waiting for Trina's car to come into view. When I saw it, I walked toward the driveway as she pulled her car in behind mine. Once the engine was off, I put my hand on the door handle and pulled it open. She grabbed her crutches and put them on the ground so that she could pull herself to her feet. When she was standing, I smiled at her even though she never looked at me.

"Hello Trina. How was church?" When she was out of the way, I pushed the door closed and listened to her speak. The smile in her voice didn't show on her face, but I was happy with whatever I got. "Hey. Church was good. How about you? It looks like that's what you are dressed for." She popped her trunk and pulled a small Nike backpack out of it. I grabbed it and nodded my head at her. "Yeah, it was good. I stopped and bought Amy some shoes and we're just getting in. When you sent the text, I was about to change." I walked away from her, motioning for her to follow me. "That's good. Has anyone else let you know that they were on the way?" I opened the front door, trying not to focus on the bruise on her cheek. It upset me that someone had hit her in the face, and I had a feeling that there was more to the story than she had told me. "No, but we still have an hour before we need to start. I was going to run to the store to get snacks after I change. You want to ride?" Trina nodded at me, keeping her eyes straight ahead. "Okay. That's fine." We walked into the family room where my mom and dad were rearranging furniture. "Trina Hart, this is my mom Aubrey and my dad Lawrence Dennison. Mom, dad, this is my friend Trina Hart."

My stepdad walked toward us, and I watched Trina tense up as he held his hand out to her. She slowly put her hand in his, shaking it for less than a second before pulling it away. "Hello Trina. It's nice to meet you." Trina looked at the ground and adjusted herself on her crutches before she spoke. "Hi Mr. Dennison. It's nice to meet you too. Thanks for allowing me to come to your home." My dad stepped out of the way and my mom stepped forward. "Hello Trina. How are you doing? It's nice to meet you. I've heard nothing but great things." Trina glanced at me and then looked at my mom standing in front of her. She grabbed my mom's outstretched hand and shook it for a few seconds longer than she shook my dad's.

"Hello Mrs. Dennison. I'm okay and yourself. It's nice to meet you too. You both have a beautiful home." My mom smiled and winked inconspicuously at me. I shook my head and acted as if I didn't see her. "I'm well thanking you for asking. Thanks for the comment on our home. We spent years looking for the perfect home for us, and when we saw this one, we knew it was it." Trina's expression stayed blank, but she looked around the room we were in, in silence.

"Jam!" I turned and watched Amelia bound toward me. "Amy stop yelling." She hung onto my leg when she saw Trina, staring at her in confusion. "Amelia, this is my friend Trina. Trina, this is my little sister Amelia." Trina smiled, the first real smile I had seen on her face in days. She stretched out her hand, waiting for Amelia to grab it. Once their hands were together, Trina spoke.

"It's nice to meet you sweetie. Your brother loves you so much. I wish I had a little sister." Amelia smiled and stepped away from my leg. "Do you have any sister's at all?" Trina shook her head no and the two of them dropped hands. "No. Only brothers." Amelia stepped closer, looking up at Trina. "How many do you have? Are they bigger than you?" I caught myself smiling at the two of them and the conversation they were having. "I have 3. Yes, they are all bigger than me. I'm the baby of the family." Amelia smiled widely and grabbed onto Trina's leg. "Me too!" Trina chuckled, the first time since I had known her to do so. "Amy, let her go so she can change. Do you want to ride to the store with us?" Amelia nodded her headed excitedly while letting Trina's leg go. "Go put on your shoes then. We'll leave as soon as Trina and I get changed." Amelia started running towards the stairs, slowing to a walk when my mom told her to stop running in the house. "Trina, you can change in our room, so you don't have to try to climb the stairs." My mom motioned for Trina to follow her, so I gave her bag to my mom and watched the two of them walk away.

    I finished changing clothes and walked out of one of the guest rooms. Just as I was about to walk down the stairs, my parents stopped me. "Jamere, what happened to her? She seems to have been through a lot." I looked at them, but I knew I couldn't tell them what I thought, so I told them what she told me. "She fell on the way to school one day last week and sprained her ankle." My parents looked at one another and focused their attention on me once more. "What about the bruise on her face?" I shook my head, knowing they were having the same thoughts I was. "She got in a fight. No more questions. I shouldn't have told you what I did. I want her to be able to trust me." I heard the sighs exit their mouths, but they respected my wishes and didn't ask me anymore questions.

Amy and Trina were sitting on the sofa when we returned to the family room, deep in conversation about something. "Are we ready?" Trina jumped so far up; she nearly fell off of the couch. "Sorry, I didn't mean to scare you." Trina shrugged her shoulders and put her Nike backpack on. "It's all good. I just didn't hear you. I've always been a jumpy person. My brothers used to tease me all the time for it." Trina used her crutches to get to her feet and then tucked them under her arms securely. "We'll be back in a few." The three of us walked away from my parents and out the front door.

Amy, Trina, and I walked the aisles, grabbing finger foods to get through our study group. After refusing to use a wheelchair, Trina was determined to look as if she weren't in pain, so I acted as if I couldn't tell. Amy stayed close to Trina, chatting a mile a minute but Trina didn't seem to mind. She kept Amy engaged, making my little sister happy. And by the smile on her face, I could tell Trina was happy too.

Once everything was paid for, we walked out of the store toward the car. My phone rang, so I answered, giving directions to my classmate who was on the other end of the phone. I loaded the trunk, and made Amy and Trina get in the car as I did so.

"Trina, there are going to be six of us total. Robert is on the way and I'm hoping the others are as well." Trina stared at her ringing phone as if she didn't hear it ringing. I couldn't make out her expression while driving, but when I stopped, I looked at her. Really looked at the expression on her face. Her phone started ringing again, so I put my hand on top of hers and spoke softly.

"Are you going to answer that?" Trina flinched, but she didn't move her hand away, so I knew that I had made progress. Fear covered her face, clouded her eyes, but she tapped the answer icon on her phone and put it to her ear. "Hello?" Her voice shook slightly, but she disguised it as much as she could. I glanced in the backseat, thankful for Amelia being asleep. I listened to the one-sided conversation, keeping my free hand on Trina's as I drove.

"Stephan, I'm running a few errands, that's why I'm not at home. I want to get them done before work." Pause. Trina shook her head and spoke again. "I did make dinner. It's in the fridge. I left some for Q too." I pulled into the driveway and shut off the engine. I squeezed Trina's hand so that she would look at me. When she did, I mouthed to her that I was going to carry Amelia into the house. "Stephan, I have no reason to lie. I cooked lasagna, made some garlic bread, and a salad as well. It's all in the fridge in your apartment." Trina held her finger up and then pressed the mute button on her phone. "Okay go ahead. I have a jealous boyfriend, so I didn't want him making assumptions about random noises." I nodded and opened the door, closing it while opening the rear driver's side door. I scooped Amy into my arms and pushed the door closed before walking toward the house.

    I walked in as my stepdad was walking toward the stairs with my mom at his side. "I'll take her." My dad took Amy from my arms and started up the steps while my mom spoke. "Where's Trina?" I nodded my head toward the car and then answered her question. "In the car. Her boyfriend called so she's talking to him." My mom's eyes widened, but I shrugged and walked outside once more.

    Trina opened the door as I walked toward the car and pulled herself to her foot with the crutches. "You okay?" The defeated look on her face gave me my answer, but I waited to hear her reply anyway. "Yeah. I'm good." I wanted to tell her I didn't believe her. Tell her that I could read the lie all over her face, but the car pulling up stopped me. So, I walked to her side, squeezed her hand gently, and spoke softly to her. "If you need me, I'm here. Always." I let her hand go and watched Robert walk toward us. I stood in front of Trina, not wanting Rob to come at her the wrong way and scare her. "What's up Rob? This is Trina." I didn't move more than two inches, just enough so that the two of them could see each other. "Hey." Trina spoke as I popped the trunk. "What's up? Nice to finally meet you." I could hear the apprehension in Trina's voice as she responded to Robert's statement. "Thanks. You too." I turned to look at her, smiling kindly while speaking. "Trina, go ahead and have a seat in the family room. We're right behind you." Trina nodded, so I turned and looked at Robert. "Will you help me get this stuff?" Robert reached into the trunk and grabbed a few bags, and I grabbed the others. I pushed the trunk closed as another car pulled up. I stood where I was and waited for whoever it was to get out. "What's up Jamere? Robert?" Our classmate grabbed her things and locked the car and walked to where we were standing. "What's up Tina? Come on. Let's go inside." Robert and Tina followed behind me to the house and we all headed to the family room where my parents and Trina sat.

"Robert, Tina, these are my parents Aubrey and Lawrence Dennison. Dad, mom, these are two of my classmates, Robert Daniels and Tina Edwards." My parents shook their hands and my mom walked to the front of the house when the doorbell bang. She returned with my final two classmates walking behind her. "Hey you guys. Mom, dad, these are my last two classmates. Kerry Grant and Johnathan Porter, these are my parents, Aubrey and Lawrence Dennison." They all shook hands, and my parents made their exit so that we could start our study session.

I glanced at Trina as everyone picked a place to sit, noticing the nervousness on her face. I walked toward her casually and sat beside her without saying anything. "You can all help yourselves to whatever snacks you want." Everyone voiced their thanks, and we started the study session by reading over notes we had taken in class.

"Okay Jamere. I'm heading out. I have to be at work in a few minutes." Before I could speak, Amy rounded the corner wearing a navy blue and white striped onesie with pink trim and a pink butterfly on the front of it. A Hello Kitty sleep mask rested on top of her head, letting us know she was getting ready to go to bed. In her left hand, she clutched a stuffed Hello Kitty that was wearing a pink dress covered in sprinkles with a matching bow on its head. In its right hand was an ice cream cone that matched the bow and dress.

"Trina!" A smile spread across Trina's face as we watched my sister run toward her. "Yes Amelia." Amy hugged Trina's legs, letting her toy fall to the floor. My parents eyes widened as they watched the toy lay on the ground. Amy never let that thing touch the floor. She acted as if something would happen to it if it did. But there it lay, ignored by its six-year-old owner.

"Are you leaving?" Trina nodded while Amy looked up at her. "Will you come see me again?" Trina looked up at me and then my parents before looking down at Amy again. "If it's okay with your parents and your brother, I would love to." The grin that spread across Amelia's face melted my heart in more ways than one. "Amy, come on. It's time for you to go to bed." Amy frowned, but did as she was told after saying her good nights. "Good night Trina." Trina moved her hand off of the crutch and patted Amy on the back gently. "Good night sweetie. It was nice meeting you. Be good for mommy and daddy okay?" Amy nodded and let go of Trina's legs and walked to me. "Night Jam." I picked up her stuffed Hello Kitty and lifted her into my arms. "Good night Amy. I'm about to leave too okay? I love you so much. Be a good girl." Amy pressed her lips to my cheek and pulled her head back. I gave her toy to her and lowered her to the ground. "I love you too Jam. I will." Amy hugged my legs and then backed away. "Go on upstairs Amy. You have school tomorrow and its getting late. I love you." Amy hugged our parents and told them both that she loved them. She hugged Trina once more and turned in the direction of the stairs.

"Trina, it was nice meeting you. You are welcome to visit anytime. "Trina thanked my parents, shaking their hands briefly before pulling away. "Bye mom and dad. I'll talk to you both one day this week." I hugged my mom and shook my dad's hand, and the two of them followed Trina and I to the front door.

"You guys be careful." Trina and I nodded and walked out on the porch, and I pulled the door closed behind me. The two of us walked side by side to her car, saying nothing until her door was opened. "You have a great family. I really enjoyed meeting them." I rested my arm on the door and tried to avoid staring at her. "Thank you. They enjoyed meeting you too. Especially Amy. She never lets that Hello Kitty touch the ground, but that's where it was the entire time she held on to your legs." A small smile spread across her face, and she looked down at the ground. "Thanks for including me in the study group. It was good to get input from other people. I enjoyed myself." Trina glanced at her phone and tossed her bag on the passenger's seat. "No problem. I enjoyed having you here." Another smile, and her eyes lifted to mine. "I have to get to work. I'll see you in class tomorrow okay?" I stepped closer to her and hugged her carefully so that I wouldn't frighten her. She tensed up, but relaxed seconds later and put one arm around me. When she let go, I did the same and backed away. "Be careful okay? Let me know when you've made it to the club." Trina smiled at me and eased herself into her seat. "I will. You be careful too." I nodded my head at her, and she pulled the crutches in the car to rest on the passenger's seat. She put her legs into the car and waved at me before starting the engine. I pushed the door closed and watched as she backed out of the driveway.

    I watched as her car drove away into the darkness until I could no longer see it. Once it was out of sight, I got in my car and headed home. Visions of a beautiful young woman named Trina Hart flooded my mind as I drove in silence. The hurt she has had to face, the strength she exudes, only making her more attractive. As each day passed, I was more determined to find out what the mystery was behind the woman I was beginning to care for.

    I laid across my bed, watching ESPN after having been home for a few minutes. My phone vibrated on my chest, so I lifted it to see what was on the screen. I opened the text and read the message that Trina had sent. **Hey Jamere. I made it to work. I got your message that you made it home.**

Okay, thanks for letting me know. I'm glad you're safe. I'll talk to you later.

I'm glad you're safe too. Sleep well. I'll see you tomorrow. I smiled at the words on the screen and put my phone on the nightstand. I got off of my bed and went in the bathroom to take a shower.

    I laid under the covers in a pair of blue Hanes boxers and some white socks. I stared at the ceiling, ignoring the sound of my T.V. playing in the background. I was tired, but sleep refused to take over me. It was barely ten o'clock, but I thought I would have been able to sleep early. That was obviously not going to happen though. The ringing of my phone brought my attention back to the present. I disconnected my phone from the charger and put it to my ear.

"Hello?" I wasn't in the mood for talking on the phone and I was getting ready to let that be known. "Hey Jamere. Do you know who this is?" That voice was one I wasn't sure I'd ever forget. The voice of my ex who up and left without a word as to where she was going. I pinched the bridge of my nose, trying to keep my mood, my attitude under control. "Hey. Yeah, I know it's you Chasity. What do you need?" The last thing I needed was to be involved with her again. No matter how much I loved her once. My love for her died when she left me a year ago.

"Well, I missed you. I haven't heard from you in a while." I eased off of my bed and started pacing the floor, memories of that day resurfacing in my mind. "Whose fault is that? You up and left me remember?" I stopped in the middle if the room and exhaled angrily. "Look Chasity, what do you want? I don't have time for childish games. Tell me why you called so, I can go on with my life. My life that no longer includes you." I started to pace again, walking the length of my room over and over. "I just wanted to see you. I want to apologize for leaving the way I did. You didn't deserve it." I said nothing for a few seconds. I just let her words sink in. I had grown so much over the past year, and I knew being bitter over something I had no control over would only hold me back.

"Thank you for saying that Chasity. I know it had to have taken a lot of courage for you to say those things. This past year, I've learned that holding on to things that hurt you, only cause you to hurt worse. I was able to move on when I released all the pain you caused when you left. I accept your apology and I hope that you can move past it as I have." "Thank you Jamere. Do you think we could get together sometime? Have dinner or something?" I sat on my bed once again and stared up at the ceiling as if the words I was about to say were printed above me. "I don't think that's a good idea. I was forced to let you go a long time ago and in order to keep moving forward, I can't look behind me. So no, I don't want to meet up with you. But I wish you all the best." I heard a soft gasp before Chasity's voice filled the line. "Okay. I can respect that. Thanks for your well wishes and I wish the same for you. Bye." I hesitated but responded with what I knew was the right reply. "Goodbye." I ended the call and shook my head; feeling a huge weight being lifted off of my shoulders.

I laid down once more, my attention going to the ceiling once again. Never in a million years would I have thought Chasity would have called me. I never thought I would even speak to her again and that was fine with me. But she had, and although I had moved past her months before, that call gave me the closure I needed. I knew now that I could love someone and not worry about whether or not they would leave me. That call let me know that I had actually moved on.

I turned my T.V. off and the room was cocooned in darkness. My eyes closed and I felt myself drift off to sleep. Images that were once filled with myself and Chasity had disappeared and for that I was grateful. I was ready to give my heart to someone else and I knew who I wanted that person to be.

When I woke up, I immediately started getting ready for my day. I made my bed and then went to the bathroom to brush my teeth and wash my face. Once that was done, I walked to my closet and searched for something to wear to school. Something I hoped, Trina would like.

Dressed in Levi's Khaki's and a denim Levi's button down. I put my feet into a pair of solid white Vans. I slipped my arms into a tan jacket, grabbed my backpack, keys, and phone, and left my apartment. My stomach growled, so I made a mental note to stop and get breakfast before heading to school.

    I walked into class with my bag that held my breakfast in my hand. I walked to the back of the classroom, smiling when I saw Trina in her regular seat. When I was standing beside her, I bent to hug her and stood up straight. "Good morning. I got you a chicken biscuit." Trina smiled and accepted the biscuit, speaking as I sat in my seat. "Good morning. Thanks. I was going to stop, but when I saw the line, I quickly changed my mind." I laughed at her, handing her a few napkins after pulling out my own biscuit. "Do you need honey or jelly?" I watched the frown on her face as she unwrapped the biscuit. "No thank you, I hate both." A smile graced my lips as I pulled a pack if grape jelly out of the bag. "You're the first person I've met who shares my hate for honey. Whenever people find out I don't like it, they look at me like I've lost my mind." Trina closed her eyes to pray over her food, and then looked at me as she took a bite. "Same. Chey swears there is something wrong with my taste buds." The two of us fell into a comfortable silence, eating our biscuits quickly before class started.

    When Trina stood so that we could leave, I looked over the outfit she was wearing. The way she dressed fit her curves, but never showed them off. She was almost always in sneakers; other than the two times I had seen her in flats or combat boots. Today her outfit consisted of a black sweatshirt with the words, 'I Woke Up Like This' printed on the front in white letters. She wore some dark blue jeans and a pair of black number 1 Jordan's on her feet. Her earrings were round and flat with some words printed on them, but I couldn't make out what they read from where I stood. Her scent wafted toward me, the soft scent of her perfume causing me to want to bury my face in her neck.

"Trina, what do your earrings say?" Trina put her bookbag on her shoulders and her messenger bag over her head to rest on her hip. Once she was done, she slid her phone into her back pocket and removed one of her earrings. "I forgot. Hold on." She put the earring in front of her face and read the words in a clear, even tone. "If you can read this you are too damn close." A laugh escaped my lips as she pushed the earring back through her ear. "That's a good point." She adjusted herself on her crutches and the two of us exited the classroom.

"You look nice Trina." Trina smiled and looked down, avoiding eye contact with me. "Thank you. When you walked in class, I had the same thought about you. Those colors suit you well." My eyes went to her, the slight flush of her cheeks letting me know she was telling the truth. "Thank you. I'm glad you think so." Trina nodded, but kept her head down as we exited the building. "I'll see you later Trina. I hope the rest of your day goes well." Trina finally looked at me, a warm smile on her face. "Thanks. Same to you. See you later." I smiled and winked at her, then turned to walk away. I felt her hand touch me, so I turned so that I was looking at her again.

"What's up? Do you need something?" I watched the uncertainty on her face and smiled as she stared nervously at me. "I don't get a hug?" My smile grew and I stepped closer to her. I put one arm around her as I stepped between the crutches and squeezed gently. I held on for a few seconds before stepping away from her. "Better?" She nodded and we said our goodbyes once again before walking away from one another.

I loaded trucks while I listened to music, memories of my earlier experience with Trina bringing a smile to my face. She was starting to trust me more and more each day and that I was happy about. I wasn't certain why her trust meant so much to me, but knowing that I was gaining it, left me feeling like it would be worth it in the end.

My mind worked overtime as I worked through the night and into the early hours of the next morning. I changed clothes and exited the locker room so that I could head home. As I was getting in my car, my phone started to vibrate in my pocket. I pulled it out, and when I saw my brother's picture on the screen, I immediately started thinking the worst. I pushed the answer icon as I slid into my seat, and I spoke into my Bluetooth headset.

"What's up Juss? Everything okay?" Engine started, I pulled out of my parking spot to head home. "Yeah, everything's good. Why?" I looked at my watch, making sure I wasn't being paranoid, and when I saw the time, I knew I that I wasn't. "Because its three a.m. and you're calling me." Juss muttered a cuss word and spoke to me again. "Sorry, I didn't look at the time. I was just calling to tell you that I was bringing Honey out there next week for her spring break. She's been bugging me about coming to visit." I got out of my car with an excited smile on my face. Ever since my brother and niece had moved back east, I had missed my niece more than words could explain. Knowing they were moving back, at the end of the year made me so happy.

"That's great! When will you be here?" I could hear the smile in his voice when he answered my question. "She gets out Friday, so we're leaving Sunday and we'll be there until the following Sunday. This will be our last trip out there until we move back in November." I entered my apartment, still smiling while walking to my bedroom. "That's great! I can't wait to see my niece. And you too. I'll talk to you later though. I have an eight-a.m. class that I need to sleep for." Juss chuckled but I knew he understood. "Okay. See you Sunday. Love you little bro." "Okay. Love you too. Tell Ang I said I love her, and I can't wait to see her." Juss agreed and we ended our call.

After I showered, I got in the bed and closed my eyes. Sleep came quickly and for that I was grateful. Even if my dreams were filled with a faceless woman whom I had started a family with. A woman I had a feeling, I knew who she was.

Chapter 5:

Trina

I shielded Stephan's blows as best I could, throwing in punches whenever I could. But whenever I hit him, his hits got harder, and he got angrier. But I was tired. Tired of the abuse. Tired of the pain. Stephan was going to have to be removed from my life.

Suddenly, the blows stopped, and I was no longer being kicked in my side. My ankle that had finally healed was now sore from the wild kicks I was using to defend myself. I opened my eyes and sat up, my eyes scanning the room for Stephan. Fearing that he would come back with a weapon, I quickly got to my feet. When I turned around, Quincy was holding his brother securely, keeping his arms restrained.

"Trina, why didn't you tell me?" I shrugged and stared at the two men in front of me. With my hand to my left side, I started for my bedroom. "Get some clothes and go stay with a friend. My brother won't hurt you again if I can help it. I'll hold him until you're gone." I shook my head and held my side tighter. "Don't have many of those because of him, but okay." I rushed past them, the pissed voice of Quincy in my ear. "She should have said something. Why didn't she say anything?"

With undergarments and clothes in a bag, I rushed into the living room and toward the front door. "Go Trina. Don't tell me where you're going. Turn the GPS off on your phone." I nodded and rushed out of the apartment and to my car.

I drove to school and parked, trying to decide on who to call. Chey and my brothers were out of the question, and I really didn't trust the handful of people besides them that I knew. Except.... I searched my contacts and tapped on Jamere's name. I listened to the ringing and waited, hoping for Jamere to answer.

"Hello?" Thankfully, he didn't sound as if he had been sleeping, so I didn't have to feel bad about waking him up. "Hey Jamere. Sorry to bother you, but I have a favor to ask." I could hear the smile in Jamere's voice as he spoke to me. "Nothing you do bothers me. What's the favor?" I inhaled, grabbing my side as the pain shot through me. "My boyfriend and I got into it. Do you think I could stay the night with you? His brother told me to get out of the apartment for the night." "Sure! Do I need to come get you? Where are you?" If I wasn't in so much pain, I might have smiled, but that wasn't the case. So, I answered his questions in the order he'd asked them. "No, you don't need to come get me. I'm at school. I just need directions to your apartment." "Why don't you just put my address in your GPS?" I rotated my ankle, trying to soothe the pain that was starting to throb. "I turned it off. Don't want him to try to track me." A noise escaped Jamere's mouth, but he started giving me directions without any more questions.

I turned into Jamere's apartment complex and drove toward his building. Once I found a parking spot, I grabbed my bag and exited the car to make my way to his apartment.

I let out a deep breath and knocked on his door, waiting patiently for him to open it. A few seconds passed and the door swung open. Jamere looked at me, anger flashing in his eyes as he stared at my face. "He did this to you?" I nodded as he stepped back and let me into the apartment. "I don't feel safe with you going back to your apartment. He may be waiting for you." I stopped and waited for him to lock the door. "We don't live together. His brother will keep him at his apartment." Jamere lifted his hand to my face, causing me to flinch. But even in doing so, Jamere still put his hand on my face gently and rubbed his thumb over my bruised right cheek. "If he has a key, it won't take much to get away from his brother. At least get your locks changed. If not for your sake, for mine. Please." I stared into his eyes, as he stared at me, his hand cupped to my cheek. "Okay, I'll call tomorrow." Jamere smiled and moved his hand, taking my bag from my shoulder. "Come on. Let's get some ice for that face." I followed him to the kitchen where he opened the freezer and pulled out an ice pack. He opened a drawer and wrapped a dish towel around it before putting it in my hand. "Thanks."

"Do you want to talk about it? When I talked to you after church earlier, I never would have thought your day would have ended like this. Are you going to work after school?" Jamere directed me into his bedroom, the room that held on to his masculine scent. "I can't talk about it now. Its five a.m. and all I can think about is pain. And I have class in a few hours. I didn't either, although I should have expected it. I don't think so. I just have to figure out what to tell my supervisors." Jamere put my Adidas messenger bag on his bed and motioned for me to have a seat. I climbed on the side of his bed, holding my side, and wincing in pain.

"Maybe you should miss school. You're struggling to walk as is." I shook my head quickly while holding the ice pack to my cheek. "That's out of the question. I would have no way to get notes. And I live by my notes." Jamere stood in front of me and rested his hands on my knees. "Well at least sleep through our eight o'clock class. I'll take your tape recorder and you can copy my notes. You know I take good notes."

"Okay." Jamere smiled in victory and moved his hands. "You want to take a shower or something?" I nodded and watched him walk out of the room. He came back with a towel and a washcloth as I dug through my bag. "In my rush, I forgot my pajamas. Do you have something I can borrow to sleep in?" Jamere sat the towel and wash cloth beside me and went to his dresser. "Sure do. It will probably be too big, but it will work for tonight. Do you want pants or shorts?" I pulled out my toiletry bag, socks, and undergarments before answering his question. "Pants." He pulled a t-shirt and pants out of the drawer and pushed it closed. "Here you go. Bathroom's right there. Everything you need should be in there. If not, just let me know. I'll be in the living room. Take your time." I started to nod and stopped, remembering what happened when I had done it to Stephan. "Okay. Thank you Jamere." Jamere smiled at me and winked while backing out of the room. "You're welcome." He walked out and closed the door behind him, so I slid to the floor and walked to the bathroom.

  I stood under the steady stream of warm water, letting the heat soothe my sore body. Jamere's concern for me, I would never forget. He didn't judge me for being in the situation I found myself in, instead he welcomed me into his home with open arms, even though he didn't have to. For that, I would forever be grateful.

  I rubbed bedtime lotion over my body and slid some boy shorts up my legs. I pulled my white Nike sports bra over my head and once it was secure, I pulled the black and red checkered pajama bottoms that Jamere had loaned me, up. The black T-shirt was next, the white letters reading, 'Do Not Read The Next Line.' Underneath that in small print, the words read, 'You Little Rebel, I Like You.' I smiled and folded my dirty clothes and sat them on the floor. I stared at myself in the mirror, the bruise already starting to turn purple on my cheek. I lifted my shirt, and although my sides were sore, they weren't bruised. My stomach area was a different story entirely. I put my shirt down and pushed my pants down to my hip. A bruise started and trailed down my thigh in the shape of Stephan's shoe print. He never seemed to tire of kicking me, and I guess this time he wanted to inflict more damage. The other side looked similar, but wasn't on my hip, just my thigh. I could feel the pain on my back, but I refrained from looking at the bruises I knew would be there. I turned on the water in the sink and rinsed my toothbrush so that I could brush my teeth. Once I was finished, I brushed my hair up into a ponytail, grabbed my things, and exited the bathroom.

"Hey, I'm kind of tired. Can you show me where I'm sleeping?" Jamere yawned, stood, walked to me, and placed his hand in mine. He led me back into his bedroom and we walked to the bed. He pulled the covers back, patting the sheet with his hand. "You can sleep in my bed. I had just changed the sheets when you called so they're clean. I'll sleep on the couch." I turned to look at him, shaking my head no.

"I am not going to kick you out of your bed. I've imposed on you enough." Jamere lifted me and placed me on the bed, pulling the cover up to my waist. I continued to sit up, looking at him as he spoke kindly. "You are not kicking me out of my bed, I am offering it to you. You are not an imposition. I want you to be comfortable. I want you to know that you are safe. So, I'm going to sleep on the couch, and you are going to sleep here. No arguments." I had no fight left in me to argue with him. I was too tired emotionally and physically. So, I conceded and took what he offered. "Alright. But I don't like it. If I weren't so tired, I'd continue this fight." Jamere chuckled and pulled his shirt over his head. "I'm going to shower. Lay down." I did as he instructed, closing my eyes when his lips touched my forehead. "Good night Trina. Sleep well." I closed my eyes, his scent on the pillows tormenting me as I drifted off to sleep.

I sat up quickly, a yell escaping my mouth as I looked around the room. "Stephan Stop!" I jumped when Jamere rushed into the room, pulling my knees in front of me in fear. "Trina, it's me Jamere. You're safe. No one can hurt you." He walked towards me slowly, keeping his eyes on mine as he spoke to me tenderly. "He can't get to you here." He reached for my hand, and I hesitantly gave it to him. He sat in front of me and used his free hand to put on my face.

"How long was I asleep?" I dropped my head to rest on my knees, waiting for my heartbeat to slow to its normal rhythm. "Minutes. I just got out of the shower." I absorbed the comfort of his hand in mine, his presence calming me more than I had ever been able to calm myself. I felt so safe with him. Something I hadn't felt in a long time.

"Most nights, I'm awakened by punches, kicks, etcetera. I guess my body was expecting it to happen." I stared at the empty side of the bed, never lifting my head to look at Jamere. "I'm sorry Trina." Upon hearing those words, I lifted my head to look at him. His thumb stilled on the back of my hand and his eyes returned to mine. "You have nothing to be sorry for. I chose the wrong guy to fall in love with. The only one to blame is myself." Jamere eyed me as if he were going to say something but stopped when my phone rang beside me. Who would be calling me at six o'clock on a Monday morning, I had no idea. But when I saw my oldest brothers name on the screen, I braced myself for the lies I was about to tell.

"Hello?" Jamere's thumb started its slow rub on the back of my hand once again as I spoke to my brother. "Hey Lil Bit. I didn't wake you up did I?" The soreness in my stomach made me put my legs down, but I didn't release Jamere's hand. I tried to ignore the pain, but that was easier said than done. "What's up Tay? No, I'm awake. What's with the early call? Everyone's okay right?" I leaned my head against the headboard and waited for the point of the call. The reason he decided to call me at six o'clock in the morning. "Everyone's good. I was just calling to see if you had any free time this week. Dylan, Ryan, and I wanted to do something with you if you're free." Here it was. The lies. The deceit. But it had to be done. When I was completely free of Stephan, I'd get back on track with them. Once my injuries had time to heal, I would be back like I'd never left. But for now, this was how I had to go about it.

"No, sorry. I'm working at the club and the hotel all this week and I have school every day. Time is just not a luxury I have right now." I heard a loud sigh exit Tay's mouth and I waited for the onslaught that was about to happen. "Trina, it has been nearly three years since we've seen you. And it's not like we even live in different states. Every time we call, you turn down our invitations. You are our little sister, and we are in the dark when it comes to you over the past few years. What is going on?" I held onto what little sanity I had left. But with every call like this, it diminished.

"There is nothing going on. I'm busy. I'm working to pay my way through school. I'm being independent. I don't want to have to depend on you, Dylan, and Ryan to make it. Mom and Dad deserve to be taken care of. They took care of me all my life, so I'm going to do everything I can so I can take care of them." Tay was silent. I couldn't even hear him breathing, but I knew that he hadn't hung up.

"Tay if you're not going to say anything, I'm hanging up. I had a long night and I'm going to have to go through my day on only minutes of sleep. I love you. Talk to you later." I heard his voice as I started to move the phone from my ear, so I waited to hear what he was going to say. "I love you too. Later." *Click* I shook my head and put my phone down beside me on the bed. I looked at Jamere, his hand still closed around mine securely. "Can I have a hug?" Jamere slid closer to me and put his arms around me carefully. "It will get easier. I'm here for whatever you need." I nodded my head against his shoulder and breathed in deeply. After a few minutes, I pulled myself away from him. "Thank you." Jamere gave his infamous wink and stood up. "I need to get ready for class. Try to get some sleep okay?" I shook my head no and watched him walk to his closet. "Doubt that will happen. Meet you in front of our professor's building?" "That's cool." Jamere winked at me again and then walked into the bathroom.

"I'm out Trina. I'll leave my key with you so you can lock up when you leave. How's your ankle? Can you walk on it?" I eased to the floor and walked to where he stood in the doorway. "All good. No pain or anything. Now if the rest of my body would follow suit, I'd be set." Jamere smiled and put my hand in his. "Lock the door behind me." I nodded and, holding my hand to my stomach as I followed him through the apartment and to his front door.

    I stood, waiting patiently for Jamere to exit the building. Random people stared at my bruised face as they walked by, and as the minutes ticked by, it was getting harder and harder to ignore. "Hey Trina." I turned slowly at the sound of the male voice coming from behind me. "Hey Johnathan. How are you?" He reached for me as if he were going to touch my face. I took two steps away from him and he stopped coming toward me. "I'm great. What about you?" He stared at my cheek as he said it, but that wasn't any of his business, so I answered him casually. "I'm fine." The two of us stood in an awkward silence until I saw Jamere walking out of the building. He smiled widely at me, so I smiled back at him. When he was close to me, I held up his house key and watched him take it from my fingers. "Thank you. Later John." Johnathan nodded and said bye to me while Jamere motioned for me to walk away with him.

"How is the pain? Any better?" I shrugged, but shook my head no. "I wish there was something I could do to help." I glanced around to make sure no one was watching us before grabbing Jamere's hand and giving it quick squeeze. "You've already done enough." I released his hand and watched him dig in his pocket. "Here's your tape recorder." I grabbed it from his hand and slid it into my pocket. "We need to get to class. Thank you for recording the lecture. I'll get your notes later, okay?" Jamere smiled and hugged me before opening his mouth to speak. "You're welcome. See you later." The two of us walked away from each other, and for once, I knew I had a real male friend.

I pulled my car in next to Stephan's, fear roaring to life inside of me. I immediately pulled my phone out and called Jamere, hoping he hadn't made it home yet.

Hello?

Hey Jamere.

Have you made it home yet?

No. I'm just now leaving school. Why?

I just got home, and Stephan's car is outside. I'm scared to go in.

I'm on the way.

No, you don't have to....

You're not going in there alone.

I'll be there in a few. For whatever reason, I couldn't argue with him. As much as I wanted to, the words wouldn't come. So, I just didn't try.

Okay. Be careful.

I will.

I stayed low in my seat while I waited for Jamere to arrive.

I jumped when I heard a knock on my window and put my hand to my chest when I saw Jamere's face. I got out of the car and looked up at Jamere's tall frame. "Thank you. For coming." "Stop thanking me. I'm happy to do it." I inhaled and let it out before leading the way to my apartment.

The two of us walked inside, but Jamere walked in front of me. Trying, wanting to keep me safe, to protect me. Jamere stopped suddenly, causing me to walk right into his back. His fists clenched, and he looked at me with anger in his eyes. "Is that him?" I looked around Jamere's body, but he wouldn't let me step away from my spot. I looked at the person he was referring to. I looked at him and released my held breath before I answered him.

"No that's Quincy, his brother." Jamere glanced at Q, and then returned his focus to me. "Is he cool?" I nodded my head at him, so he moved out of the way to let me walk by. "Hey Q. What are you doing here?" Quincy smiled at me, looked at Jamere, and then answered. "Hey, I wanted to check on you. Make sure you were okay." I wanted to talk to you too. I don't think it's safe for you to be here for the next few days." I shook my head, thinking about where I was going to go. "I'm fine. This is my friend Jamere. He let me stay with him this morning. Talk about what?" Quincy looked at Jamere and then back at me. "Go ahead. He's fine. I can trust him." I motioned for Jamere to sit down, while waiting for Quincy to speak.

"First off, I'm sorry my brother has been doing this to you. If I had had any idea, I would have gotten someone to be looking out for you. But while locked up, there was only one or two ways. I could have found out. From the bottom of my heart, I apologize. The last thing I wanted was for Stephan to follow in my footsteps. Please believe that. I'm going to try to get him on the right path. Hopefully, he's not too far gone." My eyes focused on Quincy, the sincerity of his words letting me know he wasn't heartless like his brother was. I felt like I could believe him and hope that he wasn't just trying to get over on me. "Thank you for saying that Quincy. He needs help, and hopefully you will be able to help him see that. "Quincy nodded and released a breath of air. "I hope so too. Do you know where you are going to stay tonight?" My sore body went on alert at the thought of sleeping anywhere other than my own bed, but I was going to have to get over it. "I'll probably stay at the hotel I work at. I'll be alright." Quincy dug in his pocket, pulled out a wad of cash, and held it out toward me.

"What's this for?" Quincy put the money in my hand and stepped away from me. "What you deserve. What you're owed. Consider it a gift from my brother." I held it out to him, but he refused to take it. "How did you get all this?" Stephan gave me access to his account. Ever since I got out, I have seen how he treats you. You make his dinner, he complains. Do his laundry, not so much as a thank you. Clean his apartment, he gets mad. You shouldn't be treated like that. So, every week, I have been taking money out of the account and putting it aside for you. He'll never know I gave it to you because I keep showing up in new clothes. Clothes I bought before I got locked up last year. So, take it. There is a couple thousand dollars there. Between his job at the car dealership and the drugs he sells, he'll never even miss it. I have to go. I have an interview to get to. It was nice meeting you Jamere. Treat her right. She's a keeper."

"We're not together." Jamere and I told him at the same time. Looking at each other after. "Okay. But treat her right anyway. My brother has hurt her more than enough. See you both later." Jamere and I nodded and watched as he walked out the door.

"Trina, you are not staying at a hotel. You are coming back to my apartment. Don't waste money if you don't have to. Okay? I don't mind and you're not an imposition. So, pack for the week and we can leave." I knew arguing was pointless, so I walked away from him slowly. I stopped and turned around, so that I was looking at him. "Come keep me company." Jamere stood and walked to me, following me to my bedroom at the opposite end of my one-bedroom apartment.

"What time do you have to be at work?" Jamere carried my suitcase into his bedroom while I walked behind him with my laptop. He placed the suitcase on the floor in the closet and answered as he came out. "I'm off today."

I put my laptop at the foot of his bed. I wondered if he had called out or if he was actually off, but I wasn't upset either way. "I'm going to call and get my locks changed. After I finish, I have an errand to run. Will you be here?" Jamere let me know that he would be, so I dialed the rent office on my phone and walked out of his room.

When I finished the call with the rent office, I walked back in Jamere's room to get my purse. "I'm about to go. You need anything while I'm out?" He shook his head no and walked to me with his key in hand. "Come on. I'll walk you down." The two of us exited the room and walked through the apartment in silence.

Once I was in my car, Jamere put his key in my hand. "You can let yourself back in when you get back. Be careful okay?" My head moved up and down so Jamere pushed the door closed and stepped away from the car. I rolled the windows down, the warmth of the day a far cry from what it had been a week before. I pulled out of my parking spot and maneuvered my car away from the building.

I walked through the aisles, putting the groceries I would need for dinner in the buggy. The least I could do for Jamere was make dinner for him. He was being so kind to me.

Offering me his home since I was in the situation I'd found myself in. This was the thank you I would give him every day that I had to stay at his apartment. I hoped he liked Salmon because that was what was on the menu. Broiled Salmon, mashed potatoes, steamed broccoli, and cheesecake brownies for dessert. I wasn't sure if he drank, so I got a two-liter soda and hoped that would work for the night.

    I walked back into the apartment and put the groceries in the kitchen. I went looking for Jamere and smiled when I saw him sprawled across his bed sleeping. I backed out of the room quietly and walked back to the kitchen to start prepping dinner. I made a mental note to go back to the car to get my purse before the night was over.

    I peeled potatoes and cubed them, throwing them in a pot to boil. I then seasoned the salmon and set it to the side until the potatoes were nearly done. It wouldn't take long for dinner to cook, so I was able to take my time to make sure everything was just as I wanted.

    With the broccoli and mashed potatoes done, I slipped out of the apartment to get my purse out of the car. Once it was in my hand, I locked the door and walked back to the stairs.

When I walked back to the stairs, Jamere was looking in the oven.

"I wasn't ready for you to see this yet." Jamere turned around, a wide grin on his face. "The smell woke me up. I thought I was just hungry and hallucinating. It smells amazing. What's the white and brown in the brownie pan?" I pulled the salmon out of the oven and put it on the stove. I adjusted the temperature and then answered his question. "Cheesecake brownie. I hope you like sweets." Jamere's eyes lit up and he licked his lips. "Do I? I can't wait to murder those. I might eat the whole pan by myself." He laughed, but I knew there was probably some honesty to his statement. "Are you ready to eat?" Jamere nodded excitedly, so I told him to go wash up while I got his plate ready. Once he was back, he sat down and waited for me. He prayed over the food and the two of us started eating hungrily.

Chapter 6

Jamere

My eyes focused on the ceiling that I couldn't see in the dark room. I crossed my ankles on the arm of the sofa I was laying on. Trina had been at my apartment for 4 days and I was becoming more and more aware of her presence. Knowing that she was in my bed, in my room, only feet away had my body on full alert. The way she moved, trying to hide the pain in her movements, was something that broke my heart. No one should have to endure the hurt and pain she had to. And as the days passed, I longed to find Stephan and show him what it felt like to fight a man.

I heard Trina's screams that seemed to come at the same time every night. I rushed into my room as I did every night and watched her watch me walk into the room. I sat in front of her and grabbed her hands in mine. "I'm sorry. I know this has to be getting old." I moved one hand to her face and rubbed her cheek with my thumb gently. Her free hand moved to the hand I held on to her face and rested there. "There is nothing you should be apologizing for. This is a trauma. It might take a while to get past, but I'll be here for whatever you need." I watched her yawn, knowing that she needed to get some sleep. It was almost four a.m. and seven would be here before either of us realized it.

Trina moved her hand, keeping it clasped around mine, but pulled both away from her face. I squeezed her hand in mine, staring into her eyes warmly as I spoke. "You should try to get some sleep. We have school in a few hours." I slid my hand from hers and eased to the ground. "Wait! Will you stay with me until I fall asleep? Your presence calms me." Her words made a smile appear on my face and I knew that right then, I would have done whatever she wanted me to. "Sure. I'll just pull my desk chair over and I'll sit beside the bed until you fall asleep." I walked toward my desk after Trina nodded, and pulled the chair up to the side of the bed she was lying on. "Close your eyes. I'm right here." She did as told her, her eyes drifting shut as she hugged a pillow tightly in her arms.

An hour after Trina and I had fallen asleep, I heard her moving around on the bed. I opened my eyes and watched her thrash violently in her sleep. I moved my chair closer to the bed and took her hand in mine. I rubbed my thumb across it softly and she began to calm down. Once she was sleeping peacefully again, I closed my eyes and went back to sleep with my hand still holding hers.

I woke to the sound of my name being called tenderly in the otherwise quiet room. I opened my eyes and looked around to see the person who had been saying my name. "Good morning Jamere." I rubbed my eyes and stretched, noticing my hand still clasped with Trina's. "Good morning. Sorry about the hand thing. You were tossing and turning in your sleep, so I held your hand to calm you." I let her hand go, immediately feeling a rush of cool air pass over my hand. "There is nothing to apologize for. I appreciate you doing what you did. Thank you." I stood and smiled at her, stretching again before looking at her. "You're welcome. I guess we should get ready for school." Trina nodded and slid to the floor, the legs of her shorts falling from their bunched position. I returned my chair and tried to shake the image of Trina's thighs from my mind. Even with the faint bruising, they were still amazing to look at and I knew the image would be stuck in my head for days.

Trina and I rode in my car to school, listening to the weather report. I maneuvered through the streets, glancing at Trina when I was at a red light. "Want some breakfast?" Trina shook her head slowly and leaned her head against the headrest. "No thank you. I don't have an appetite." My heart ached for her, but I left her alone in her thoughts. When she wanted to talk, she would. Her mood was extremely somber, and I knew she was heading for a ridiculously dark place inside. If I could, I was going to stop it before it got to that point.

I pulled into a parking spot and killed the engine. Once I had retrieved our book bags from the backseat, I walked around the car to open Trina's door. She put her feet on the ground and stood, stepping out of the way so I could close the door. With the doors locked, the two of us walked to our morning class.

"You okay Trina?" Trina looked at me, shaking her head back and forth while tapping her desk absently. "I'll be alright. It has just been a long week." I was silent for a few seconds, trying to think of some comforting words to say. "I won't say I understand your pain because I don't. But I will say I admire your strength. Even with everything you've been through, you refuse to play the victim. That is a quality most people don't have these days." Trina's tapping stopped and she sat up straighter, her eyes landing on mine once more. I watched her eyebrows raise, the surprise evident on her face. The small smile that graced her lips let me know that I had said something that she needed to hear.

"Thank you. Thank you for saying that." I returned the smile and spoke to her kindly. "Are you working at the club Saturday?" Trina looked up as if thinking about it, and then responded. "Club yes. Hotel no. Why?" Just as she asked, the professor walked into the room. I put my finger to my lips and pointed at our professor as she started to lecture.

"Meet you at the car after your last class. Okay?" Trina slung her book bag onto her back when I handed it to her. I put an arm around her shoulders and squeezed her body to mine gently. "Okay. See you then." I let her go, winking at her playfully before we walked away from one another. She had the sweetest personality, but no one knew because of her life over the past three years. I am determined to bring that person out. I hated to see her in the shell she was in. Afraid of what she was so used to, so she kept people at a distance. Afraid that everyone was going to hurt her like her boyfriend had done for years. As painful as it is to see, I can't even imagine how painful it must be for her. My thoughts were interrupted when my phone rang as I walked to class. I pulled it out of my pocket and looked at the name on the screen. I pressed the answer icon and stuck one of the phones from my Bluetooth in my ear and spoke.

"Hello?" I waited for a reply, listening to Lloyd's voice when he spoke. "What's up Jamere? Are you busy?" I walked into the building my class was in and headed in the direction of it. "Nope, just walking to class. You need something?" Lloyd spoke once again, the sound of his radio ringing in my ear. "Yeah. Are you off tonight? I know you're usually off on Thursday's." I walked into my classroom and found a seat in the back. "Yeah why?" I waited for his reply and pulled out my materials for class. "Do you think you could pick L.J. up from daycare at around noon and watch him until I get off at 3? I'm working a double and I have to be at work at noon." I smiled because I was excited to see my nephew. I hadn't seen him since he got here, and this was the perfect opportunity to spend time with him.

"Of course, man. It's not a problem." I stood when my professor walked in and walked to the front of the class. "I'm on an emergency call. I'm going to step out and finish it." My professor nodded but started to teach as I walked into the hallway. "Great man. Thanks. I'll pick him up after I get off." I shook my head although I knew he couldn't see me. "No, you go home. I'll drop him off at daycare before school. That way you can get some sleep." I leaned against the wall and put one foot against it and waited again for his reply. "He doesn't have anything to wear though." I cut Lloyd off and spoke before he could finish. "I'm uncle Jamere. I'll pick up what he needs. Get him some stuff to keep at my apartment. He'll be good. I have a question for you though. Be honest okay?" "Okay. What's the question?" I thought about Trina and asked my question without hesitation. "My friend Trina has been staying with me this week so we can study together. I'm letting her sleep in my bed and I'm on the couch. Do you have a problem with L.J. sleeping in the bed with her? It will only be for a few hours because she works at a club and doesn't get off until 4 a.m." Lloyd was quiet for a few seconds but spoke to me as a concerned father would. "That's fine, but you have to stay in the room. I know you wouldn't bring anyone dangerous around my son, but I don't know her. So that's my one condition." I nodded to no one and stood up straight. "No problem. I understand. Let me get back in class. I'll let you know once I've picked L.J. up." "Cool. Thanks again man. Talk to you later." "Later." I ended the call and walked back into class, hoping I would be able to pick up on what I'd missed.

Trina and I walked to my car, where I held her door open and waited for her to get in. "Trina, I have to go pick up my nephew from daycare, what time do you have to be at work?" After I closed Trina's door, I walked to my side of my car, and she answered my question with a smile. "2. Uncle Jamere. That is so cute." I smiled and shook my head, easing into my seat as I replied. "Yeah whatever." When the two of us were situated, I started the car and headed to pick up L.J. "He's going to spend the night so do you want to go with me to pick him up the things he's going to need? We can be back at my apartment in time for you to get ready for work." I watched her smile. The same smile she had when she was near my little sister. "Okay. That's cool with me. How old is your nephew? What's his name?" Trina adjusted the volume on the radio and waited for me to answer her. One thing I noticed about her after seeing her interact with my sister was that she loved children. One day, I believed she would be an amazing mother.

"He's 4 and his name is Lloyd Jr. But everyone calls him L.J." I turned into the parking lot of the daycare that wasn't too far from my school and pulled into an empty parking space. "Oh okay. Well, I can't wait to meet him." I grinned at her and opened my door to get out. "I'll be right back." Trina shooed me away, so I chuckled and closed the door.

    I walked to the front desk and spoke to the woman sitting behind it. "Hi. I'm here to pick up Lloyd Anderson Jr." The woman nodded and asked for my license. I gave it to her and signed him out on the paper she told me to use. "Relation to the child?" She asked me in a dry tone. "He's my God son." She nodded her head and put my license back in my hand. "If you wait right here, I'll go get him and be right back." I nodded and looked at the artwork that was plastered all over the walls. It was obvious the children had done the artwork and the teachers plastered them all over the walls for everyone to see. I smiled when I saw L.J.'s name and turned when I heard his small voice. "Uncle Jamere!" L.J. rushed to me and jumped into my waiting arms. "What's up little man? I missed you." I waved at the woman and walked out of the building, carrying L.J. in my arms.

    I opened the door to the backseat and placed L.J. on the seat. As I buckled him in, I spoke to him tenderly. "L.J., this is my friend Trina. Trina, this is my nephew L.J." Trina looked at him, a sweet smile on her face. "Hey cutie. How are you? It's nice to meet you." L.J. smiled shyly at her, looking at his hands as I closed his door. "Hi. I'm fine. Are you fine too?" I chuckled as I eased into my seat and heard Trina's reply. Trina glanced at me, but said nothing before looking back at L.J. "Yes I'm fine too. How old are you?" I glanced in the rearview mirror as I pulled out of my parking space and watched L.J. hold up four fingers. "I'm four. How old are you?" Trina laughed, but answered his question anyway. "I'm twenty." The two of them continued to chat while I drove, listening to the conversation that was going on.

    We walked into the mall at around twelve forty-five and we walked into Finish Line to find L.J. some shoes. I only planned on buying him one pair from Finish Line, but I ended up with four. But at least I knew he would have some things at my house. We walked out and I led the way to Gap kids. L.J. had become comfortable with Trina and he refused to hold my hand. Instead, he kept his hand clasped tightly in Trina's. I found more than a few outfits for him and the three of us walked back to the car.

    Trina rushed in the apartment to change and lock up so that she could go to work. L.J. and I waited in the car for her to bring the key back to me. "Uncle Jamere, I like Trina." I smiled at L.J.'s innocent words and spoke to him in a kind tone. "That's good. I like her too." I rolled my window down and grabbed my keys that Trina was sticking through the window. "Where else do you have to go?" I thought to myself, watching Trina check the watch on her wrist. "Wal-Mart. I need to get him a car seat, some pajamas, toothbrush, toothpaste, and underwear. And some socks too." Trina nodded her head at me and stuck her head in the window. She pecked my cheek and then unlocked the doors of her car. "Yall be careful. See you when I get off." I nodded, still surprised that she had kissed me, even if it was only on the cheek. "You do the same. Let me know when you get to work." Trina nodded at me and started her car. She waved and pulled out of her parking spot, and I followed her through the complex.

    I carried L.J. to my apartment and laid him on the sofa, locking him inside while I went to retrieve my purchases. I probably spent a week's pay on him, but he was worth it. I am good at saving money, so that wouldn't harm my bank account in any way. I unlocked the door to my apartment and piled all the bags on the floor by the door. I locked it again and went outside to get the plastic dresser that I bought to put his things in. I locked my car and made my way back to my apartment. Once I was inside, I locked everything up and lugged everything to my bedroom. I put L.J's things away and walked into the living room.

I stared at him as he slept, the innocence that covered him something I wished he could hold onto forever. I sighed and rubbed his head, walking away from him and into the kitchen. With a child over, I was going to have to cook something that I knew he would eat. I looked at what I had in stock, and decided to make some cube steak, cabbage, mashed potatoes, and English peas. I went to the freezer and took the cube steak out so it could thaw. The small pack I bought would be defrosted within an hour, so I would start dinner when it was thawed.

I sat on the couch where L.J. slept and turned the TV on. I knew I would have to wake him up soon so that he would sleep when it was time for him to go to bed tonight. I hoped he would wake himself up soon, because I hated to wake him up when he was looking so peaceful.

I flipped channels and just as I set the remote down, L.J. popped his head up and looked around the room. "Did you have a nice nap?" I watched as he stretched his small body and nodded his head. "Is Trina coming back?" I smiled at his question, amazed at how quickly he had taken to her. "Yeah, you'll probably be asleep when she comes though. You'll see her in the morning." L.J. dropped his head but said nothing for a number of minutes. I knew how he felt. But I could only admit that to myself.

I returned to the kitchen to start dinner, smiling as I saw L.J. trailing behind me. I washed my hands and turned to look at him sitting at the table. "You want to watch me cook?" A sad look appeared on his face, and he answered my question. "I used to watch my mommy cook every night. I've missed her since she went to heaven." Those eight words, that one sentence broke my heart when it exited his mouth. Four years old and he was already down one parent. As heartbreaking as it was though, I know God makes no mistakes. "I know you have little man. But you still have your daddy and me too. I know it's not the same as having your mommy, but we both love you so much. We'll make sure you always remember her." L.J. nodded his small head slowly and I got started on dinner.

I got L.J.'s plate ready and sat it on the table. He went to wash his hands and came back to his place at the table. He blessed his food out loud and then started to take small bites of it. I made my own plate and sat in front of L.J. I prayed over my food and started to eat hungrily. With everything that had gone on today, I didn't realize that I hadn't eaten all day.

"Uncle Jamere, this tastes good. Daddy doesn't cook like this." I chuckled while watching him continue to put food in his mouth. "What kind of stuff does he cook?" L.J. didn't look up from his plate as he answered me. His tone was casual as if he didn't realize he had just clowned his father. "Hamburgers, hot dogs, pizza, and spaghetti." I knew that Lloyd could cook, he just cooked like a bachelor. I guess he had to get used to the fact that he had a four-year-old living with him now. Whether or not he cooked it from scratch, hamburgers and pizza were not the meals for a four-year-old to eat all the time.

"Oh okay. Are you full? Do you want anything else?" I watched as he stood and grabbed his plate from the table. "No. I'm full." He carried his plate to the sink and sat it down. "Are you ready to take your bath?" He nodded at me, so I took my plate to the sink and led him to my bedroom. "Stay right here. I'm going to go run your bath water. You should feel special; you're the first person to take a bath in my tub." L.J. grinned and then looked at me in confusion. "What about Amy?" He pulled his shirt over his head and dropped it in the hamper by my closet door. "Nope, when she spends the night she has already taken her bath at home." I walked into the bathroom and ran his water and when I turned around, he was standing there in just his underwear. "Get in. I'll bring you everything you'll need." I walked out of the bathroom chuckling when I heard the splash of water when he got in.

With L.J. clean and ready for bed, we walked into the living room, and I sat him in front of the TV. **"What do you want to watch?"** **"What time is it?"** I looked at my watch and answered his question. **"A little after eight."** **"Grey's Anatomy."** I raised my eyebrows trying to figure out how he could have become interested in a show like that. And then, it hit me. His mom probably watched it, and my heart broke all over again. If that helped him deal with the pain of his loss, then I was more than happy to turn the TV on the show for him. "I'm going to clean up the kitchen. Holler if you need me." L.J. nodded but kept his attention on the TV. I smiled at the back of his head and walked to the kitchen without another word.

I eased off of the bed when Trina walked into the room and turned on the lamp that sat on the nightstand. I had gone to unlock the door minutes before, knowing that she would be arriving shortly. That was our nightly routine, but it probably would have been easier to just have her a key made. But I didn't want her to think I was trying to get something from her. She smiled at L.J. who was laying on the opposite side of the bed and spoke softly. "Hey. I didn't wake you did I?" I walked to the closet and pulled a comforter down. "No, I wasn't asleep. I was just waiting for you to get here. I didn't want you to be shocked when you saw me asleep on the floor." Trina raised her eyebrows in confusion, glancing at the comforter I was holding. "Why would you be sleeping on the floor?" The expression on her face, I had to force myself to make my statement without smiling at her. "Lloyd told me he didn't mind if you slept in the bed with L.J. but he wanted me to be in the room. So, I'll sleep on the floor. That way I can keep my word." Trina shook her head and placed her phone on the dresser. "You can sleep in the bed; I'll go sleep on the sofa. It's not a problem." I shook my head at her, before letting her know that that was not going to happen. This was an argument we were not going to have for the hundredth time. "Not going to happen. You are not sleeping on the couch, or the floor so get that out of your head now." Trina rolled her eyes at me and retrieved her pajamas from her duffle bag. Pajamas that she had actually stolen from me.

"Well just sleep on the opposite side of the bed. We'll put L.J. in the middle and everyone will be happy." My eyes froze on her, trying to determine if she was being serious. Her eyes locked on mine and didn't stray at all. "Are you comfortable with that?" I watched her shrug her shoulders and resume digging through her bag. "Its fine. I'm going to take a shower. Be back shortly." I watched her walk away, trying to determine whether or not she would have flashbacks of the abuse she has had to succumb to for years.

"Are you sure you're okay with this?" Trina slid onto the bed, pushing L.J. gently to the center of the mattress. "Its fine. I think I know you well enough to know you won't do anything to hurt me. Get in and lay down. We only have a few hours of sleep left." I shrugged and slid on the opposite side of the bed. I usually slept shirtless, but I didn't want to make Trina uncomfortable, so I left it on and pulled the comforter up to my waist. "Good night Jamere." I smiled as I turned the light off and replied with a smile I knew she couldn't see. "Night Trina. Sleep well." We were both silent after that, but I knew I wasn't going to get any sleep. Not with a beautiful girl in my bed. Even with L.J. between us, all I could see myself doing was moving him and getting in his place. So, I stared out of the window, doing everything I could think of to try and fall asleep to no avail. I knew at that moment; it was going to be a long night.

My alarm went off as I stared at the door to my closet. I sat up automatically only to see Trina doing the same. "Sleep okay?" Trina slid to the floor and ran her hand over L.J.'s head before lifting him from the mattress. "I would have had to sleep to be able to answer that question. You?" Trina was either no longer in pain or she was ignoring it because she carried L.J. to the bathroom as if he weighed nothing. "My answer is the same as yours." I listened to her talk to L.J. sounding exactly like my mom did when I was growing up. "Use the restroom, brush your teeth, and wash your face. We'll have your clothes ready when you finish." I smiled and watched as Trina walked out of the bathroom and over to the already made bed.

"Where is his outfit? Or did you get him one out yet?" I walked past her and into the closet, pulling the hanger that held L.J.'s outfit from the bar. I laid it across the bed and watched Trina pull out his socks, undershirt, and shoes. A pair of khaki slacks, a blue and white striped Polo sweater, and blue and white Polo boat shoes was good enough for a four-year-old to wear to daycare. No jewelry other than his black Adidas watch and silver cross that once belonged to his mom. A wave of sadness crashed over me, but when I saw L.J. coming out of the bathroom, I pushed it away. "Trina, I'll get L.J. ready. You go get ready for school." Trina nodded and grabbed what she needed and walked to the bathroom.

We all got into my car, and I drove to L.J.'s daycare. He unbuckled himself from his seatbelt when I stopped in a parking spot and climbed over the seat and into Trina's lap. "See you later Trina." He put his arms around her and squeezed her tightly. "Okay little man. Have a good day at school. It was nice meeting you." Trina hugged him back, rubbing the top of his head gently. The two of them let each other go and L.J. crawled over into my lap. "I'll be right back." Trina nodded and before I opened the door, L.J. leaned over and kissed her on the cheek. "Bye." He told her with a wave. Trina smiled at him and returned the wave, speaking as I opened my door. "Bye little man." I pushed the door closed and sat L.J. on the ground and we walked to the entrance of the daycare.

I returned to my car and started the drive to school. The silence that filled the car was deafening, so I spoke to fill the void. "Do you want to get the study group together Sunday? It would be at my parent's house again because they're having Sunday dinner there." Trina replied almost instantly, relief in her voice when she spoke. "Yeah. I'm working the morning shift at the hotel, so I'll get off at one. I'll be free until eight or so." I figured she was happy to have an excuse to get out of something, and I couldn't necessarily blame her. She hadn't had the best week and it was obvious she didn't want to be bothered. "Cool, so from about 2 until when? 6? That way you can stay for dinner." I felt her eyes on me, but I kept my eyes on the road in front of me. I knew she loved Amelia, so I figured why not. This was as good a time as any to get the two of them together again.

Trina stayed silent for a few minutes but answered my question when she finally spoke again. "Do you think your parent's will be okay with that?" My eyes cut in her direction, but I didn't turn my head. "Yes. They like you and Amy loves you." I caught a glimpse of her smile before returning my eyes to the front. "Okay. Find out if I need to bring anything." My parents would probably have enough stuff to fill a store, but I would ask just to ease Trina's mind. I parked my car and looked at her sitting beside me. "Will do. Come on, let's get to class."

I held my breath as I watched the semi blow through a light. I slammed the brakes but didn't turn the wheel, because I knew that would cause more harm. When my car stopped, I was in the middle of the intersection. I put my arm across Trina's chest as the car jerked to a stop, trying to keep her body from jerking forward. The light on our side turned red and I prayed that nothing would hit us and that we would be able to get out of the intersection safely. Just as the prayer left my lips, the light turned green once again. The other side was still red, so I moved my arm and drove under the green light. My heart pounded in my chest as I continued the drive to my apartment.

"Are you okay Trina?" I felt her hand grab mine, so I looked over at her. "Me? Are you okay? That scared me and I wasn't even driving." My heartbeat returned to its normal rhythm, and I answered her question honestly. "It scared me too, but I'm worried about you. Are you okay? I'll be fine as long as you're okay." Trina continued to hold my hand but said nothing for a few seconds. "I'm fine. Just shaken up." I felt her fingers tighten around mine and relished in that. As long as she held my hand that is where it would be. I refused to let it go. If she wanted it gone, she was going to have to break contact. "Good. I'm glad." I turned into my complex and drove toward my apartment.

"I'll see you later Jamere. I made some chili while you were on the phone. It's on the stove." I nodded and followed her through the apartment and out the door. The two of us walked to her car where I held her door open for her. "Be careful." Trina winked at me, and I had to grin at her as she eased into her seat. "I will. Have a good night at work. Be careful." I gave her the thumbs up sign and pushed her door closed and watched her drive away.

Once I'd had my fill of the delicious chili Trina had made, I left home for work. It probably wasn't the best decision to eat so much, but the damage had been done. Now if I could just get through the next ten hours of work. With no sleep the night before and a stomach full of chili, I could practically feel the sleep at my back. As much as I wanted to be in my bed, I knew I had money to make. Bills didn't pay themselves and this was the cost of being a grown up.

I walked into the locker room, raising my eyebrows at Lloyd as he grinned at me. "What? Why are you grinning at me like that?" Lloyd continued to grin, walking to me, and putting his arm around my shoulders. "I talked to L.J." I looked at him as if he had lost his mind and waited for him to continue. When he didn't, I spoke. "Okay and?" I pulled my long-sleeved shirt over my head and waited for him to reply. "He told me about Trina. About how much the two of you like her." I shook my head and continued to get dressed, trying to make him believe that there was nothing going on between Trina and me. Which was true, we were just friends, but that is a common statement. "He's four Lloyd. Trina and I are just friends." Lloyd shook his head and put his shirt he wore to work on. "Okay. Well, when do I get to meet her?" I shrugged my shoulders and the two of us exited the locker room. "She's staying for Sunday dinner at my parent's house. We have a study group there at two so she's going to stay when we finish." I watched Lloyd smile and the two of us stopped in the middle of the hallway. "I'll be there. See you later. Thanks again for watching L.J. Now, I'm going to pick him up. Why he had to be picked up so early yesterday, I'll never understand." I laughed and the two of us shook hands. Once our goodbyes were said, we walked away in different directions.

My eyes were getting heavier and heavier as the minutes ticked by. So, I dragged myself to my car, praying that I would get home without falling asleep at the wheel. The weather outside was finally getting warmer and I knew that in a few weeks, the warm weather would take over the colder the weather. I was ready for the warmer weather but not ready at the same time. But I had better get ready because soon the heat would arrive, and I would have no choice but to deal with it.

I knew that I was tired because I was thinking about the weather. Something I only seemed to think about when I was tired. I realized that I had made it home, and I knew that I had never been that happy to see my apartment. I rushed inside and took a shower before going to the living room and collapsing on the sofa. Before my eyes were even closed good, I was out like a light.

I felt a soft touch on my forehead, but I didn't move from my comfortable position. The scent of perfume and smoke clouded my nostrils, but I ignored the smell and fell deeper into my slumber. I dreamed of Trina, her smile that lit up whatever room she was in. The way she interacted with my nephew and sister touching a part of me that had never been touched before. The way she cared about those she loved made me ache for her in ways I couldn't explain. Her heart was so big and knowing that she had a heart like that after being abused for years, let me know what kind of person she was. And as much as I wanted her to be the girl I took home to mom so to speak, I knew that right now, she wasn't ready. I wasn't going to pursue her, just be there for her. That was what she needed the most. And since she refused to tell her brother's or Chey what was going on, I would be the one to make sure that punk never hurt her again.

    I woke up when my alarm went off and stretched on the couch. I opened my eyes spotting Trina sitting on the floor with her head leaning against the couch. Her soft breath sounds let me know she was asleep, but I wondered how long she had been there. I shook her gently and said her name, not wanting to kick her when I moved to get off of the couch. Her eyes fluttered open, and she turned to look at me. "What are you doing in here? Why aren't you in bed?" Trina stood and folded the cover that was once over her body and waited for me to stand. "Bad dreams. Couldn't shake them. I haven't had one in two days; I don't know why they started tonight." "I'm sorry. Don't come out here and sleep on the floor though. Just wake me up and I'll sleep in a chair or something okay?" Trina nodded her head and led the way to my bedroom with the comforter clutched in her arms.

    "I'll drive today. I need something to do with my hands that won't end up with me having stitches." I raised my eyebrows at Trina but nodded my head as we walked out of my apartment. With each day, I dreaded the fact that she would be going home soon. Sunday was coming too fast, and I had already become used to having her around. But it was almost time for her to return to her apartment, and that I was not ready for. Knowing that Stephan might pop up on her at any given moment worried me in more ways than one. Although she wasn't mine to protect, I couldn't ease the knot that formed in my stomach. The thought of her being alone in her apartment, shook me to my core and I couldn't think of a way to protect her. All I could do, was hope that she knew I would do whatever she needed me to whenever she needed me to do it.

Chapter 7

Trina

I rang the doorbell of Jamere's parent's house and waited patiently for someone to open the door. I clenched my bag that had my changing clothes in my left hand, smiling when I saw Jamere's face on the other side of the door. "Hey Trina. Come on in. How was work?" The smile on his face was as gorgeous as ever and I didn't think I would ever tire of seeing it. "Work was work. How was church? Where is Amelia?" "Church was great. I have a surprise for you." I looked at him in confusion, looking down at my hand as he took my bag from it. "What kind of surprise?" We turned into the kitchen and my eyes landed on Amy and L.J. When they saw me, they both jumped up from their seats and rushed towards me.

"Trina!" I grinned as L.J. jumped into my arms and Amy held onto my leg. I squeezed L.J. and rubbed Amy's back as she kept her arms clenched around my leg. My heart swelled just being able to see the two of them. "Hey guys. How are you?" L.J. pulled back and kissed my cheek, the two of them responding at the same time. "Good. We missed you." I smiled even harder, setting L.J. on the ground so that I could hug Amy. "I missed you guys too. Have you been good?" They nodded their heads rapidly, lifting their heads to look at me as I stood up straight. "Good. Let me go change clothes and I'll play with you for a little while okay? Finish your lunch." They smiled and rushed back to the table to finish their food as I looked at Jamere. "Where are your parents?" He nodded his head toward their bedroom and led me to the stairs. "They're getting changed. They had to stop at the store after church."

I climbed the stairs in front of Jamere, stopping when I reached the top landing. He walked around me and directed me to a room to the right of the stairs. "You can change in Amy's room. I'll be downstairs." He turned to walk away, and I slid my hand into his. When his eyes were on mine, I let his hand go. "No hug?" He grinned at me and let my bag drop to the floor before putting both arms around me. I no longer flinched or jumped when he went to touch me which was an accomplishment for me. It meant I was learning to trust him, and if I had to start somewhere, I was glad it was with him. The two of us separated and Jamere winked at me. "See you downstairs." And with that, he turned and started his descent down the stairs. I walked into Amy's room and closed the door and proceeded to get changed.

I returned to the kitchen, smiling when I saw Mr. and Mrs. Dennison embracing one another. "Excuse me." The two of them turned, smiling when they saw me standing in the kitchen. "Hi Mr. and Mrs. Dennison. How are you doing?" I watched them walk toward me after they broke their embrace. "We're doing good sweetie, how about you? It's nice seeing you again." My attention strayed when a set of arms went around my leg, but I returned it to the Dennison's. "I'm okay thanks for asking. It's nice to see you again as well." I looked down once again when I heard L.J. say my name and lifted him into my arms. "Trina?" I bumped our foreheads together gently and shifted him to my hip. "Yes L.J." He rested his head on my shoulder as if he were embarrassed and spoke just loud enough for me to hear him. "You said you were going to play with me and Amy. Did you forget?" I glanced at the Dennison's who were both smiling at the child in my arms. "No, I didn't forget. I just wanted to speak to uncle Jamere's parents. I'm going to put my bag in the car and then we can play. Okay?" L.J. wiggled so that I would put him down and took my bag out of my hand. "I'll take it." I chuckled at him but stopped him before he could run off with it. "Wait for me at the front door, but don't open it. I'm coming." L.J. nodded his small head and rushed off to the front door. I returned my attention to Jamere's parents and smiled my apology.

"Sorry about that. That's children for you." The two of them chuckled quietly before Mr. Dennison spoke. "Is today your first time meeting him?" I shook my head no and let my keys jingle in my hand. "No, I met him the other day when Jamere picked him up from daycare." Smiles graced their lips as they looked at each other and then back at me. "I know you said you didn't have any younger siblings, but do you have any nieces or nephews?" I shook my head no, looking in the direction that L.J. had gone. "Not yet. He's a sweet kid, I would love to have a nephew like him. Let me go before he drags me away. I'll talk to you both later." They both nodded and walked to the counter as I walked toward the front of the house. When L.J. saw me, he opened the door and walked out, anticipating that I would be behind him. "Where is Amy?" L.J. glanced back at me, waving his hand behind him. "She's in the back yard with uncle Jamere. That's where I want to go." I popped the trunk and watched him sit the bag inside. "Alright, let's head back there." I pushed the trunk closed and put my keys in my pocket. L.J. put his hand in mine and led the way to the back of the house.

Jamere and I played kickball with Amy and L.J. for an hour or so but stopped when our classmates arrived. I held the ball under my arm and walked beside Jamere to the front of the house. "I'm going to have to leave early to shower for work. I didn't plan on getting sweaty today." Jamere grinned, leaning toward me and sniffing. "Well, you don't stink so that's a plus. Did you get your things from my apartment already?" His mood shifted, but I wasn't sure why. So, I answered his question with a shrug. "Yeah why?" Amy and L.J. ran ahead of us, bounding into the house while talking to one another. "Just take a shower here. My parents won't mind and I'm going to do the same. We'll probably eat right after the study group, so you can take one now or we could end early." I thought about what he said and figured why not. I wasn't in a hurry to go home, and the longer I could prolong it, the better I would feel. "Okay. We can just end early. That way I won't miss anything." Jamere nodded and we greeted our classmates before walking into the house. Jamere took the ball from me to put it up and I went to the bathroom to wash my hands. Once I was in the family room, I sat down, and we started to study.

  I walked out to my car after the study group ended and got what I would need for my shower. When I walked back into the house, Mrs. Dennison walked up to me. "Trina, Jamere told me you wanted to take a shower. Come on, I'll show you where everything is." Mrs. Dennison led the way up the stairs and stopped in front of a door in the hallway. She pulled it open, and I saw the shelves lined with linens. She retrieved a towel and a washcloth, handed both to me and closed the door. She walked to another door and pushed it open and turned the light on, illuminating the dark bathroom. With the light on I could see the decorations that screamed little girl.

"Ignore all the Hello Kitty and pink stuff. I refuse to let Amy wear cartoon characters on her clothes, so I figured I could at least do her bathroom in it. She's the only one that uses it. We're renovating the guest bathroom, so that one is not usable right now." I entered the bathroom and looked back at her. "It's okay, this bathroom is fine. Thanks Mrs. Dennison." She smiled at me warmly and backed away. "You're welcome. Take your time. See you downstairs. I nodded and she pulled the door closed, and I locked it behind her before walking to the bathtub and starting the shower.

I put on some lotion and then my underwear before proceeding with my outfit.

Black jeans and a white crop top because I was finally able to show my stomach again. The bruises weren't entirely gone, but in the dark club, no one would notice unless they were looking for them. I fitted a white belt to my waist and then put my sock covered feet in a pair of white Dr. Martens. I put on a black cardigan to cover my stomach while at dinner and sprayed on some Crystal Noir by Versace perfume. I checked myself in the mirror, nodding at my appearance as I turned to look at the back of my outfit. When I was satisfied, I picked up my bag, opened the door, turned the light off, and walked out of the bathroom.

    I slipped out the front door to put my bag in the car and re-entered the house again. I walked into the family room, searching the room for Jamere's face. L.J. walked to me and grabbed my hand, pulling me toward where he and Amy were sitting. "Trina, are you wearing a cardigan to a club? That doesn't seem like something you would wear to work." I chuckled and shook my head while answering Jamere. I caught a quick glance at the familiar face sitting next to him, trying to figure out where I had seen him. "No, I'm wearing a crop top. I have the cardigan on to be respectful. I'm sure your parents don't want to look at my stomach." I heard them laugh from behind me, and then Mrs. Dennison spoke. "It doesn't bother us. We were young once too. Working at a club, you had to get your tips whatever way you could. You don't have to wear the cardigan. Thank you for showing the respect though." I smiled at them and nodded my head as L.J. crawled onto my lap and played a game on someone's phone. "Thanks, but I'm okay for right now. You're welcome." I looked at Jamere when he said my name, watching him stand and walk toward me with the unfamiliar face. When they were in front of me, I moved L.J. to the sofa and stood in front of them. "Trina, this is my best friend and L.J.'s dad, Lloyd. Lloyd, this is my friend Trina." Lloyd looked at Jamere with wide eyes and then back at me.

"The same one from the other day?" Jamere stopped him with a look in his eyes telling Lloyd to shut up. Lloyd nodded and then smiled at me. "It's nice to meet you. I've heard nothing but great things." I returned his smile, flinching slightly when he held his hand out for mine. I stared at his hand before putting mine in it, pulling it away after my up and down motion. "It's nice to meet you too. You have a great son. He is so sweet." A smile filled with love formed on Lloyd's face as he looked down at his son still playing on the phone in his hand. "Thank you. That's my big man." The two of them walked back to their seats and I sat back down, Amy and L.J. both perching themselves on one of legs. I looked over L.J.'s shoulder and watched him swipe the screen while playing Subway Surfers. I smiled at his small fingers swiping at the screen to avoid the obstacles that were in his way. I looked over at Amy, smiling widely as she read from the book that was in her hands.

"What are you reading Amy?" She kept her eyes on the pages of her book and answered my question without lifting her head. "The Indian In The Cupboard." I raised my eyebrows and looked at the Dennison's before looking back at the book in her hands. "What reading level are you on? You're only six, right?" Amy nodded her head and then looked at me. "Yes, I'm six. I'm reading at a fourth-grade level." My eyes widened and I looked over at her parents. "That's great. You both must be very proud." The pride showed on their faces as they nodded their heads up and down. "Tremendously. And she pretty much taught herself. We started teaching her the alphabet at about two. Once she had that down, Jamere taught her the sounds the letters made, and on her third birthday, she had read 'The Cat In The Hat' by herself. By five, she was reading second grade chapter books. I'll never forget the day she came home after being in kindergarten for two months. She had gone to the library at school and picked out Matilda by Roald Dahl. The teacher didn't believe that she could read it so she asked me to record her so that the teacher could see her read it. Her teacher was so shocked, she couldn't teach that day. Within two weeks, she was in an advanced reading class. Now, she's in the gifted program and she is about to move up another grade level in English and reading."

  I didn't know what to say, but I stood up and watched Amy read quietly, seemingly oblivious to the fact we were talking about her. "Wow! That's amazing." Mrs. Dennison stood, and spoke so that everyone could hear her. "Guys go wash your hands so we can eat. The little ones, Jamere, and Trina have school tomorrow. Trina has to be at work in a few hours also." Everyone who wasn't already standing stood and walked to bathrooms, while Mrs. Dennison walked into the kitchen. "Do you need help with anything Mrs. Dennison?" She stood at the kitchen sink washing her hands, her eyes going to mine when I spoke. "No but thanks anyway. Everything is already set out like I want it." With a nod of my head, I turned and went to wash my hands.

I stood behind the bar, people watching and serving drinks. After spending the majority of the night on the floor, I got sick of getting hit in the stomach, so I switched areas with someone else. From my position behind the bar, I could see the entrance of the club. I watched as people continued to flood into the building, even with it being after two a.m. I had no problem with that, because the more people that came in, the more tips I was liable to make. Those tips would help me in my move that I desperately needed to make. My lease was up in two months, and I didn't intend on renewing it. I needed to free myself from any memory of Stephan, and my apartment was filled with horrible memories of my time with him. So, it had to go as well.

I handed a patron his drink, smiling when I looked into the eyes of my best friend. "Hey Trina." I glanced at another patron, smiling at him when he told me what he wanted. "Hey girl. Still mad at me?" She knew not to lie, because I could read her like a book. So, she nodded and spoke over the music that was blasting through the speakers. "Yeah, but I should have never just stopped talking to you. We've been friends too long for that. So, I'm sorry. Not for being mad but refusing to talk to you for as long as I have." I retrieved the money from the patron, smiling my thanks at the ten-dollar tip he left me. I waited for him to walk away before replying to Chey. Just as I started to speak, someone else walked up to the bar and ordered a drink. "It's cool. I know why you were mad, and I don't blame you. I figured you would talk to me when you were ready." Chey nodded as I gave the girl her drink and accepted her payment. "I came by your apartment earlier, but you weren't there." I kept my eyes on the bar I was wiping down and replied to her statement.

    Thankfully, I wasn't going to be lying this time. "I worked the morning shift at the hotel and then I had a study group with Jamere and four other people from class." Chey sipped from her drink and turned her back to me and watched people dance. Seconds later, she turned around with a grin on her face. "What?" I asked her in confusion. She nodded her head behind her, so I looked in the direction she was motioning to. When I saw Jamere walking toward the bar, I had to force myself not to grin.

    Jamere's ever present smile was plastered on his face, and I had to admit to myself, that I was glad he was in my life. If for no other reason, so I could see that gorgeous smile on a regular basis. When he stopped in front of me, I gave him a casual smile and nodded my head toward Chey. "Jamere, you remember my friend Cheyenne. Chey, you remember Jamere." Jamere's eyes stayed on me, but I acted as if I didn't notice as he spoke. "Yeah. What's up? How are you?" Cheyenne nodded her head and grinned inconspicuously at me. "Nothing much. I'm good. What about you?" This was an awkward conversation for them to be having in a club, but hey what could I do? "I'm cool." Cheyenne nodded and looked back at the crowd again.

"What are you doing here?" His grin returned to his face, and he mouthed his answer. "Missed you?" I rolled my eyes, but his words touched me on an intimate level. One I had never before experienced with anyone. "Sure, you did. You just saw me a few hours ago." Jamere chuckled, but I could barely hear it over the loud music. "Really though. Why are you here? Do you want something to drink?" I looked over at the guy that walked to the bar and took his order. Once he had his drinks and he had paid, I returned my attention to Jamere. "I just want to make sure you get home safely." I felt the smile form on my face, knowing that Cheyenne was listening as much as she could. I knew, before the end of work the following day, she would have interrogated me as if I were on trial.

"Well, I don't get off for a little over an hour. I'll be alright. Go home and get some sleep." Jamere shook his head at me and sat on an empty barstool. "Not going to happen. Can I get a Sprite?" I nodded and grabbed a glass and went about the process of making his drink. "How much do I owe you?" I shook my head at him and sat the drink on the bar. "Nothing. It's on me." He winked at me and picked the glass up and sipped from it. "Thank you." I nodded at him and went back to work, waiting for the next hour and a half to pass by.

Chey, Jamere, and I exited the club at 4:30 and walked to our cars in the parking lot. "I'll see you at work tomorrow Chey. Be careful going home." Chey smiled and nodded, waving at Jamere while opening her door. "Later Cheyenne. Be careful. Let Trina know when you've made it home." Chey gave him the thumbs up sign, sat in her seat, and started the engine before pulling away from her parking spot. The two of us walked toward my car, looking up when we heard some thunder in the distance. "The rain is coming. I knew it would be here this week. It's been too long since it last rained." I pushed the unlock button on my key fob and nodded my head at Jamere. "Yeah. I have a feeling it's going to flood. That's what happened the last time it went this long without raining." Jamere opened my door and waited for me to get in the seat. "Yeah, I'm going to put some clothes and stuff in my car before school in the morning. I don't want to get stranded in only what I have on. I sat on my seat with my feet on the ground and looked up at Jamere standing in front of me. "That's a good idea. Even if I get stranded at the hotel, at least I'll have clothes and stuff. I doubt I'd go to the club if the weather got that bad." A yawn escaped my lips and Jamere grinned. Come on, let's get you home so you can get some sleep. I nodded and put my legs in the car. Jamere pushed my door closed and walked to his own vehicle.

    I drove the short drive to my apartment, Jamere trailing behind me. When I was in front of my building, I parked and killed the engine. I got out of the car and popped the trunk to retrieve my bag. I saw Jamere pull his car in a few spaces away before he got out of his car and walked toward mine. I pulled my suitcase from the trunk and sat it on the ground before reaching inside once again for my small Nike duffle bag. I closed the trunk and turned around to see Jamere gripping the handle of my suitcase. He grabbed my duffle bag from me and hung it from his shoulder, leaning the suitcase so that he could pull it behind him. "You don't have to help me. I've got it." He continued to hold my bags, staying silent while waiting for me to walk toward my apartment. I smiled to myself and led the way to my apartment with him following closely behind.

The two of us walked into the apartment, Jamere leading the way to make sure no one was there. I'd had the locks changed and told the apartment manager that Stephan was no longer welcome, but the manager couldn't guard my apartment 24/7, so He was still able to get to my apartment even if he couldn't get in. The changed locks weren't enough reassurance for Jamere though. He walked into my bedroom and sat my things in front of the closet before checking out the rest of the apartment. When he returned to my room, I was in a T-shirt that stopped at my belly button and a pair of pajama bottoms. "Everything is all good. If you need anything call me. Okay? I don't care what it is." I nodded at him, smiling as he turned to walk out of my room. "Come lock the door behind me." I followed him through the apartment to the front door, watching him open the door and turn to me. "Good night Trina. Sleep well." He hugged me closely and pulled away so that he could kiss my cheek. "Good night. I'll try. Let me know when you've made it home." Jamere smiled at me, holding the doorknob in his hand. "Lock the door as soon as it's closed. Don't try to wait for me to get in car. We don't know if he's lurking somewhere." I nodded my head, closing my eyes as he kissed my forehead quickly. "I'll see you in class. Later." He waved at me and pulled the door closed, so I immediately locked the door behind him. I rushed to the window in the living room and watched him get in his car. I waved when he looked at me, watching him wave back before sliding into his seat. I waited until he had driven away before leaning against the wall and shaking my head at myself. How I let myself like him after the relationship I was still technically in, I would never understand. The technicalities of that were about to be over though. I was about to break up with Stephan, officially, over the phone. And not just over the phone, but through text. I returned to my room and picked up my phone from the dresser. I sat on my bed and started the text that would end the horrible relationship I'd allowed myself to be in for the past three years.

Stephan, this is just a courtesy, but at this point you should already know what I'm about to tell you. This relationship is OVER, in every sense of the word. You know the reasons why, so I won't belittle

myself by summarizing the things you have done to me over the past three years. As you have probably already noticed, I've changed the locks as well as informed the manager that you are no longer welcome. So, if you are caught anywhere near my building, the police are going to be notified. I will mail your things to you, along with the key to your apartment. If I never see you again, it will be too soon. Goodbye.

    I didn't expect a response, especially not at five in the morning, so I put my phone on the charger and laid down. I stared at the ceiling, waiting for Jamere to let me know that he had made it home. Fear crept in, and I knew that I would never be able to sleep alone in this apartment again. My phone vibrated, so I picked it up, expecting it to me Jamere. But when I saw Stephan's name attached to the text, I began to fear the worst. I opened the text and read the words that he had typed.

    This is not the last you will hear or see of me. You will learn to respect me, even if I have to beat it out of you. The fat excuse of an apartment manager can't, new locks can't stop me, the police can't stop me, and YOU WON'T STOP ME! I will get to you, and you will be mine and no one else's. Just wait for it.

And just like that, I was wide awake. I hadn't expected to get a response, especially not one like the one I had just received. So, sleep was out of the question. I jumped when my phone vibrated in my hand indicating a text from Jamere. I opened it, and read the words on the screen, hoping they would calm me, even if only slightly. **Hey Trina. I made it home. I'm going to bed. See you in the morning.** My hands trembled as I sent my reply, wishing that I had just told Jamere to stay with me overnight. **Okay. Thanks for everything. Sleep well.** I got off of my bed and went to the closet. I pulled out clothes to pack in the event it flooded. I unpacked my clothes that had been with me at Jamere's and replaced them with the clothes I had just taken from the closet. I put a few pairs of pajamas and socks inside, shoes, and then underwear. I zipped the bag up and stood it by the door so that I could grab it before walking out in the morning. I sorted my clothes from the previous week and took them to the laundry room to wash. That was sure to help the time pass until it was time for me to go to school. If only I could get through the next few hours without looking over my shoulder in fear.

"Did you get any sleep after I left?" I yawned as Jamere spoke to me loud enough so only I could hear him. "No." I yawned again, while trying to keep my eyes open. "Here, drink this. The sugar should keep you awake at least long enough to get you through class." I shook my head no, stifling another yawn as he held out the bottle of orange juice out to me. "Jamere, I'm not going to drink your juice. I'll be fine once class starts." I watched him open the bottle and hold it out to me again. "I bought this for you. I got you some breakfast too, but at this point that may only serve to make you sleepier. Drink it." I took the bottle from his hand and took a few sips, grabbing the lid that he held out to me. "Thank you." Jamere winked at me, his face filling with concern. "Why didn't you sleep last night? Nightmares?" I shook my head and thought about lying to him, but I was sick of all the lies. And I refused to start lying to Jamere, so I pulled up the message from Stephan and handed my phone to him.

"Read the last two messages." Jamere looked down at the screen and read the words, his fists clenching tightly in anger. "Why didn't you call me? I would have come back." My shoulders moved up and down as I opened the bottle and sipped from my juice again. "I've occupied too much of your life as is. I wanted you to be able to sleep in your own bed again." I gripped the bottled tightly in my hand, avoiding eye contact with him. I knew what he was going to say, but I couldn't continue to invade his life the way I had been.

"I don't have a problem with you, 'occupying my life' as you put it. I want you in my life, and when stuff like this happens, I want you to come to me. I looked at Jamere, the sincerity in his eyes melting my heart. Something that I had never before experienced. "Sorry." Before I could say anything else, Jamere was replying. "You have no reason to be sorry. Just know that I am not, nor will I ever be like Stephan. I want to be here for you, and I want to help you. But you have to let me. Okay?" He grabbed my hand that was closest to him and gave it a gentle squeeze. "Okay. Thank you." The entire class flinched when a crack of lightning illuminated the sky, and the power went out. Within seconds, our professor was entering the classroom.

"Everyone go home. School is canceled until further notice. There is a flood coming so everyone be careful. Get home as quickly and as safely as you can. If you don't have to stop, don't." Everyone grabbed their things and rushed out of the classroom as quickly as possible. "Jamere, come to my apartment with me. We don't know how far out this flood is and I don't want you to be caught in it. Did you get your stuff like you said you were going to?" When I saw him nod, I nodded my own head. Come on. We can go the back way." Jamere nodded and followed me, to the parking lot. We couldn't get to each other with the traffic, so I called him and told him what way to go. When I saw him in my rearview mirror, I pulled off and led the way to my apartment.

  Jamere and I retrieved our bags and locked up our vehicles. The rain had already soaked our clothes, but at least we would be able to change when we got inside. We walked, trying to power through the wind and rain that was whipping past us, causing us to stumble a few times. Just as we were about to walk into the breezeway, we heard a loud cracking sound. We turned our heads just as a tree started its descent toward the ground. My eyes widened and I looked at Jamere, yelling his name as I tried to get to him through the rain that was making it hard to see anything around me.

Chapter 8

Jamere

"Jamere!" I turned my head in the direction of Trina's frightened voice but was only greeted with rain. I felt around in front of me, until I felt an arm in my hand. "Jamere, are you okay? I saw the tree fall but I couldn't see you." "I'm fine. Let's get inside before anything else happens." I pulled her arm gently so that she would move, only moving when she was in front of me. We fought through the heavy rain, thankful when we made it to the door of her apartment. The two of us rushed inside and pushed the door closed, our wet clothes dripping water on the floor. I watched Trina pull her shirt off and drop it on the floor. She looked at me and then at the bag I held in my hand. "Are any of your clothes dry, or did the water soak through too much?" I pulled my shirt over my head and dropped it before opening my bag and checking the clothes inside. "It all seems to be dry." Trina nodded her head and picked up our wet shirts. "Good. Come on." I followed her through the kitchen to the attached laundry room. "Take your wet stuff off and put it in the washer and when the lightning and thunder stops, I'll wash them. I'm going to go get some dry clothes to wear." I nodded my head and unbuttoned my pants while Trina dropped our shirts in the machine. After doing so, she exited the room and walked in the direction of her bedroom.

Visions of Trina standing in front of me topless played over and over in my head. I don't think I had ever seen a body more beautiful than hers. I knew that tonight, as well as many future nights, that sight would keep me up. The smooth caramel skin, the tattoo on her right shoulder blade. That was sure to haunt me for days on end. I stepped into some dry boxers and basketball shorts just as Trina walked back into the laundry room. If she had walked in seconds earlier, she would have seen me completely naked. The thought of that, sent a distinct feeling of heat throughout my body. "Everything in there? The lightning and thunder have stopped for the time being." I dropped my soaked boxer briefs in the machine and nodded my head. "That's it. You look comfy." A grin appeared on her lips, and she dropped her clothes in on top of mine, added detergent and fabric softener, and then closed the lid to start the washer. She stood wearing one of my school hoodies and a pair of purple sweatpants. Colorful socks covered her feet, and her hair was pulled back into a low ponytail. How she had managed to sneak my hoodie out of my apartment, I didn't know. "Nice hoodie. Looks familiar though." "It should. I took it from your closet while you were working a double the other day. The nightmares wouldn't stop, so I put it on because it smelled safe. Like you." The two of us stared at each other for several minutes before Trina grabbed my hand and pulled me out of the laundry room.

"No homework, too early to make dinner, so we can watch a movie." I nodded and sat on the sofa while she searched her collection quietly. I adjusted the T-shirt I was wearing, watching each of Trina's movements that were probably not meant to be sexy. There wasn't much that Trina could do that wouldn't come off as sexy to me though. "The Maze Runner?" I nodded my head, waiting for Trina to put the movie in. Once the previews started to play, Trina stood. "I'll be right back." She walked away from me, and I had to force myself not to follow her with my eyes. Every passing moment, I was more and more thankful that I was given the opportunity to be a part of her life in whatever capacity possible.

Trina plopped down on the sofa next to me, resting her feet on the coffee table in front of us. "Do you want something to drink or eat?" Her focus was on the T.V., her hands rubbing together absently. Although her question was directed at me, you wouldn't know by looking at her. "No, I'm good. I stopped for breakfast on the way to school. I brought you some too, but the rain ruined it. Sorry." Trina glanced at me, a slow smile easing onto her lips. "I appreciate the thought. That's what counts. Thank you." She went back to looking at the T.V., her hands rubbing together once again. Whether it was nerves or fear, I wasn't sure. Looking at her stiff body, I knew that I was going to use this time to find out. I stared at her for a number of seconds before parting my lips to speak.

"Trina, do I scare you?" Her head spun around until she was looking at me with wide eyes. "Of course not. Why would you ask me that?" I ignored her question and asked another question of my own. "Well, am I making you uncomfortable?" Trina stared at me for a few seconds, shaking her head and looking away. "No. Why?" I stared at her, watching as she dropped her head. There was so much about her that I didn't understand. So much that I desired to learn. But the closer we got, the harder I realized it would be.

"You seem nervous. You're stiff and you won't look at me for more than a few seconds. Tell the truth. If I make you uncomfortable or afraid, let me know. As soon as the storm breaks, I'll leave." Trina looked at me and slid closer, taking my hand in hers. She gazed into my eyes, her expression letting me know she was going back and forth with herself in her mind.

"Jamere, you don't scare me, and you don't make me uncomfortable. Honestly though, you do make me nervous." My mind started to come up with reasons why I would make her nervous. Tried to figure out why I couldn't realize that I made her nervous. "How do I make you nervous?" Trina's hand loosened in mine, a sigh escaping her lips as her eyes locked on something behind me. "I don't know. Before I met you, I was pretty much afraid of every male I came in contact with. But I have never been afraid of you. I feel safe when I'm with you. And that makes me nervous. The fact that you don't scare me. The fact that I'm not uncomfortable around you. The fact that I like you, even though I shouldn't." My thoughts rushed through my mind, trying to make some sense of what Trina had just revealed. The words she said, I never expected her to verbalize. I thought she was too hurt and too filled with memories to even think of me in any way other than friends. But I was obviously wrong on more than one level. My happiness couldn't be denied though. At least I knew I had a chance. At least I knew, that with time, she and I could develop our relationship on a more intimate level.

"Trina, look at me." Her eyes came back to land on mine. She let her hands slide completely out of mine, the empty feeling making me reach for them again. Trina made no effort to grab them, so I took the initiative and grabbed them myself. "You know I would never push you to do anything. I would never go there, knowing what you are just coming out of. Hard as it may be, I respect you too much to go where I know you're not ready to go." Trina's eyes became low, almost to the point of being closed. I could read the sadness in them and knowing that she thought I didn't like her hurt me in a deep part of my heart. "Make no mistake, I like you too. But there is a time for everything. Right now, is not our time. But when our time comes, believe me, it will be well worth the wait." Trina's eyes became brighter, some of the sadness washing away. Her next words were soft, but sincere, and I knew that she was happy with my words.

"I can honestly say I believe you. You're right, now is not our time. But as long as I have you in my life, even as just a friend, I'll be happy." She smiled when I winked at her, and I reluctantly let go of her hand. "Ditto. We can watch the movie now." Trina looked at me with a smile and pressed play on the remote.

She slid herself back on the couch until her back was touching the cushions.

Trina's sleeping body was curled into mine, her head resting on my chest. Knowing she trusted me enough to curl into me as she had, warmed my heart. I tried to move her, but she curled closer to me and continued her much needed slumber. Since it was obvious I wouldn't be turning the television, I leaned my head back and closed my eyes in an attempt to fall asleep.

My eyes fluttered open and when I saw Trina's face in front of mine, I raised my eyebrows at her. She rubbed her thumb over my bottom lip, resting it on the scar I knew was there. The heat that accompanied desire pooled in my stomach and it was impossible to ignore it. "How did you get this scar?" I forced myself not to lick my lips and pull her thumb into my mouth. A few seconds later, I was able to answer her question. The memory I hated but with everything I had witnessed with Trina, I knew this was something I could share with her.

"When I was about 14, my brother and I walked in on our biological father abusing our mother. So, we rushed in to defend her. He then pulled a knife out and tried to stab her. I pushed her out of the way, and because of it, he came at me with the knife. My brother and I fought him, but I got distracted and ended up with a sliced lip. Four stitches later, I'm left with this scar and the memories that go along with it." Trina's thumb rubbed over the scar once again before she pressed her lips to it in a fleeting kiss. A kiss so quick, it was almost nonexistent. But it was a kiss I would feel for days. "What was that for?" Trina backed away from me, plopping back onto the sofa. "Just for being you. Your strength, your compassion. It's not every day you meet someone with all of those qualities. I'm glad that I have met someone who does." In just a few seconds, our relationship had shifted once again. And each time it shifted, the harder I knew it would be to keep my word.

    Trina stood and looked at her phone, pulling my hoodie over her head. The white tank top she wore underneath it bunched up, exposing her beautiful skin. My eyes stared at her, not hiding the fact that I was looking at her. I didn't care that she may have seen me staring because she was beyond beautiful to me. Even with the barely there bruises, she was more beautiful than anyone I had ever seen before. I don't think I would ever tire of looking at the beautiful woman I had come to know. "I'm going to see what I can whip up for lunch. Any food allergies?" I shook my head back and forth watching her drape my hoodie over the back of the sofa before walking away.

    Trina was once again curled into my side, sleeping peacefully after the two of us had eaten lunch. Trina jumped when someone started banging angrily on the door. "Trina! Open the god damn door!" My head turned in her direction and her body stiffened. "Stephan." She told me in a soft tone. My fists clenched at my sides, and I stood to my feet. I felt Trina tug on my arm, so I put my focus on her again. "I don't want him to hurt you. I care about your safety more than I am afraid of him. Please, just let me get rid of him." Trina stood, preparing to walk to the front door. "Not going to happen. I'm not going to risk you being hurt again. I'm going to get rid of him and he won't bother you again. Stay here. I've got this." I waited for her to sit down, listening to the banging on the door. I took my time walking to the front door because I knew he wasn't going anywhere, no matter how long I took. I stopped at the door with my hand on the knob, inhaling deeply before unlocking it and pulling it open.

    I looked at the guy in front of me, the anger on his face increasing when he saw that I wasn't who he expected. Stephan tried to push past me, but that was not going to happen. Years of playing football taught me how to block and he wasn't going to get anywhere near Trina. I didn't care what he tried. "Who the hell are you? Move out of the way! Where is my girl?" I kept myself as calm as I could, stepping out of the apartment and pulling the door closed behind me. He was seething, but I knew his anger didn't top mine. His face was twisted in anger, his light complexion a dark shade of red. He clenched his fists tightly at his sides as if he were preparing to swing at me.

"Look Stephan, if it weren't for my friend in there, I would be kicking your ass all over this complex. I don't care about the rain or the floods, as long as I know Trina is safe, I would risk any and everything to make sure you never hurt her again. But because of my friend in there, because I respect her and her home, I'm not going to do that unless you push me to. Now, Trina is no longer your girl. I saw the message she sent as well as your reply. Come near her again and I'll kill you myself. This is the last she is going to hear from you. No one respects a man who beats and abuses women. The apartment manager might not be able to stop you. The police and new locks may not be able to stop you. But believe me when I say this. Listen and I mean listen well. I will stop you, by any means necessary. Trina is no longer your concern and if I hear anything informing me that you have done anything to her, I will hunt you down. Now leave and don't come back."

Stephan's anger intensified, but I knew he wouldn't try to hit me. Usually if a man would hit a woman, he wasn't man enough to hit another man. "Who the hell are you to tell me what I can and cannot do? Where is Trina?" I stuffed my hands in my pockets, trying to stop the overwhelming need to punch him. The wind blew the rain into the breezeway, soaking my once dry shirt. I ignored the wetness, keeping my eyes focused on the disgusting boy in front of me. "I'm a man first. A friend second. That's all you need to know." Frustration surged through him, and he squared himself up at me. "Tell that bit-." Before he could finish his statement, my fists were out of my pockets. My right hand swung and connected with his right jaw and my left fist followed suit and connected with his left jaw. I watched his body fall to the ground, a splash of water signaling his landing.

"This is my only time saying this. Get the hell out of here!" I watched as he got to his feet and stared at me with fury all over his face. "Disrespecting Trina will not be tolerated around me. Take heed to that." After my last word had been spoken, I walked back into the apartment and locked the door. When I turned around, Trina was standing there, looking at me with tears welling in her eyes. "I take it you heard that?" She closed the space between us and put her arms around my soaked body. "Trina, let me change. I'm soaking wet." Her grip didn't loosen, and her next words had me fighting for control of my emotions, among other things. I put my arms around her, relishing in the way her body fit against my own. I didn't think I would ever feel the way I felt with her, with anyone else in my arms. And as I stood, holding Trina with my lips pressed against the top of her head, realization hit me. I never, wanted to hold anyone other than Trina Hart as long as there was breath in my body. That simple realization had my heart thumping rapidly in my chest. Trina was no doubt feeling it, but I couldn't do anything to stop the rapid beating of my heart that she caused.

Trina let go of me, so I pulled my wet shirt over my head. Trina kissed my cheek, speaking softly as her eyes trailed down my body. "Thank you Jamere." My lips burned to meet hers, to show her the desire, the passion that she filled me with. But as much as I wanted to, I couldn't rush her. I would give her time to move past the abuse she had been through, and I would be waiting for her the second she was ready.

"There is no need for you to thank me. As long as I'm around, no one will hurt you again. And I put that on everything." The way she stared in my eyes, the way the fire flashed in them, I knew we were in for a long day. Being trapped in her apartment was not the best place for me right then, but what could I do? "I'm going to take a shower." Trina grabbed my hands and inspected them carefully before speaking. "Your hands are bleeding and slightly swollen." My head shook from side to side as I watched her fingers trail gently over mine. "It's not my blood. I'll be back in a few. If I don't get away from you right now, I won't be able to control my actions." Trina released my hands, a sexy smirk appearing on her gorgeous face. "See, that right there is why I'm going to shower. By the time I'm home, I'll be the cleanest person in America." I watched her wink at me, so I turned quickly and walked away from her.

I sat on the sofa and Trina stood and walked away. I was curious as to where she was going, but I didn't ask. I stared at the TV screen and tried not to count the seconds until Trina was beside me again. Commercial after commercial played, but I paid no attention to them. There was one thing, or rather one person on my mind. Trina Hart was where my mind was, and nothing else would take it off of her.

Trina re-entered the room and sat next to me while holding a towel in her hand. She reached for my swollen hands and placed them on her lap. The towel was obviously filled with ice, so she rested the towel on top of my hands and left them there as she turned her attention to the television.

Minutes after placing the hand towel on my hands, Trina lifted it and pressed my knuckles gently with the tips of her fingers. "Any pain, numbness, or anything?" I opened and closed my hands slowly while responding to her. "Pain is minimal. Nowhere near unbearable. No numbness or anything though." Trina put the towel on my hands once again, nodding to herself and then reaching for the remote.

My eyes took in every inch of her, memorizing every inch of her face as she flipped channels absently. Without thinking, I opened my mouth and let exactly what was on my mind flow from my mouth. If I were going to stop, it was too late because the words spilled out and despite my best efforts, I couldn't catch them.

"You are beautiful. If I had to pick one word to describe your beauty, your heart, your mind, and your body, that word wouldn't do you justice. If I had your heart to protect, you would never have to worry about it being broken again. You are beautiful from the inside out. No one has ever filled my heart the way you have, and we're not even together. I just wanted to tell you that. I wanted to make sure you knew that you hold a place in my heart that no one else ever has."

Tears welled in her eyes, but she quickly blinked them away. "No one has ever said anything like that to me. And hearing it come from you, makes me want you that much more. As much as I know I shouldn't want you this much, I can't stop myself. The pull you have on me is stronger than anything I've ever experienced before. I have to get away from you now. If I don't, there's no telling what I may do." Trina stood and pulled my hoodie over her head. "That is covered in your scent. That will only make matters worse right now." I nodded my head and watched her walk out of the living room and towards her bedroom. I forced myself to stay in my seat, which I realized was harder than it should have been.

Chapter 9:

Trina

"Cheyenne. I need your advice. I'm falling and I mean hard! I'm trying not to, but it's not the easiest thing to do. Especially when I'm flooded in with him right now." Cheyenne was quiet for a number of seconds before she spoke to me. "I'm alright. Bored as hell though. This flood sucks. What about you?" I heard her giggle, so I rolled my eyes to myself. "How are you Chey? I'm sorry you're bored. The flood is not a problem for me right now though. Now help me!" Cheyenne hesitated briefly and spoke to me in a tone that let me know she was being serious. "You've been with Stephan for 3 years. I'm surprised you hadn't fallen for him before now. "Guilt seeped in, but I refused to let it take over. I owed Chey an explanation, but now wasn't the time for it. "I broke up with him the other day. He's not who I'm falling for." "If it's not Stephan then who is it? In the past three years, I've never seen you show interest in anyone but him. And as much as I don't like him, I chose to respect your decisions, even after seeing how he changed you. And not for the better." I took in Chey's words and discovered that maybe I had changed more than I realized. And for her to say something about it, I know it must have been a change no one liked. "I'm sorry. I didn't realize that. But it's over now, I promise. Help me though. I can't fall for someone less than three days after breaking up with Stephan." The tone of Chey's voice let me know that she was about to get very serious, so I listened to her words and responded when it was needed. "You have to tell me who this guy is, even if I don't know him. I want to know what his name is." I stared at my bedroom door as if I could see through it. As if I could see Jamere sitting on the sofa where I had left him. "You've met him before. At the club." Before I could say his name, Chey spoke it with a smile in her voice. "Jamere? The guy in your class?" A smile spread across my face, and I was thankful Chey couldn't see. She would definitely know I had it BAD!

"Yeah." Cheyenne giggled like a schoolgirl with a crush, easing a chuckle out of me. "If you really feel that seriously for him, let yourself fall honey." My head shook from side to side, and I replied before she could finish her statement. "But that's not right." I stared at a picture of Stephan that was on the wall, my feet carrying me to where it was. I took it off of the wall and dropped the picture and its frame in the trash and repeated the process with each one I saw. "Says who?

Look girl, if you find one that makes you fall that hard, you let yourself fall. Because if you wait too long, you may miss out on him. At the very least, just give him a chance. He seems like a good dude, and I know he has to be better than Stephan."

On that, I couldn't argue. At this point, almost anyone would have to be better than Stephan. He abused me physically and emotionally, and that I knew Jamere wouldn't do. His heart was too big. Too kind. But fear still shook me. Although I knew Jamere wouldn't hurt me, I was afraid Stephan would go to whatever lengths to make sure I was hurt. And that made me worry about Jamere's safety above all. "I see what you're saying, but I'm afraid. Afraid of being hurt. Afraid of having my heart broken." What I told Cheyenne wasn't really a lie, it was more of an omission. One day after the flood passed, I would tell her everything. But right now, I couldn't deal. My thoughts were too focused on Jamere, and I would only deal with one situation at a time.

"That's a risk you're going to have to decide whether or not to take. In every relationship you're in, heartbreak is a possibility. But you have to decide whether pursuing the relationship is worth the risk or not." My best friend, my sister, always knew exactly what to say. Listening to her, I knew that she'd made a valid point. If I was going to pursue the relationship with Jamere, I was going to have to take the risk, no matter how afraid I was. "You're right. Thank you sister. You told me what I needed to hear. I'll call you later. I have some thinking to do. I love you." I looked at my walls that were now void of anything related to Stephan. A huge weight had been lifted from my shoulders and for that, I was grateful. "You're welcome. You know I have your back even when we're mad at each other. I love you too sister. Let me know what you decide. I'll talk to you later." "I will. Later." I sat my phone down after finding some music to listen to. I stood and started removing Stephan's things from various places in my room and threw them in his luggage that sat in my closet.

 I pulled my bedroom door open and slowly walked toward the living room. I was calm enough to be near Jamere, without jumping on him. Or at least I thought I was. As soon as his eyes landed on mine, all the heat I felt when I left the room two hours before, rushed back full force. "Better?" I exhaled, ignoring the fluttering in my stomach as I sat with him on the sofa. "I thought so, but now, not so much." Jamere nodded, more to himself than me and spoke softly. "Trust me. I know what you mean." The two of us were quiet for more than a few minutes, but I knew we couldn't continue walking on eggshells so to speak. I mustered up all my courage, and spoke to Jamere, being as honest as I knew I needed to be.

"Jamere, I think you; we have made a mistake. I think it is our time to pursue our relationship. I truly believe, deep down in my heart, that you were placed in my life when you were for a reason. God knew my pain and I believe He sent me the one who would show me the one I was with had to go. I think this is our time." Nervousness filled my body when I saw the expression on his face. And as I sat there, looking at him and expecting the worst, I just knew that I had really embarrassed myself.

"I don't know what to say. Those words sound like heaven pouring from your mouth. But if I'm going to be honest, I'm afraid you're going to resent me because of the relationship you're just getting out of. As much as I want to be with you, I refuse to hurt you by getting in a relationship too soon and having you resent me for it. I would be no better than Stephan if I allowed that to happen." The honesty in his words touched me, and that gave me even more confirmation that this relationship was meant to happen. "I would never, could **never** resent you. The way you've helped me, opened me up when no one else could lets me know that. I like you Jamere. I believe we could have something built to last, but you have to want to. I'm falling for you. Hard. Harder than I have with anyone else. But if I fall, if I jump, I need to know that you'll be there to catch me." Jamere was silent for less than ten seconds, when the words started to spill from his mouth.

"I like you too. I only did what I thought you needed. I believe we could have something built to last as well. Trust me, I want this. I want you. Fall, jump. Whatever you need to do, just know that I'll be waiting with open arms to catch you. That's a promise."

My heart banged against my chest as I tried to figure out what I needed to do or say next. As soon as I opened my mouth, Jamere placed his soft lips on top of mine. He moved slowly, probably making sure I was okay with it. The truth of the matter was, I was more than okay with it. My hand rested on his chest as he pulled away and I caught his bottom lip between my teeth before letting it go.

"Those lips have taunted me for weeks. I had to do that." The grin that slipped onto my face was sneaky. Full of untold truths, because I had wanted him to do the same since the first time he complimented me. "I'm glad you finally did it. Its bugged me for a while as well." Jamere grinned at me knowingly, sending shivers throughout my already heated body. "We'll take this as slowly as you need to. There is no rush. Take the time needed to get back to you. I'm going to help your heart to heal, and right now, that's what I want the most."

My hand went to his heart, my eyes focusing on his eyes with honesty in my own. "As long as I know I'm in here...." I tapped the spot under my palm with my fingertips and continued to speak. "That will heal me faster than you know. Just carry me in your heart, and everything else will fall into place." Jamere closed his hand on top of mine and kissed the back of it gently. This time, I hoped I had it right. I hoped that I'd finally found someone who wouldn't hurt me. That would definitely be a welcome change.

Jamere leaned against the sofa cushions, talking to his parents, and letting them know that he was safe. The past two days had been eventful, but I wouldn't change the outcome for anything in the world. I slid to the edge of the sofa, preparing to walk away when I heard the conversation shift. I wanted him to have his privacy so that he could speak freely to his parents. Jamere had a different mindset though. As soon as I stood, he grabbed my hand and tugged me gently until I was sitting beside him once again. He pressed his lips to my forehead and continued his conversation. I smiled at his responses, and the shakes of his head that went along with them.

"Ma, I told you I'm at Trina's house. The storm hit while we were at school, and she invited me to stay with her so I wouldn't get stranded in the flood." Jamere pinched the bridge of his nose, easing a chuckle out of me. "All due respect Ma, but this is not your business. I'm an adult, and while I know I'm your son, you have to let me be one. My relationship and my non-existent sex life with Trina is not your concern." I looked at Jamere with wide eyes, the smile slipping from my lips. Jamere mouthed the words I'm sorry and continued to talk to his mom. He was quiet for a few minutes and then he spoke again. "I know that, and I appreciate it. I love you Ma, you know that. But you have to let me grow up. I care about Trina too much to ever hurt her. Lord willing, I'll be able to prove that to her for the rest of my life." My heart swelled with emotion, and I put my hand on Jamere's stomach and rested my head on his shoulder. There would never be any other man that would touch my heart the way Jamere had in such a short time period. If I could just continue to heal and grow with him, I know my life would be so much better. Jamere made me feel better, made my life better, and I knew over time, our lives would get, would be filled with so much happiness. "Yes ma'am. I understand. I love you too. I will. Bye." Jamere shook his head and looked at me, angling his head so that he could peck my lips. "My parents said hello." I chuckled and curled into him, rubbing my hand over his abs. "Tell them I said Hello the next time you talk to them." His head bobbed up and down, and he tossed his phone on the coffee table. "Parents right?" Jamere nodded again, dragging his hands down his face.

Jamere and I spent the day talking and learning about each other things we didn't already know. Despite my best efforts, I couldn't hide my tiredness and from Jamere's yawning, he couldn't either. I looked out of the windows at the dark sky, the stars twinkling brightly upon their dark canvas. "I guess we should call it a night baby. Sleep well okay?" I nodded slowly, holding onto him tightly as he hugged me. "You too." I pressed my lips to his cheek and stepped away from him. A quiet sigh escaped my mouth, and I made my way to my bedroom alone. The nightmares I knew were bound to haunt me throughout the night. I pulled off my socks that I had put on after my earlier shower and put on a fresh pair. I sat on the bed, a yawn escaping my mouth, causing me to shake my head. Once the covers were pulled back, I slipped under them and turned off the lamp beside my bed.

    As soon as my eyes closed, images of Stephan flashed through my mind. I tried for an hour to push them away, but it didn't work. I eventually eased to the floor and walked to the living room where Jamere was sleeping. Jamere sat up when I appeared at the edge of the couch. The outline of his body was all I could see, but his voice caressed me as if he were touching me. "What's wrong? Bad dream?" I grabbed his hand and tugged it gently until he was standing. I led the way to my bedroom in the dark, stopping at my bed when we were inside my room.

    "I just need you to hold me while I sleep. I need to know Stephan can't get to me. Can you do that?" Jamere patted the mattress and once I was laying down, he walked around the bed and got in behind me. He pulled my back to his front and held me close and pressed his lips to the back of my head, rocking me slowly until I fell asleep.

Chapter 10:

Trina

I watched Cheyenne as she got out of her car and walked toward my apartment. The floods had stopped and Jamere had gone home, much to my dismay. Cheyenne and I were having a much-needed girl chat. There were sure to be lots of tears coming from her before the day was over. We both had to be back at work the following day, so this needed to happen now. As hard as I knew it would be, I knew it had to be done. Tears or not, my sister deserved to know the truth.

The two of us embraced one another and I let her walk past me and into the apartment. Cheyenne walked directly towards the kitchen and pulled open the refrigerator door. "What do you have to eat? I'm so hungry I could eat a cow." I leaned against the counter and watched as she stared into my refrigerator with a hand on her stomach. "There is some beef and potatoes leftover from our dinner last night. It's in the blue container. Help yourself." Cheyenne pulled the container out and walked to the sink to wash her hands. "I'm going in the living room." I exited the kitchen and entered the living room to wait for Chey. The sofa was covered in Jamere's scent which brought a smile to my face. He refused to sleep in my bed, so for four nights he camped out on my sofa. He wanted to make sure I knew he wasn't going to rush me into anything. But truth be told, I didn't want to sleep in my own bed, knowing what had happened there. For that reason, I usually camped out in the living room with him for all night movie marathons. I mean we were flooded in, so there wasn't much more we could do.

"This room smells like a man." I shrugged and tucked my legs underneath my body. "Does it stink?" Cheyenne's head shook back and forth, and she forked some more food into her mouth. Jamere was here for four days so I knew what she was referring to. The scent of his body wash clung to everything and a smell that was just him did as well. I smiled so hard, I had to bite my tongue to stop it. Thankfully, Cheyenne didn't seem to notice.

"Girl this is BOMB! You have a serious gift." "Thanks, but Jamere made that." The smile that graced my lips made her grin at me. "He cooks too!! Oh, he's definitely a keeper." A soft laugh escaped my lips, and I shook my head at her. "So, what is this chat we need to have about? You're not hurt or sick, are you?" She continued to eat, her eyes checking over me to see if she could see anything that may be wrong. "No, I'm not sick. And I'm not hurt. Not anymore anyway. Finish eating and we can get into it." Cheyenne raised her eyebrows but did as I had told her. "I'll be right back."

I returned with the hoodie I had stolen from Jamere clutched in my arms. Cheyenne stood and walked into the kitchen to clean her dish. A million thoughts rushed through my mind as I tried to figure out how to start this conversation that was at this point, inevitable. Nerves filled me and I tried to push them away as best I could. However, when I heard my name, I knew nothing would make them go away. I just had to ready myself for what was about to happen.

"So, what's up Trina?" I pulled Jamere's hoodie over my head and let out a deep breath. I still had no idea where to start, but I knew I had to. So, I just started from the beginning and told her my story. My truth. As hard as that was proving to be.

"Well, I guess I need to start at the beginning." Chey waited patiently for me to continue. "As you know, when I got with Stephan, months after our relationship changed. We didn't see each other as much as we usually did with the exception of work. For years I told you it was simply because I was busy. I guess you've figured out that that wasn't completely true. I stopped calling you and stopped spending weekends with you. What I'm about to tell you is the reason why." Cheyenne nodded, waiting for me to continue. "About six months into my relationship with Stephan, he became abusive physically as well as verbally. It started with him telling me hated me and would kill me for one thing or another. When that didn't get the response he wanted, he told me that no one loved me but him." I pulled the neck of Jamere's hoodie up to my nose and inhaled deeply. I looked at Chey whose fists were beginning to clench in anger. "Those words weren't giving him the response he wanted either. So, one evening after I had gotten out of the shower, he told me that my phone had rang a number of times. Of course, I went to check to see who it was. I returned the call and talked long enough to find out the purpose of the call. When I hung up, Stephan asked me who it was. I told him it was my brother as he snatched my phone out of my hand. 'Who the hell is Ryan and why does he keep calling you?' That's what he asked me when saw the name on my call log. I told him that Ryan was my big brother and he punched me in the face. He thought I was lying. He said I told him my brother's name was Dylan. My eyes went to the ground, and I rolled my eyes as I forced away tears.

I told him I had three brothers and proceeded to name them. When he still didn't believe me, I pulled up pictures them in my phone and showed him a group text we'd had a few days before." I watched as angry tears fell from Cheyenne's cheeks, knowing that there was no point stopping at that point. "Once he was sure I was telling the truth, he hugged me and then looked down at me. 'Sorry, but it's not like I hurt you. So, you'll be okay.' That's what he told me, and it's something I haven't been able to forget." I released a sigh, shaking my head as the memory plagued me once again. When I looked at Cheyenne, I could tell that she was beyond angry. As much as I wanted to stop, I knew I had to keep going.

"Anyway, that was only the beginning. Over the years the abuse became worse. I cut myself off from my friends and my family because I didn't want them to be angry about the situation I had allowed myself to get into. I knew that if I told my brothers, they would be upset with me. I know that they always told me not to get in a relationship with anyone who would hurt me in any way. But I thought he loved me. I thought I loved him. Now, after meeting Jamere, I know that what I thought I felt was not love. Over the past few weeks since I met Jamere I've realized exactly what I want in my life. So, as you probably noticed my lies about my injuries over the past few weeks were because of Stephan. The bruise on my face, he punched me because I came in late. The crutches I was on when I told you I fell down a small hill, he beat me up for some reason I can't even remember. When I met Jamere, for some reason it was him that made me realize I deserved more. I knew that if I didn't get out of that relationship, Stephan would probably kill me. At that point I didn't even know him. I only knew that he was a boy that sat next to me in class. He helped me without even knowing he was doing so. Stephan's older brother got out of prison a few weeks ago and walked in on Stephan abusing me. Q was upset that he did not know what Stephan had been doing to me. So, he told me to stay away from my apartment for a few days and Jamere was nice enough to let me stay with him." Cheyenne cut off my statement and looked at me with hurt eyes. "Why didn't you call me? You know you could have stayed with me for as long as you needed to." I put my hand on Cheyenne's, squeezing it gently in my own.

"Honestly, I was afraid, and embarrassed. Although Stephan didn't know you, he knew about you. I didn't want him to track you down to try to get to me. At the time, he didn't know Jamere existed. I felt like right then, that was the safest place for me to be and even now he doesn't know Jamere's name. The next day, I went home, and Stephan's car was in the parking lot. I called Jamere and he came to make sure I wasn't hurt again. He led the way into the apartment and saw Quincy standing in the living room. Once I assured him Q wasn't Stephan, he let me walk around him. Quincy told me to stay away for a few days, just to be on the safe side. I was planning on staying at the hotel, but Jamere told me that was out of the question." I smiled at the memory, warmth filling my stomach as I thought about the concern behind his demand.

"The comfort that Jamere made me feel let me know that being abused by someone who was supposed to love me was unacceptable. So Chey, this is what I have been hiding from you. I know we have been friends for too long for me to have lied to you this way. But I hope you can forgive me for leaving you out of it for so long. I'm so sorry Cheyenne, I will never lie to you about something this serious again. I promise. Forgive me?" Cheyenne was quiet for a number of seconds, tears rolling down her cheeks. I gave her the box of Kleenex that was on the end table beside me. She swiped her cheeks with the tissue and slid her body closer to mine on the sofa.

"I am truly sorry you had to go through that alone and I'm sorry you felt like you couldn't come to me. You're my best friend and I would never, will never judge you for anything that happens to you. I hope you realize that I love you and I will always be there for you. I hope you hold to your promise that you won't ever lie to me about something that serious again. I forgive you Lil Bit. Thank you for finally letting me know what caused the change in you, but I can already see you getting back to your old self. Are you ever going to tell your brothers what happened?" I shrugged my shoulders inhaling the scent on Jamere's hoodie once again. "I don't know. I mean, I know I should but how do you tell your brothers that you ended up in a relationship they told you to never find yourself in?" I brushed a few tears away from Chey's face and shrugged my shoulders again. "I get it, but they need to know why you have been the way you have. They won't be mad they'll just be glad you're no longer in the relationship. I have your back whatever you decide."

A grin formed on Cheyenne face, and I had a feeling I knew what she was going to ask. "So, Jamere huh?" I grinned, covering my face with my hands as my body started to heat up again. "Yeah. He's a great guy." Cheyenne ran a finger over my cheek and laughed playfully. "Aww! You're blushing. I've never seen you blush before. You must really be feeling Jamere." My hand pushed hers away, but she just laughed again. She had spoken true words though. I liked him more than I planned to, and that scared me a little.

"Yeah, I am. He makes me tingle all over. You know that feeling you had when you met Michael Greer in the sixth grade? For reasons I still don't understand, he was your first crush. You thought he was the best thing since sliced bread, and you said he gave you tingles in your belly." Cheyenne laughed exuberantly while shaking her head at me. "That was a serious lapse in judgment. I think it was his long hair. I used to love playing with it in math class." I rolled my eyes at her but continued my statement. "Well, that's what I feel whenever I think about Jamere. I don't know how it happened, but he stole my heart without me even knowing. Not until it was too late anyway." The humor left Cheyenne's face and she spoke to me with honesty in her voice. "Believe me I've been there. I know the feeling. I hope things with you two work out well. Lord knows you deserve to be happy, and if Jamere is the one the Lord has sent for you, I couldn't be happier. I smiled at Chey, knowing in my heart that I had done the right thing by telling her. She was always the sister I never had and times like this I was reminded of that. "Yeah well, we're not rushing into anything, but I'm not going to fight it either. I fought my attraction to him for weeks, and I refuse to go back to that." Chey nodded her head at me, but she didn't say anything. Her support was what mattered to me, and I was glad to know that I had it.

"Okay let's get out of the apartment. I've been cooped up for four days, and as enjoyable as it may have been, I need to get out." Cheyenne looked at me, squinting her eyes playfully. "Well, you might have told me that before I left the house in sweats." I laughed at her and stood, pulling her to her feet and dragging her behind me to my bedroom. "I had no idea the talk would end the way it did. It's cool, you can borrow something from me. But, I guess it will have to match your shoes because my feet are smaller than yours." I let Chey go through my closet first, and once she had an outfit, I searched for my own to wear.

Cheyenne and I checked ourselves in the mirror, making sure we looked okay before we left. Cheyenne was wearing a pair of black

True Religion jeans, white cami, and a green V-neck sweater. Silver hoops were in her ears and a black watch was secured around her wrist. What she wore on her feet, was a pair of black, green, and white number 1 Jordan's. I nodded my head at her and then looked over myself one final time. White long-sleeved crop top, dark gray waist tapered joggers, and a pair of all white number one Jordan's on my feet. White studs were in my ears and a white watch was on my left wrist. I put my purse over my head so that it rested on my hip, and I was ready to go.

"Are you ready Chey?" Cheyenne pulled a comb through her hair and then sat it back on the dresser. "Yep let's go. Who's driving?" I led the way through the apartment and out the front door. "I'll drive, but let's take your car. In the event you know who stops by." I locked the door and turned, holding my hand out for her keys. The anger in her eyes reflecting everything I felt on the inside. "Let's ride." I unlocked the door when her key was in my hand and slid behind the steering wheel. I started the engine and let it warm up a little before pulling off.

Cheyenne and I walked around the mall, looking in different stores, looking at things we may have wanted to purchase. At the moment, I hadn't seen anything I wanted, but I knew as soon as we entered Foot Locker, that was going to change. Cheyenne had four bags already and we had barely been in the mall for an hour. But she was a definite girly girl. Now I can't say I wasn't girly, but I was nowhere near the level of girly that Chey was on. "Chey, I'm going Foot Locker, are you coming?" Cheyenne adjusted the bags in her hands, putting the three smaller ones inside the one big one. "Yep, I want some Huaraches. Let's see if they have some in my size. I've gone to four other stores and none of them had my size. How hard is it to have a size nine in your store?" She shook her head and the two of us entered the shoe store.

I walked to the wall and started eyeing shoes, trying to figure out which ones I wanted to buy. One thing I knew I had a problem with was my indecisiveness. Even if I knew exactly what I was going to get, I had a hard time picking what I wanted. I reached for a pair of Lebron's, jumping slightly when I felt a set of arms wrap around my waist. I turned around quickly, my fear turning into happiness when I saw Jamere standing in front of me.

His hands rested on my hips and an adorable grin was plastered on his face. He kissed my lips softly and glanced down at his side. Amelia and L.J. stood there quietly with wide smiles on their faces. "Hey Trina!" I grinned and knelt down to hug the two of them. "Hey baby's. How are you both doing?" When I stood up, L.J. jumped up in my arms. "Good. How about you?" I smiled at Amelia and turned my head when Chey stopped beside me. "I've been good too. Amy, L.J., this is my best friend Cheyenne. Cheyenne, you remember Jamere. Well, this is his little sister Amelia and his god son Lloyd Jr." Chey greeted the children, smiling as I sat L.J. back on the ground. "It's nice to meet you cuties. How old are you?" Jamere removed his hands from my hips and leaned forward to hug Chey. "I'm six and L.J. is four. How old are you?" Cheyenne laughed at Amelia's question and pinched her cheeks gently.

"Amy, that is rude." Jamere stated while looking down at her. "She asked me how old I am." Jamere shrugged and asked her what her point was. "If she can ask me how old I am, why can't I ask her how old she is?" Jamere shook his head, trying not to smile at his little sister. "Because she's an adult and you're a child that's why." Amelia looked down and nodded her head slowly. "Okay Jam. I'm sorry." Jamere nodded, but Cheyenne spoke. "It's good that you listen to your brother, but I didn't mind your question. I will tell you my age, but that doesn't mean you shouldn't listen to him okay?" Amelia nodded her small head, her ponytail bobbing with the motion. "I'm 21." I'll be 22 in a few weeks." Amelia smiled and looked up at Jamere and spoke to him.

"She's older than you Jam." I turned around and continued looking at the Lebron's. I wasn't feeling them, so I continued to look. I knew I wanted a pair of all white Huaraches, but I needed some all-black shoes as well. I looked until I saw a pair of Jordan 7 Bordeaux. I knew they weren't all black, but I had to have them. I motioned for an employee while holding the two shoes in my hand. When he was in front of me, I showed him the shoes in my hands. "Can I get the Bordeaux in a 6 and the Huaraches in a 6 ½?" The guy nodded and walked away, so I sat down on the bench I was standing in front of. Amy and L.J. each perched themselves on one of my knees and Jamere looked down at me.

"Hey babe, I'm about to go over to get my shoes. The guy that was helping me is coming out from the back. Come on yall." I watched Amy and L.J. frown before I spoke. "They're good. Go get your shoes. We'll be right here." Jamere smiled at me and then looked at the two children that were still in place. "Are you sure?" I nodded so he looked at them with seriousness in his eyes. "Amy, L.J. I'll be right back okay?" They nodded and

L.J. rested his head against my chest. Jamere winked at me and walked away to the opposite side of the store.

"Did you get your Huaraches?" I looked at Cheyenne's hands, looking for the shoe box that should have been there. "No. All they had was a ten and that was way too big. Although they run small, I still should only need about an 8 ½ or a 9. I might have to order them from online. I was trying to avoid that because I didn't want to pay the possibly ridiculous shipping charge." I nodded and looked down at L.J. who was asleep.

The guy, who was helping me, brought my shoes to me and sat them next to me, pulling one of the Huaraches out first. "Amy, sit on the bench so I can try the shoes on." Amy did as I told her, and I took the shoe from the guy's hand. I wrapped my arm around L.J.'s stomach and leaned forward to put the shoe on. Chey sat her bag on the bench and knelt down in front of me. She pulled the tongue on the shoe and tied it before easing back. "Stand up." I did as she told me to, holding on to L.J. securely. Chey pressed her thumb to the top of the shoe and pressed my big toe. "How does it feel?" I gave her the thumbs up sign, so she nodded her head at me. I sat down again, and she untied the shoe so that I could take my foot out of the it. "That one's good, I'm keeping it." I handed the shoe back to the guy and he gave me the Jordan. I put my foot inside and Chey went through the same process once again.

"How's that feel?" I moved my foot from side to side and put it flat on the ground once again. "It's a little loose, but not enough to go down a size. I'll just have to wear thicker socks when I wear these." Chey untied the shoe and pulled it off of my foot. "Where's your debit card? I'll pay for them for you and then when Jamere comes back we can leave. You weren't getting anything else right?" I shook my head no and pulled my wallet out of my purse. "I'm paying cash. Just take my whole wallet." Chey nodded and walked away, so Amy knelt down in front of me.

I pushed my foot into my shoe and Amy tied it up for me. "Thanks Amy." She nodded and sat on my knee once again. "Are you going to come to dinner on Sunday?" I looked down at her and shrugged my shoulders. "I don't know. I haven't been invited." Amy furrowed her eyebrows at me and spoke. "I just did." I chuckled softly and rubbed her smooth hair. "I know, but an adult needs to invite me. Your mom or dad." Amy nodded and I could practically see the ideas churning in her head. She reminded me so much of Chey when we were little it didn't make sense.

Chey and Jamere made it back to us at the same time and they both smiled when they saw L.J. sleeping with his head on my chest.

"Come on Amy, let's get out of here. I have to get you to choir practice. Tell Trina and Chey bye." Amy stood and hugged me and then shook Chey's hand. See you later." I nodded my head and stood with L.J. in my arms. Jamere took him and leaned down to kiss me. He enveloped me and I had to force myself not to latch onto him like a piece of tape. When he pulled away, he winked at me and looked at Cheyenne. "It was nice seeing you again Cheyenne. We should all do something one day." Chey nodded her head at him and rubbed L.J.'s back gently. "Call me Chey, and that sounds like a plan." "Cool. Later baby. I'll call you later." I squeezed his hand in my own and nodded my head. I kissed L.J.'s smooth cheek and watched as Jamere and Amy walked away from us.

Cheyenne looked at me, a grin on her face that caused my cheeks to flush. "I've never seen you like this with a guy. It's like you've found happiness." The two of us walked side by side, a grin forming on my face. "It's a welcome change. I really like him and it's nice to be with someone who really cares." Cheyenne nodded at me, adjusting the bag she clutched in her hand. "I can see that.

He seems like a good guy and as long as he makes you happy, I'm happy for you." The two of us walked into another store and fell into a comfortable silence as we walked around. After the silence had lasted a few minutes, I looked away from the rack I was standing in front of and focused my attention on Chey.

"So, you know all about my love life, how's yours going?" Cheyenne shook her head, and rolled her eyes at me, but she answered my question honestly. "Slow girl. Really slow." She laughed briefly but became serious once again. "I mean I've gone out with a few guys, but none of them are able to hold my attention past our date. I decided to take some time for myself and when the right guy comes along, God will let me know." I looked at my sister with a newfound respect. She was finally growing up and out of that 'I have to have a man' stage. For that, I couldn't be happier. "That's good Chey. Get back to you. Work on yourself and everything else will fall into place. I know that doesn't have much validation coming from me, but that is something I'm finding out is very true." Cheyenne stopped walking and stared directly in my eyes. "It has validation. Everything is a learning experience and listening to you now confirms that. Don't put yourself down, even if you feel it's true. Not in front of me." I turned away from her and shrugged, agreeing to her demand quietly. "Alright Chey." She turned around after staring at me for a few more seconds, leading the way to Bath and Body Works.

The Semi-Annual Sale I knew was far off, but I couldn't wait until the time came. All of those fragrances would be on sale for little to nothing and that was when I would buy the bulk of my purchases. Right then though, I would get a couple scents I knew I would like. As we were going through the different scents, my heart started to beat nervously. I looked up and around, freezing when I saw Stephan staring at me. I grabbed Chey's arm, clenching it tightly in fear. "Ow Trina. What was....?" Cheyenne looked at me and then in the direction my attention was in. Her eyes locked on Stephan, and she grabbed my hand, leading me to the front of the store. "Give me your phone." I did as I was told and placed my iPhone in her hand. I watched her unlock it, then her fingers went to work on the screen. She put my phone to her ear, waiting for an answer with an angry frown on her face. After a few seconds passed, she started to speak into the phone.

"Jamere, this is Cheyenne. Trina is going to stay with me tonight. We just saw Stephan and he had been watching Trina and we don't know how long. I don't want her to be home by herself. There's no telling what he might do. If you would just meet us at her apartment so she can get what she needs for work tomorrow, I would appreciate it. If you want to stay with us you are more than welcome to. I just want her to be safe." Cheyenne listened to Jamere talk, nodding her head to no one as he spoke. "Okay that's cool. We'll meet you there. Bye. And thank you." Cheyenne nodded once more and ended the call before giving me back my phone. "He said to meet him at yall's school, and he'll follow us to your apartment. He just dropped Amelia off at church with their mom and he should be there within the hour." I nodded my head at Chey, the two of us walking towards the exit.

    Chey and I pulled into the parking lot of my school, spotting Jamere's car as we did. Cheyenne honked her horn and he waved before starting his car and following her. "Jamere is going to stay with us tonight in the event that Stephan is following us. He said he's going to take you to file a restraining order against him before work tomorrow." I nodded my head at her, my heart beating fearfully in my chest. Jamere was ten times the man Stephan was. He refused to leave me if he thought I may be in a dangerous situation. Now adding Chey into the mix, he refuses to let her be hurt either. With every day that passes, I fall harder and harder for him. I know that in the future, he'll prove to be, the man I have been waiting for.

Cheyenne and Jamere parked their cars, and Cheyenne put her hand on the door handle. I grabbed her arm, and she turned her attention to me. "Don't open the door. If you do, Jamere is going to fuss and tell you to let the man be the man." Cheyenne grinned but moved her hand away from the door and sat waiting for Jamere. He pulled my hand when my door was opened, keeping it clasped around mine as he pushed the door closed. We walked around the car and he used his free hand to open Cheyenne's door. He reached for her hand, and when it was in his, he helped her out of the car. He let go of her hand when she was out of the way and pushed the door closed. Once the car was locked, the three of us walked toward my apartment.

Jamere held his hand out for my key, so I gave it to him. He unlocked the door and stepped inside, ushering Cheyenne and I in behind him. He closed the door but didn't lock it as he looked at us. Don't lock the door. Stay here until I come back. Don't move from this spot. Okay?" His eyes bounced between the two of us until we both told him okay. He walked cautiously through my apartment, entering, and exiting rooms slowly before coming back to the front where we were waiting. "Okay, it's all clear. Lock the door and come pack your bag baby." I turned around and locked the door, trying to stop the trembling in my hands as I did so. Cheyenne sat on the sofa and looked at her phone as I walked past her towards my bedroom.

 "Cheyenne told me you're staying too. Do you have to stop and get clothes from home?" Jamere sat on my bed, watching me as I got my things together for the night. I pulled out one of my work suits and hung it on the closet door as he spoke. "No, I bought some new boxers and pajama bottoms earlier. My gym bag is in my car and that has all my toiletries and some socks inside. When I take you to file the restraining order in the morning, we can stop by my apartment, and I'll put some clothes on." I stuffed Jamere's hoodie in my small Nike duffel and went back into the closet for my shoes. I grabbed the appropriate box and walked out, removing my suit from the closet door. I put the shoe box in the duffel bag, zipped it, and watched Jamere grab it. He held his hand out for the suit, so I gave it to him, and we both walked out of my bedroom.

The three of us walked into Cheyenne's apartment and locked the door behind us. I flipped on the light and the semi dark room illuminated. "That's a big couch!" Jamere told Cheyenne as we walked deeper into the living room. "Yeah. My grandmother had it custom made for my grandfather. He was nearly seven feet tall, and when he watched the game he liked to stretch out. But his legs either hung off of the couch or were bunched underneath him, so she had it made. He passed a few years ago, and she couldn't bear to see it every day, so she gave it to me. It was murder trying to get it through the door, but we managed." Jamere nodded his head, running his hand along the deep blue fabric. "I love it. I'm sorry about your grandfather's passing. I know how it feels." Cheyenne smiled and motioned for him to follow us. "Thanks. Same to you. Its comfortable and since I only have one bedroom, this is where you can sleep. Is that okay?" Jamere nodded and followed us into her room, setting my bag on Chey's bed and laying the suit on top of it. "Yes that's fine. Thank you." "No problem. The bathroom is the door to your far right, everything you need should be there, if not let me know." Jamere nodded and looked around the room.

"It's only seven o'clock, so we could order some food and watch tv or something if yall want. It's too late to be trying to cook a meal now though." I moved my things to the closet and closed the door, listening as Jamere spoke. "That's cool. But I'll go pick up something to eat. What do you both want? Do you still have a taste for Popeye's baby?" I nodded my head at him, and he looked at Chey while speaking. Okay, I know what to get you. What about you Chey?" I listened to Chey tell him what she wanted and watched him nod his head. "Okay ladies. I'll be back shortly." We both nodded at him, and I followed him so that I could lock the door behind him. He pulled it open and then turned to look at me. "I'll be back in a few. Don't worry baby. I'll never let him hurt you again." He leaned toward me and pecked my lips, sending heat from the top of my head to the bottom of my feet. "Lock the door." I nodded and he pulled the door closed, so I locked it and stood there for a few seconds before turning back to the living room. "Chey, I'm going to change. I'll be right back." The tv came on and Chey waved her hand as I walked toward her bedroom.

Chey went to take a shower while I sat in the living room, staring blankly at the tv. I pulled my arms into Jamere's hoodie and rested my head on the arm of the sofa. I could hear Cheyenne moving around in her bedroom before the door closed to block out the sound. There was a knock on the door, and I flinched before standing to go see who was there. I looked out of the peephole, and when I saw Jamere standing there, I unlocked the door and pulled it open. Jamere walked into the apartment as I closed the door and locked it once more. Cheyenne's bedroom door opened, and she walked out wearing a pair of orange pajama bottoms and a blue baby tee.

"Perfect timing Chey." We all got our food and followed Chey into the living room. "Yall want something to drink? I have some juice, Pepsi, Sprite, and water in the fridge." Chey started to back towards the kitchen as Jamere and I told her we wanted Pepsi's. She turned and walked into the kitchen, coming back minutes later with three cans of Pepsi and 3 straws in her hand and a roll of paper towels under her arms.

Cheyenne and I said our good night's to Jamere, with me lingering for a few minutes after Cheyenne had entered her room. Jamere wrapped his arms around me, rocking us gently from side to side. "Sleep well baby. I'll see in the morning." I nodded my head against his chest, inhaling his masculine scent for a few more seconds before we let each other go. Jamere pressed his lips to mine, resting his hands on my hips as our mouths mated. When we pulled away, he looked down into my eyes. "Good night baby." I sighed and pecked his lips once more before speaking again. "Good night. Don't let the bedbugs bite." Jamere chuckled and turned my hips, kissing my neck before sending me towards Cheyenne's bedroom.

    I walked inside and climbed on the bed beside Cheyenne. She was laying on her back looking up at the ceiling in silence. "Night Lil Bit." I curled into a ball and turned my body so that I was facing Chey. Night Chey. Sleep well. See you in the morning." Cheyenne turned so that she was facing away from me, and the two of us settled in for a good night's rest.

    I sat up quickly on the bed, muffling a scream as I looked beside me to make sure Cheyenne was still asleep. When I saw that she was, I slid to the floor and exited the room, closing the door behind me soundlessly. I released a sigh and walked over to the sofa where Jamere was sleeping peacefully. I moved the cover that was draped over him and slid onto the sofa in front of him. I let the cover fall over us, pulling one of his arms gently until it was resting on my hip. I rested my head on the pillow with his and closed my eyes, knowing that I could sleep now that I was in his arms.

I felt Jamere's lips brush my cheek, so I opened my eyes from my slumber to look at him. "Bad dreams?" I nodded my head at him in the not quite dark room. "I'm sorry. I'm right here. Go back to sleep. We can sleep a few more hours before going to file the restraining order." I turned my body so that I was facing him, closing my eyes while resting my head on his chest. Jamere kissed my forehead and put his arms around my body and rubbed my back slowly.

I felt a hand touch my head, so I opened my eyes to see why. "Hey. Are you okay? When I woke up and you weren't in bed, I got worried." I sat up slowly, looking at Cheyenne already in her work uniform. I glanced at Jamere's phone for the time and returned my attention to Chey. "Bad dreams. I'm okay though. Why are you dressed so early?" Cheyenne handed her house key to me and glanced at Jamere's sleeping form. "I have a doctor's appointment at 11. I won't have time to come back and change. So, lock up when yall leave and give me my key back at work. Okay?" I nodded and stood, following her to the front door. "Be careful Chey. I'll see you at lunch." I stepped out of the door behind her and watched her look back at me. "I will. Go back inside. I'll see you in a few hours." I nodded as she started down the stairs and walked back into the apartment and locked the door behind me.

"Morning baby. Where is Chey?" I walked toward where Jamere was sitting up on the sofa and kissed his head softly. "She had a doctor's appointment. She told me to lock up when we leave." I pulled the blanket off of Jamere and started to fold it up. "I'm going to shower. Be out in a few." Jamere nodded and handed me the pillow I held my hand out for and watched me as I walked away from him.

I stood in front of the mirror combing my hair with a towel wrapped around my body. I put my hair in a ponytail up top and left it hanging down in the back. I had already brushed my teeth and washed my face, so I gargled with some Listerine before walking out to go put on some lotion. I pulled the bedroom door open and told Jamere I was out of the shower before sitting on Chey's trunk at the foot of her bed to rub the lotion on my legs. Jamere walked through the room, avoiding eye contact with me as he rushed into the bathroom and closed the door.

I checked my appearance in the mirror behind Chey's door, and then adjusted my name tag on my blazer. I stepped into a pair of black pumps and turned my head when the bathroom door opened. Jamere walked towards me with his gym bag hanging from one shoulder and a grin on his face. "You look beautiful. This is my first time seeing you in heels, and I have to say, I don't hate it." I grinned at him in the mirror, a slight blush creeping onto my cheeks. "Thank you. Well, now that I can wear them again, you'll probably see me in them a lot more." I walked away from the mirror and zipped up my bag. "I'm ready. Are you?" Jamere lifted my bag and nodded his head at me. Once my purse, phone, and keys were in hand, I led the way to the front door. "I'll take you to work at the hotel. If you can get Chey to take you home to change for the club and then drop you off, I'll stop by and get you from the club when I get off at three." I locked up Chey's apartment and nodded my head at him. "Alright. I can do that." Jamere opened my door for me and helped me into my seat. Once the door was closed, he went to the back of the car and put our bags in the trunk.

Jamere and I rode in silence to the police station. The closer we got, the more nervous I seemed to become. I didn't know why. I was making the necessary steps to be rid of Stephan for good. That should have been great motivation, but I felt like Stephan would be able to wiggle himself out of this like he does everything else. And that realization sent a new sense of fear rushing through me.

Jamere interrupted my thoughts by speaking into the silence. "It would have been great if you had pictures of the bruises he has given you. Or even your hospital bills." I looked over in Jamere's direction, grabbing his free hand before I spoke. "I do. I took some after each time he abused me. I have them in a hidden folder in my phone." Jamere squeezed my hand as I continued to speak. "And I brought the hospital bills with me. I thought they may come in handy." Jamere glanced at me, a small smile appearing on his face and then quickly disappearing. "That was very smart of you. Every day you find new ways to impress me. That I am beyond happy about." Jamere let my hand go and rubbed the back of his along my cheek gently.

The two of us walked slowly into the police station, my hand clasped tightly around Jamere's. I knew what I was about to do was necessary, but fear shook me as we stepped closer and closer to where we needed to go. "You don't have to be afraid. I'm right here and I won't let him hurt you again. You deserve to be able to move on with your life, and the further you can get from him, the easier the transition will be." Jamere touched his lips to my forehead, and I allowed a small smile to grace my lips. "You're right. Thanks for being here for me. I appreciate it more than I can express." I inhaled deeply and released it before stepping closer to the front desk with my head held high.

After filing the restraining order, I felt as though a huge weight had been lifted from my shoulders. I let out a breath that I had obviously been holding in for years and looked at Jamere walking beside me. He glanced at me, but he didn't say anything. We just continued our walk back to his car in silence.

When we got to the car, Jamere maneuvered me so that I was standing in front of the passenger side door. I watched his chest rise and fall before he parted his lips to speak. "Baby, I want to ask you something. I don't mean it in a judgmental or offensive way, so if that's how it comes across, I want to apologize in advance." I nodded my head at him and waited for him to ask whatever it was that he needed to know the answer to.

"I heard you telling them that he would...." He stopped and shook his head, a flash of anger on his face before he pushed it back and continued. "He would make you have sex with him, even after you told him no." I dropped my head and waited for him to continue. "Baby, look at me. I told you, I'm not judging you. I just want to know if you have been tested for AIDS and HIV? Because the times he didn't get it from you, I can just about bet he was getting it elsewhere. Believe me when I say this doesn't change anything between us. I'm in too deep. I've fallen too hard to pull back now. This is just coming from a place of concern." I released a sigh and placed my hand on his face gently. "Yes I have. I go at least twice a year. The last time I was tested was when you took me to the E.R. Every time I get tested; the results come back negative. Thank God. So, it seems as though he at least had the decency to protect himself if he was stepping out. And we didn't have sex unprotected either. Early on after we got together, I knew I didn't want to chance getting pregnant by him." I watched Jamere nod and then he put his arms around me. "That's great. I'm glad he didn't jeopardize your health among everything else." I inhaled his scent as I held onto him, hoping, and praying it was one I would never tire of. "I am too. More than you know." We released each other and Jamere pulled my door open. Once I was seated, he pushed the door closed and walked away.

I watched Jamere walk in front of the car, going over the many reasons I was glad to have him in my life. Not many people had an effect on me as he does, family or otherwise. And knowing I had found someone as special as him, made me more and more grateful each day. He was an amazing man, and one day he would raise an amazing son. His gentleness, his concern for others, his protective instincts. I knew, just as well as I knew God had placed us together for a reason, that he would be an amazing father one day. The realization that I wanted to be the one to carry his unborn children in my body, hit me with a wave of passion I had never before experienced.

"Baby, you still have over an hour before you have to be at work. What do you want to do?" I let my mind come back to the present and glanced in Jamere's direction. I looked at my phone for the time, thinking about what I could do. "I guess we can just go drop my stuff off at home. By the time I get everything sorted, it should be about time for me to make my way toward work." Jamere nodded while starting the car and heading out of the parking lot. I looked out of the window and grabbed his free hand absently, keeping it loosely held in my own.

I watched the trees go by, resting my head on the window and letting my eyes drift shut. My apartment search was going well, the only problem I was having was finding somewhere close to my jobs. But if it came down to it, I'd just have to move a little farther away. Because in two months, I planned on moving into a new place free from the nightmares the past few years had left me with. I put a down payment on a new bedroom suit while Chey and I shopped the day before. The money Q gave me, left me with plenty of money for a down payment and security deposit on a new place. All I needed to do now, was wait for God to show me where my new place would be.

I opened my eyes and turned my head so that I was looking at Jamere. "Did you have a nice nap?" I grinned at him and shook my head no. "I wasn't asleep. I was thinking. 2 questions though." Jamere nodded at me as he turned down the street leading to my apartment complex. "Question one is?" I smiled at him and let my thumb rub over the back of his hand. "Do you know of an inexpensive storage facility? I'm selling my bedroom suit, so when the new one comes, I'll need somewhere to keep the other one until its sold." Jamere shook his head no but spoke as he did. "No. Not off hand. But I can ask my parents if you can store it in the empty room in their basement. That way you won't have to spend all that money for storage." I shook my head, looking at the light we were stopped at. "I can't impose on them like that. I'll figure something out when the time comes." Jamere squeezed my hand tightly in his, driving under the light as it changed from red to green. "I'll ask anyway. If it's an imposition in any way, they'll let me know, and the two of us will figure something else out. Okay?" I smiled at him and nodded, knowing that arguing with him would be futile. "Whatever you say baby." Jamere grinned at me and turned the car into my complex. "Question 2?" My mouth went dry as Jamere removed his hand from mine and let it rest on my thigh absently. I focused on what I wanted to ask, and after a few seconds, I was able to voice my question. "Will you help me move in a few months? I don't really talk to a lot of guys other than you and my brothers, so I'll need all the help I can get. I tried to ignore the lazy circles Jamere was drawing on my thigh and tried to keep from fidgeting. "You don't even have to ask. I'll be there, and I'll recruit Lloyd and my dad too. Are you going to ask your brothers?" I nodded slowly, painfully aware of the desire that was flooding through my body. "Cool. So, six men. I think that should be good. And as soon as you are out of here, the better we can both sleep." Jamere turned off his car in front of my building, the swift removal of his hand from my thigh sending a rush of cool air through my suddenly overheated body. He opened the door and walked around to my side to let me out. Once I was standing, he pushed the door closed and walked to the trunk to get my things.

Chapter 11:

Jamere

"Baby, your phone is ringing!" I looked towards the bathroom door where she had gone to fix her hair for our date. "Answer it for me sweetie." I picked it up and read the name, speaking into it after pressing the talk icon. "Hello?" There was a pause and then an angry male voice spoke. "Who the hell are you and why are you answering my sister's phone?" I kept my tone calm and spoke to Trina's brother respectfully. "Hi. My name is Jamere. I'm Trina's boyfriend. She's in the bathroom doing her hair and she asked me to answer her phone. She is safe, I promise you that." A sigh left his voice, and this time when he spoke, it wasn't laced with anger. "I'm sorry. My initial tone was rude. My name is Tayler. I'm Trina's oldest brother. How long have you two been together?" I walked toward the bathroom and knocked on the closed door, listening to Trina tell me to come in as I answered Tayler's question. "6 weeks." My throat became dry as I looked at Trina standing in front of the mirror in her jeans and bra. "That's nice. Hopefully, I'll get to meet you soon. Lord knows, she never introduced us to anyone else she dated. Maybe you'll be the exception." I barely heard what he said, as I stared at Trina, who acted as if this was an everyday thing. As if she didn't know I was standing there, feeling a tightness in my jeans. "I hope I am. Would you like to talk to her?" I was surprised I could speak over the cotton in my mouth, and I knew I needed to get off of the phone before I said something he didn't want to hear. "Yes please. Take care of my little sister man. She's a special one." I smiled as I entered the room, knowing how true his words were. "Believe me I am, and I will. I know how special she is. She is truly a gift from God. Have a good one man. Here's Trina." I listened to him say okay and held Trina's phone out to her. "Your brother Tayler wants to talk to you." Her eyes widened slightly as she turned her head to look at me. I held her phone out to her and she puckered her lips out to me. "I pressed my lips to hers, fighting to pull away from the soft flesh. "I'll be ready in five baby." I nodded and walked out of the bathroom, letting my legs carry me to the living room slowly.

    I paced the length of the room a few times, thinking of anything I could so that my straining erection behind my zipper would go away. But with each thought of Trina's smooth brown skin, full perky breasts held in that lacy blue material, and the snug jeans that fit her slim waist perfectly, that was harder than it should have been.

I walked to the front door and stepped outside, hoping the cold air would squash the heat that was flooding every inch of my anatomy. I stood at the edge of the breezeway and looked up at the sky, inhaling the cold air slowly. It dulled the ache a little. Enough to ease the hardness in my jeans slightly, but it was able to be hidden. The stars twinkled above me, something I seemed to always be too busy to actually look at. Each one so different, yet so similar at the same time. Not wondering if its neighboring star was shining brighter than it was, just happy to be able to shine at all. If that were the mindset people could have, a lot of problems would cease. But people were not stars. With the exception of the beautiful star, I had come to know over the past few months. People just have to have a reason to fight, even if it's over the most trivial thing. And that, I wasn't sure would ever change.

I turned and walked back towards Trina's apartment, smiling when I saw her standing in the doorway watching. The smile that graced her lips was one I didn't think I would ever tire of seeing. I walked to where she stood gazing into her eyes and watching her look away nervously. I lifted her chin with my index finger so that she was looking at me again. "You don't have to be nervous around me. Everything about you is beautiful to me. I would do anything, give anything, just to keep that beautiful smile on your face." A grin appeared on her face, and she nodded her head slowly. A low rumble formed in my stomach, and I couldn't stop myself from pressing my lips to hers. Trina gripped my shirt in her fists, pulling me unbelievably closer to her body.

    I hesitantly broke the kiss, pulling her hands from my shirt and breathed heavily on to her gorgeous face. "We have to stop. My control is slipping away, and I don't want to rush this. I want us to take our time. Share something beautiful. But not before you're ready. When it happens, I want us to be making love, and not just having sex. And when our time comes, you'll know exactly what I mean." Trina's breath brushed across my face, the sweet minty scent starting a slow, rumble in my body. A rumble of desire, of passion, I had never before experienced. "I understand. And thank you for being patient. I know this has to be harder for you than it is for me." I shook my head and let my words tumble from my mouth. "It may be hard. But it will be worth it. I believe that with everything in me. I don't mind waiting until you're ready. As long as I know you've healed. Gotten back to you. That's what you need, and that's what I want for you." Trina lifted herself to her tip toes, even in the boots she wore, she was still a few inches shorter than me. Her lips brushed mine softly and she slid her hand in mine. "We should probably go. Let me get my purse and lock up, and we can do that." I used my free hand to turn the doorknob, and she walked into the apartment. I followed behind her to grab my coat, watching her grab her own coat and purse from the sofa beside mine. With her keys in hand, the two of us walked out of her apartment once again.

    I retrieved our blankets and hoodies from the trunk of my car and Trina walked beside me as we found a place to sit in front of the huge movie screen at the outdoor cinema we were at. This probably wasn't the best place for date night, as far as the weather was concerned. But it was what Trina wanted to do, and as long as she was happy with it, I would be too.

    Once we found somewhere to sit, we got our blankets situated and then took our coats off. We pulled our hoodies over our heads, then put our coats back on. Gloves went on our hands, and then we sat down and wrapped the blankets around us as we sat as close as we could to one another. "I'm starting to think this wasn't my smartest idea." My eyes went to Trina's, a chuckle escaping my mouth as I grinned at her. "It was a smart idea, just maybe not in the best season. It's all good though. I'll keep you as warm as I can. How it manages to be in the low seventy's, high eighties during the day, and in the thirties and forties at night, I'll never understand." Trina's cheeks flushed and her body trembled against mine as she chuckled at me. But somehow, I didn't think it had anything to do with the cold.

The movie started and Trina rested her head on my shoulder. We watched the actors on the screen, nowhere near as cold as we thought we would be. That was something to be grateful about. I gripped Trina's hand in mine, the feel of her skin restricted from the gloves we both wore. I didn't care though, as long as I could touch her, I would take what I could get. Just knowing she was close to me, made me that much happier. I pressed my lips to her forehead softly, watching as she turned to me and smiled. She pressed her lips to mine in a fleeting kiss, and returned her attention to the screen, her hand squeezing mine gently.

"That was a good movie. Good pick baby." Trina smiled as we folded the blankets and walked back to the car. "I didn't pick the movie. Just the venue." She answered with a chuckle, clutching one of the blankets in her arms. "Still, I enjoyed myself. Want to go get something to eat?" I watched Trina shake her head back and forth as we dropped the blankets in the trunk. "No. I made us some soup and cornbread for this very reason. All we have to do is head back to my apartment and dig in." My eyes brightened and I pushed the trunk closed. "You know what? You're alright with me. I think I'll keep you around." I watched a sexy grin appear on her face and she winked at me. "I'm glad." Once she was in her seat, I closed the door and walked around the car to the driver's side.

"Do you have enough boxes for us to get started packing up your apartment this weekend? Next weekend you'll be moving into your new place." Trina nodded excitedly and spoke as I drove. "Yeah. We'll be able to get a lot done since finals are this week, and then we're out for the summer. Even with me working both jobs." I nodded in acknowledgement listening to the subtle excitement in her tone. "Sebastian has been saving some for me at work too. When I go in every night this week, he said he'll have some more for me." That was nice of him. She seemed to have a nice manager. The few times I had met him, he was nice and seemed to enjoy what he did. And he had the utmost respect for Trina. So that alone, made him okay in my book. "Okay cool. So, what time do you want me to come over Saturday morning? I don't have to be at work until one, so we could get some stuff done before then." Trina was quiet for a number of seconds, before she spoke in response to my question.

"Well, how about you just come over Friday evening and spend the weekend and the following week with me. That way we can sleep at least an extra hour. My vacation for both jobs will be the following two weeks. Sebastian gave me the time because of the move, and the hotel gave me two weeks since I haven't taken a vacation in the three years I've worked there. So, we can get packed up in the morning and work our regular schedules. Move Saturday, and Sunday I can get unpacked." When she finished speaking, I turned to look at her briefly and returned my attention to the road in front of me. "Okay. Well, I get off at 3:30 a.m. Saturday morning, so I'll come by the club and follow you home when you get off. My last final is at eleven Friday morning, so depending on how long it lasts, I may be able to drop my bag off before going to work. Is that cool?" I watched her nod from the corner of my eye and then listened to her smooth tone. Mine is at 10, and I have to be at work at 12:30, so I'm heading there once I finish my final. I'll meet you somewhere on campus Friday morning and give you my key in the event that you do finish in time. I would give you my spare key, but Chey has it, and she'll probably head to my apartment after she gets off Friday evening." With my car in a parking spot, I nodded my head while opening the door. "Okay cool. That works. So after tonight, we'll see each other for our final Thursday morning, but not again until I get your key from you. I miss you already." I laughed playfully as I got out of the car, but I was actually serious. Trina made me want to be with her, be near her. And when I wasn't, I was more aware of the fact than I should have been. I waited by the open door for Trina to grab my hand, relishing in the feel of it once it was wrapped around mine securely. I guided her out of the way and closed the door, and the two of us headed for her apartment as I locked the doors to my car.

Trina and I sat in the living room in front of the TV with our soup bowls in our hands and our cornbread on saucers in front of us. "Baby, you've done it again. This is delicious." Trina used a hand to put in front of her mouth and then spoke. "Thank you. I'm glad you like it." Her phone rang, so she picked it up from the arm of the sofa to answer it. "What's up Ryan?" She put the last spoonful of soup into her mouth and then ate the last of her cornbread. I stood with my bowl and saucer in hand and spoke to Trina. "Baby, if you're finished, I'll take your dishes in the kitchen." I watched as she nodded her head and handed both dishes to me. "Thanks baby." I nodded my head at her and walked away as she continued her conversation. "My boyfriend Jamere. Is there something that you need? Because we are on a date." A smile touched my lips as I walked into the kitchen and started to wash our dishes.

Trina walked in minutes later and started to put up the remnants of our dinner. "Sorry about that babe. Ryan offered to help us start packing this weekend." I shook my head at her and pressed my lips to the top of her head. "You don't have to apologize. What did you tell him?" Trina smiled and shook her head as if clearing her thoughts and then spoke again. "I told him to come by Saturday at nine. He said he'll stay after we leave for work and get the kitchen packed up and drop my keys off at the hotel when he finishes." She dried her hands on a paper towel and then grabbed my hand to lead me back to the living room.

"You're not ready to leave are you?" I shook my head quickly and plopped down on the sofa, bringing her with me. "Good. Because I'm not ready to let you go yet. Find something for us to watch while I change." I nodded and let her go hesitantly, scanning Netflix for something to watch when she returned.

Trina returned and my mouth lost all moisture when my eyes saw what she was wearing. A tiny pair of white shorts, that exposed her smooth thighs, a black cami that had my attention on her full, round breasts. Her shorts weren't the shortest I'd seen, but on her, to me, it was as if she weren't wearing any. I swallowed past the cotton in my mouth, watching as she walked towards me while putting her hair into messy bun. "So, what did you find?" I shook my head, trying to remember what I was supposed to be doing when Trina sat down beside me and looked at the tv. "Oh. Nothing yet. What genre do you want to watch?" Trina shrugged and grabbed the remote from my hand. "Horror okay with you?" My eyes trailed over her body once again, my voice coming out in a dry whisper. "Yeah that's fine." Trina glanced at me, a smile gracing her lips when her eyes landed on mine. "If you get scared, you can always hide in my chest." That statement eased a chuckle out of me, and the two of us eyed the movie choices that were displayed on the screen.

Trina pulled the throw from the back of the sofa and rested her head on my lap. I drug my hand down her cheek gently, relishing in the smoothness of her skin as she stared at the screen. She was so beautiful. The innocence she showed a far cry from what I was used to. She seemed to be unaware of the affect her outfit of choice had on my body. With each absent touch, every casual move, each breath she took, my body was consumed in heat. A heat I had never before felt. One I never wanted to feel again, unless it was with the woman with me right that second.

I stared at the tv, unsure of what the movie was about. The desire that consumed me kept me from focusing on anything other than Trina. She was no longer laying her head on my lap, she was now sitting beside me, her fingers gripping my shirt in fear. I put my arms around her, but her attention stayed on the screen in front of us. I shifted so that I could look at her, each curve of her face, each blink of her eye. Every move of her mouth. "Baby, if you're scared, why don't you turn it off?" Trina adjusted herself in my arms and spoke, keeping her attention on the movie she was obviously afraid of. "I'm not scared." I suppressed a chuckle, raising my eyebrows in her direction. "With the way you're grabbing my shirt, you sure had me fooled." Trina slowly turned her head in my direction, stopping whatever I was going to say. "Maybe I just wanted a reason to be in your arms." The husky tone in which she said it, along with the mischievous grin that was on her face, confirmed everything I thought I knew about our relationship. I knew right then that I had fallen in love with the beautiful woman in front of me. I watched her lick her lips slowly and I had to resist the urge to pull her tongue into my mouth. I lifted her chin and locked her eyes on mine. Stared into the brown depths that seemed to go on forever.

"Baby. You don't need a reason to be in my arms. They are always here and waiting for you. Never, ever think you need to come up with any reason to be where I love for you to be. Okay?" Her voice came out in a hoarse whisper, the one word she spoke filled with desire and passion. "Okay." As soon as the word left her mouth, my lips covered hers, and her body came apart in my arms. Her body shook with desire, each tremble more intense than the one before. I lifted her body and laid her on the couch, holding myself above her as her hands eased up my shirt. I took my lips from hers and peppered her face with kisses, each area of soft flesh sending a flood of heat through my body.

I pulled away from her, using every bit of control I had left to do so. "Baby. I have to go. If I don't, I don't think I will be able to control myself. The way I ache for you, desire you, want you. If I don't leave now, I won't be able to keep myself from being inside you. I'll call you when I get home. I promise." Trina's chest rose and fell rapidly, each gasp coming out in succession with my own. "I don't think that would be a bad thing. But you're right. As much as I want you here with me, I think it may be too soon." I stood and helped her to her feet. I then picked up my coat and stepped back into my shoes. She followed me to the front door and stood in the doorway as I stepped out. "I'll call you in a few." She nodded and stood on her tip toes to press one last lingering kiss to my lips. "Okay baby. Be careful." I nodded and hesitated before speaking again. "I will. Go inside and lock the door." I watched her nod before she stepped back into the apartment and closed the door. Once I heard the click of the lock, I made my way to my car.

    I drove the streets, my mind overflowing with thoughts of Trina and my love for her. The sight of her body, the desire in her eyes, the passion she filled me with sending an ache of longing through my body. Her beauty was like no other. Her smooth brown skin, her toned arms and legs, her long eyelashes. Each time I looked at her, something new captivated me in a way I had never before experienced. Her heart drew me to her. Her personality grabbed my attention, and her body was just an added bonus. As each day passed, I was happier than I was the previous one, simply knowing she was in my life. In my heart, as I hopefully was in hers.

As I stepped out of my car, I pressed Trina's speed dial and made my way to my apartment. I listened to the ringing as I walked up the stairs that led to my apartment. Just as I unlocked my door and pushed it open, Trina answered the phone. "Hey baby. Are you home yet?" I locked up and walked to my bedroom, keeping my phone to my ear as I turned on the light. "Yeah, just walked in. Are you in bed yet?" I walked around my room, getting the things I would need for school the following morning together. My bookbag was against the wall with my books and my tablet inside. 3 more days, and school would be out for the summer. This was a difficult year, so I was more than happy for a break. Especially now that I had Trina as a part of my life. "Not yet. I just got out of the shower. That's what took me so long to answer. I'm putting on my lotion right now." Images of Trina naked played in my mind like a slideshow, even though I had never seen her naked before. My imagination was showing it as if I had though.

"Maybe you should have left that part out. Now, I'm imagining you naked." I heard Trina's sharp intake of breath and then her voice played in my ear. "Sorry. I didn't think about it before I said it. I'm just comfortable around you. I don't have to filter my words when I'm talking to you. You are the only man I've ever been able to do that with." I was silent for a few seconds, trying to digest what she had just told me. And with each conversation like this one, I fell even harder for her. If that was at all possible.

"Baby, there is no reason for you to apologize. When I said what I said I didn't mean it in a way that should make you feel bad or ashamed. I don't mind picturing you naked, as much as I would like to see the real thing. I'm happy you can speak your mind with me. You've had to hold your words back for years, and I'm glad you know that with me, you don't have to do that anymore. You can tell me whatever you want and know that I will never hurt you for it." I listened to the silence that invaded the line and waited for Trina to say something. Her breathing was labored, but I knew she was just taking to heart what I said. I laid across my bed and held my phone to my ear, waiting patiently for her to speak.

"Baby, I don't know how to respond to that. All I can think to say is Thank You. I know that you would never hurt me emotionally or physically. Not intentionally anyway. There is no malice in your heart whatsoever. That I have noticed about you first-hand. You are an amazing man and person, and I am enjoying having you in my life." Trina's heart was so big and so full of love, I would never understand how anyone could treat her any way other than with love. And with each conversation like this, I knew she was destined to be an amazing mother, should she ever decide to have children. "You are more than welcome sweetheart. I wouldn't say it if I didn't mean it with everything in me. And thank you for what you said about me. You are right. I would never do anything to intentionally hurt you in any way, shape, or form. And I'm glad you know that." I paused for a few seconds and then spoke again. "Sweetie, I'm going to take a shower and call it a night. I have review classes for my finals on Thursday tomorrow. I'll try to call you before you go to work. Okay?" There was a shuffling sound on the line and then Trina spoke in a soft tone. "Okay Jam. I just climbed in bed myself. Good night. Sleep well. Sweet dreams." I smiled at her words, holding back a chuckle as I replied. "My dreams will be filled with you, so I know they will be. Good night baby. Sweet dreams to you too." The line grew silent, and Trina spoke after a minute or so. "I'm hanging up now. Talk to you later." "Okay. Later." "Later."

    I listened to my professor drone on and on about material I already knew. If I had known he was going to talk endlessly like he was, I would have stayed home and used my own devices to study. I read the words he had written on the board, not bothering to write them down, because I had them written among the notes I had written over the course of the semester. All I wanted was for the remaining twenty minutes to go by, so that I could go home to eat and study before I had to be at work at three. But with each tick of the clock, it seemed like each minute was transformed into an hour.

    As soon as my class ended, I walked to my car to go home. Once I was in my seat, my phone vibrated in the pocket of my cargo shorts. I removed it and tapped the answer icon, smiling as Trina's face lit up the screen. "Hey baby. What's up?" I maneuvered my car through the parking lot, waiting for her to reply to my question. "Hey babe. Nothing. I just wanted to talk to you before work. I just got out of class and I'm on the way there now. What about you? How was class?" I ignored the vibrations my phone was making and continued to talk to Trina. Whoever it was, I would call back. "Class was boring. More boring than usual. But it will be worth it in the end. I just got out too. I'm heading home to get something to eat and study before I have to go to work." My phone vibrated again, and I glanced at the screen to see who it was. When I saw my brother's face, I made a mental note to call him back once I hung up from talking to Trina. "I feel you. That's how I felt. But it's almost over. Two more days." A smile lit up my face as I thought about what she said. These two days couldn't go by fast enough. "Yeah. You're right." "Baby, I'm at work now so I'll talk to you later. Be careful going to work." "I will baby. Talk to you later. Have a good day at work." I turned into my apartment complex and waited for Trina to respond. "Okay. You do the same." We ended the call and I pulled into a parking spot, grabbed my bag, and got out of the car.

   Once I was inside, I called my brother back to see what he wanted. The phone rang a few times before he answered the phone. "What's up Juss? I was on the phone when you called. What do you need?" Juss let out a breath and then spoke into the phone. "Both times? I called you twice a couple minutes apart." The last time I checked I was grown, and I was allowed to be on the phone however long I wanted, but I didn't go there. I just answered his question in hopes he would tell me the reason he called. "Yes both times. I was talking to my girl. What did you want?" Juss whistled and then laughed, before finally telling me what he wanted. "Yeah, we're coming in town on Sunday. For real this time. Since we had to cancel when Honey got sick right before her spring break, I decided to make up for it. We'll be there for two weeks." A grin spread across my face and excitement filled me. "That's great. What time are yall getting in? I'm off on Sunday so I could come pick the two of you up if you need me to." Juss spoke to my niece, telling her to go put up her toys before answering my question. "Our flight gets in at 11:06 a.m. So yeah, you can come get us if you don't mind. I was about to call mama and daddy to see if we could just use the basement. I don't see a point in getting a hotel room if they'll let us stay in the basement while we're in town." I nodded to no one and looked in the fridge for something to eat.

"Cool. I'll be there. Well, you can just stay at my place. I'm staying with my girl next week to help her pack up her apartment. She's moving next Saturday, and she works two jobs, so I'm helping her out. The following week, we'll figure out sleeping arrangements though. That way, you can come and go as you please." Juss was silent for a few seconds, thinking over whether or not he wanted to do that. "Okay cool. I'll help her move and pack up if she wants. Not like I'll be doing much of anything else. What's her name? How long have you two been together?" I smiled just thinking about her, answering his questions in the order he asked them. "Okay, I'll ask her. You don't have to though. Her name is Trina and we've been together seven weeks. It will be two months on Tuesday." I could hear the smile in his voice as he spoke to me with happiness in his tone. "It's no problem. I don't mind. If she wants or needs the extra help, I'll be there for her. I'm happy for you little bro. I can hear how happy you are, and I can't wait to meet the woman my little brother is so in love with. And don't tell me you're not. I could hear the love in your tone when you said her name." I chuckled, but I knew how serious he was. "I wasn't going to. But don't say anything to her about it because I haven't told her yet." Juss chuckled as if that just tickled him so much. "I won't. That's my word. I'll let you go though. I know you have to get ready for work and so do I. Love you little bro. See you Sunday." "Okay big bro. Love you too. Give Honey a kiss for me and tell her uncle Jamere loves her." "I will. Later." "Later."

As many times as I looked in the freezer and fridge, I didn't see anything that I wanted to eat. So, I went to the pantry and checked there to see if I wanted anything from there. I stared at the contents, shaking my head before closing the door. I exited the kitchen and went to the living room to study before work. An hour of my time was already gone, so I needed to use the time I had left to refresh my memory. With all my notes and my textbooks, I knew that everything would be covered between the two. And I knew, I would ace my final the following day. I opened my notebook and started to read over my notes, making sure I knew everything that would be on the exam the following day.

When I arrived at work, my stomach started to growl from its lack of food. I shook my head and walked to the locker room to get changed. "What's up J? I called you last night, but you didn't answer. I figured you were in bed already." I suppressed my grin and replied to Lloyd's statement honestly. "No, I was on a date with Trina. We went out and then got some dinner. So, I didn't get home until late. When I finally did, I just showered and went to bed." Lloyd grinned and pulled his work shirt over his head and dropped it in the hamper. "Oh okay. Well, I wanted to see if you wanted to go out this weekend. Go get some drinks or something. My parents are keeping LJ and I have the entire weekend off for once." I stripped out of my street clothes and nodded my head. "Maybe Sunday. I'm off and Trina is working but Juss is coming in town. So, depending on whether or not Honey spends the night with my parents, he may want to come too. I'll let you know though." Lloyd nodded his head at me and pulled his jeans up over his basketball shorts. "Okay cool. I can't wait to see my niece. I'll see you tomorrow though. I'm going to pick up LJ and go home. See you later." I nodded my head at him, and he walked out of the locker room while putting his phone to his ear.

  With each hour that passed, it seemed like time went slower. With my growling stomach and tired eyes, all I wanted to do was eat, talk to Trina, and go to sleep. Each truck I loaded pulled off on time, but it seemed as though the more I loaded, the more I had left. I was getting impatient while waiting for three a.m. so that I could clock out. With the way my night was going, it seemed as though that was never going to happen.

Chapter 12:

Trina

The club was busier than usual, and for that I was grateful. Any opportunity to make some extra tips, I was happy about. I walked around the bar and started my drink orders, since all of the other bartenders were swamped with patrons. My eyes glanced at my tickets, and I began making the drinks and sitting them on the tray in front of me. My head lifted to count the drinks, and when I had all of my orders, I picked up the tray. Just as I was about to walk away, a smile covered my face and I winked at Jamere as he stopped in front of the bar. "Hey baby. Give me a few minutes to take these drinks. Find a table and whatever person comes, tell them I'm already helping you." Jamere nodded his head and watched me walk away from behind the bar.

I walked up to Jamere's table, and he stood to hug me, kissing my cheek when he pulled away. "Baby, you remember Lloyd. But this is my big brother Justus. Justus, this is my girlfriend Trina." Lloyd stood and hugged me briefly, causing me to freeze for a few seconds. As he let go, Juss stood and held his hand out for mine. Once in his, he pumped it a few times and we let go. "It's nice to meet you Trina. I've heard nothing but great things." I smiled at him as he sat back down and spoke. "Thanks Justus, it's nice to meet you too. I've heard great things about you as well. I heard you have a daughter. What is her name?" I spoke loudly over the music thumping, just to be sure he could hear me. "Call me Juss. And her name is Angela, but we call her Honey." I nodded my head while pulling out my order pad. "Okay. I would love to meet her if it's okay with you. But for right now, let me get your orders." They nodded and looked at each other as he spoke. "It's not a problem with me. I'll see what I can arrange." I nodded and listened to them tell me what they wanted and then walked away from their table.

  I waited for one of the bartenders to give me my drinks, and then pulled some money from my pocket and gave it to her. "Thanks Teri." She nodded her head at me and glanced at another patron. "No problem Trina." I maneuvered around the club to go back to Jamere's table and placed their drinks in front of them. "Here you go fellas. I'll be back in a few to check on you." I dropped my hand with the tray in it to my side, turning my head when Jamere's hand slid into mine. "How much do we owe you?" I winked at him and shook my head, watching the grin appear on his face. "Don't worry about it. It's on me." Jamere attempted to speak, but I turned my body away from him. I felt his lips touch the back of my hand before he let go and let me walk away.

My hand tingled, the feeling of Jamere's lips on my hand filling my body with heat. I shook my head and walked around, taking orders from patrons as I did. With my pad in my hand, I sang along to the music playing and swayed my hips in time to the beat. I stopped and gave Teri my orders and we chatted while she made them. "Table eight is full of gorgeous men. I saw them when they came in. Times like this I wished I worked the floor so I could flirt with them." I grinned and glanced in the direction of Jamere's table. If you get a free minute, I'll introduce you." Confusion appeared on Teri's face, and she looked at me for a few seconds. "You know them?" I nodded slowly and watched the grin return to her face. "Yeah, the one with his back to us is my boyfriend Jamere. The one on his left is his brother, and the one on the right is his best friend." She slid my tray to me and nodded in approval. "Nice. Well, If I can break away, I'll definitely take you up on that offer." I gave her a nod and thanked her, picked up my tray, and walked away to deliver them.

My body throbbed each time Jamere touched me when I would stop at their table to check on them. He would do something as simple as place a glass in my hand, and when our fingers brushed, heat encompassed my body. The dull ache between my legs let me know just how much I wanted him. And as much as I craved him, desired him, I wasn't sure if I was in the right head space to give my body to him in that way. But I knew, that in time, it would come, and it would be well worth the wait.

The DJ announced last call, and I made my rounds to see if any of my remaining patrons wanted anything else before we closed for the night. Everyone was starting to file out of the building and for that I was grateful. I wanted to go home and get in bed and curl up beside Jamere. That is, if I could get him to share the bed with me instead of sleeping on my couch. It hadn't worked so far, but maybe tonight would be different. With the exception of the nights, I had nightmares when he was over, he stayed on the sofa, no matter how hard I tried to convince him that it was okay for him to sleep in the bed with me. I had to respect that quality. Most men wouldn't do as he does.

I walked to Jamere's table as they stood and prepared to leave. "Are you all heading out?" Jamere smiled and put his arms around me, pressing his lips to my forehead. "Yeah.

I'm going to take Juss back to my apartment. Lloyd left his car in front of my building, so once Juss is inside, I'll make my way to your place okay?" I nodded while putting my arms around him, pressing my lips to his quickly. "Okay baby. Yall be careful. It was nice meeting you Justus. Good seeing you again Lloyd." The two of them smiled at us still wrapped in each other's arms. "It was nice meeting you too Trina. And I told you, call me Juss." I smiled at him, and Lloyd pulled me from Jamere's arms gently and gave me a brief hug. "Nice seeing you again too. I'll see you this weekend. Keep my brother in check." I chuckled as he let go, watching Jamere punch him on the arm. "I will. Be safe going home." Lloyd nodded his head at me and glanced around as the lights came on. "I will. You do the same." I smiled and watched as he and Juss headed for the exit. "Okay baby. I'll see you shortly." Jamere pressed his lips to my cheek and then turned around, walking in the direction Justus and Lloyd had gone.

 I rubbed lotion into my skin after my shower and then sat on the bed to wait for Jamere. The tv was on, but all I was doing was flipping channels absently. I pulled at the sleeves on my shirt, trying to fight off the cold. I didn't want to get under the covers, because as soon as I did, I would be dead to the world.

And I knew I wouldn't have heard Jamere knock. So, until he got here, I was going to have to be cold.

A yawn escaped my mouth, and I leaned my head against the headboard. With a shake of my head, I looked around at the few boxes I had already packed in my room. It was a process, but it would be done by the time moving day got here. The walls were the same white they had been when I moved in, the carpet a beige color, that I thankfully had never had to have cleaned. My mahogany furniture stood out against the bland walls and plain carpet, and now that all pictures were off of the walls, my room seemed empty. But my new room, would be completely different. Life would be breathed into it, and I would never allow myself to be in the situation I had been in for the past three years.

I jumped when I heard a knock on the door, shaking my head when I realized it was probably Jamere. I slid to the floor and walked through the living room and to the front door. "Who is it?" I called through the door with my hand on the doorknob. "It's me baby." I knew the light in the hallway was flickering, so it was pointless to check the peephole. I took in a deep breath and eased the door open, peering around to see if it was actually Jamere. When I saw his gorgeous face, I pulled the door open and let him walk in. "Sorry baby. My phone died, otherwise I would have called to let you know I was on the way. He pushed the door closed and locked it securely and then followed me toward my bedroom. "It's okay. I figured it was you. No one else should be stopping by at five a.m." I jumped on my bed as Jamere went through his bag. "I'm going to shower." I nodded, following his retreating body with my eyes.

    Jamere walked out of the bathroom minutes later, shirtless with a pair of basketball shorts on his legs. He walked to the trunk at the foot of my bed and lifted the lid, so I opened my mouth to speak. "Baby, sleep in the bed with me tonight. I want to be in your arms." Jamere stopped what he was doing and looked over at me. One hand still rested on the lid of the open trunk, but his eyes stared into mine. "Baby, are you sure you're okay with that? I don't want you having any flashbacks." I slid to the floor and walked to where he was, closing the lid on the trunk. "Have I ever had any flashbacks when you held me through the night, when my nightmares plagued my mind? You make me feel safe, protected. I just want to be close to you. To touch you. I'm okay with it. So, let's lay down and get some sleep. Okay?" I watched his eyebrow raise briefly, before he nodded his head. "Okay baby. Let's get some sleep." We each walked to our sides of the bed and slid under the covers. I looked at the tv, smiling to myself when Jamere grabbed my waist and pulled my body to his. I turned so that I was facing him and trailed my fingers over the outline of his face. "Good night Jamere. I.... See you in the morning." I felt his lips press against mine, smiling behind the kiss and causing him to chuckle. "That felt weird. But good night Trina. Sleep well." He pulled me closer to him and I rested my head against his shoulder as another yawn escaped my mouth. "You too." That was the last thing I remembered before sleep pulled me under.

    The sound of my alarm woke me the next morning, so I turned it off and scooted closer into Jamere's warm body. I felt him shift and try to sit up, but I wrapped my arms and legs around his slim body like a vice. His chest vibrated as he chuckled, and he slipped his arms around my waist securely. "Good morning to you too. Did you sleep okay?" I nodded my head against his bare chest, inhaling his masculine scent as I spoke. "Yes. What about you? I didn't crowd you, did I?" Jamere pressed his lips to the top of my head and then moved his hand so that he could lift my chin. "Never have you crowded me. I sleep better than ever when you are in my arms." I smiled as he spoke with his mouth angled away from my face. "Now, can you release me so I can brush my teeth and get my good morning kiss?" He wiggled his eyebrows at me playfully, causing me to chuckle. "I guess so." I removed my arms and legs from around his body and sat up on the bed. Once I was on the floor, I rushed to the bathroom to brush my teeth.

    I made some breakfast for Jamere, and I while he got himself together in the bathroom. We both had to be at work in a few hours, so we were going to try to get as much done as we could before we left. But first, we needed to eat. We would get a lot more accomplished if we had the energy we would gain from eating. "Okay. Just let me know. Talk to you in a little bit." Jamere ended his conversation as he walked into the kitchen and put his arms around my waist. He kissed my neck softly, sending shivers through my body as he did. "Juss is on the way. He should be here in twenty minutes or so." I nodded and turned away from the food, stood on my tip toes and pressed my lips to his. Jamere's tongue slipped into my mouth, mingling with mine, the taste of mint prominent on his skilled tongue. His hands went to my thighs, and he lifted me onto the counter, never breaking the kiss. I moved my arms to his neck, holding him close to me, until we finally detached our mouths.

"You make me lose control. I haven't figured out if that's a good or a bad thing yet." A smile graced my lips and I looked down when I heard his phone ring. "Hello?" He stepped back but continued to look at me as he talked to whoever was on the line. "Okay. Get out. I'm coming out now." I watched him end the call, and back toward the front door. "Juss is outside. Be right back." He quickly walked back to me and lifted me from the counter, placing me gently on the floor. I walked back to the stove and stirred the grits, grinning when he winked at me and walked to the front of the apartment once again.

I placed some sausage in a pan and turned when I heard the door open. Justus smiled at me, so I returned the gesture. "Good morning Justus. Want some breakfast?" He walked to me and hugged me, nodding his head as he spoke. "Sure, thanks. And I told you to call me Juss." He smiled as he said it, so I knew he wasn't upset that I hadn't called him that. "I know, I just have this thing with first names. Especially ones that I like. Yours is one that I like. There are only five or six people I call by anything other than their first name. Those people being, my three brothers, my best friend, sometimes Jamere, and sometimes Amelia. Oh, and L.J., but that's only because he shares a name with his dad. So, don't be offended. Sometimes I may call you Juss, but most times I won't. It's just the kind of person I am." Justus smiled at me and then looked at Jamere, so I went back to cooking.

"I like her bro. She's a keeper." I smiled at his statement but kept my attention on the pancakes and sausage I was cooking. "Yeah I do too. She is definitely that." I felt Jamere put his hands on my waist, so I turned my head so that I could see him. He pecked my lips softly and looked down at the food on the stove. "Need some help?" I shook my head and continued what I was doing. "No babe. I'm good. You and Justus can watch TV or something. I'll let you both know when everything is done." He slid his thumb under the cami I was wearing and moved it in a slow up and down motion. "Are you sure?" I tried to suppress my gasp and I hoped I was successful. "Positive." I let out, trying not to squirm at the feel of his thumb rubbing my side. "Okay. Holler if you need me." I nodded and he kissed my temple, removed his hand, and then walked away.

I listened to the sound of Justus' feet walk out of the kitchen, knowing that Jamere was with him. With only socks on his feet, I know there was no way I would have heard his feet touch the ground. My body trembled as I finished the pancakes and sausage, but not from fear. This was a completely different emotion, and it was one I don't think I would ever get used to if Jamere made me feel it. That, I was definitely not upset about.

I answered my ringing phone, as I sat Jamere and Justus' plates on the table. "Jam, Juss, breakfast is ready." After calling them, I answered my phone while making my own plate. "Hello?" I put what I wanted on my plate and leaned against the counter. "Hey sis. I just wanted to let you know that I was on the way." I watched Jamere walk to me, pressing his lips to mine before speaking. "Thanks baby." I winked at him, and he opened the fridge, pulling some cheese and orange juice out as I spoke. "You're welcome sweetie. I'll be there in a minute." He put the juice and cheese in one hand, and grabbed my plate with the other, nodding his head and then walking away from me.

"Okay Ryan. How long will it take you to get here? Jamere and his brother are here already. We're eating and then we're going to get started." I grabbed three cups and then walked to the kitchen table with the others. "No kissing on the phone with me. But I should be there in thirty minutes or less.

Depending on traffic." I nodded to myself and sat the cups on the table. "That was just a peck, so whatever. See you when you get here." We said our goodbyes and then I prayed over the food in front of me. "My brother is on the way. He should be here by the time we finish eating." Jamere nodded and started to eat his untouched food. "Which one? Ryan?" I nodded and started to eat, doing so as fast as I could so that we could get started.

  The knock on the door made me turn my head in the direction of the sound. I stood, but Justus stopped me. "I'll get it for you. That way you won't have to maneuver around all these clothes." I nodded my head as Jamere walked into the room from starting the dishwasher. "Okay. Thanks, it's probably my brother Ryan." Justus nodded and exited the room as Jamere sat on the floor and started to put clothes from the floor in a box. "Where is he going?" I taped a box up and pushed it out of the way as I answered his question. "Someone was at the door. He went to answer it. You probably didn't hear the knock over the sound of the dishwasher." Jamere nodded and a few seconds later, I heard my brothers voice.

  "Lil Bit!" I flinched but looked up in time to see my brother lifting me from the floor. He spun me around, squeezing me tightly while kissing my cheek. "I missed you." He put me down and removed his arms from around my body. "I missed you too R.J." Jamere stood, smiling at me as I reached for his hand. "R.J. This is my boyfriend Jamere and his brother Justus. Jamere, Justus, this is my big brother Ryan." Jamere smiled and shook his hand while keeping the other clasped in mine. "Nice to meet you Ryan. I've heard nothing but great things." Jamere let go and let Justus shake his hand. "It's nice to meet you too. You can call me R.J. though. Trina is the only person who calls me Ryan." I watched Justus and Ryan release hands and Justus spoke. "Yeah, she told us she has a thing with first names. You can call me Juss." Ryan chuckled and nodded his head. "Cool. That's true. She's been like that all her life. Lil Bit is the only nickname she let us call her growing up, and Cheyenne initiated it because she was so tiny." I rolled my eyes and sat back on the ground to finish my task. "It's okay baby. I like your name." I looked at Jamere and grinned, pressing my lips to his for quick kiss. "Thank you, sweetie." I winked and listened to the other two guys make gagging noises. "Shut up, or I'll kiss him for real." They both stopped the gagging noise, sending Jamere into a fit of laughter. "Let's get to work, I have three hours before I need to get ready for work." They all started to pack boxes and I played some music on my phone, the four of us making small talk the entire time.

I exited the bathroom and stepped into my shoes that I had left outside of the door. Ryan looked at me and Jamere slid to the floor, still in his basketball shorts. "Okay fellas, I'm out. Thanks for your help and I'll see you later. Ryan, don't forget to drop my key off when you leave." Jamere slid his hands onto my waist and turned me toward the door to my bedroom. "I won't. Have a good day at work. Love you." I smiled and started to walk away, my body tingling as Jamere kept his hands securely on my waist. "Love you too. See you Justus. Yall be careful going home." Justus stood and hugged me and then sat back on the floor. When they told me they would, Jamere slipped his hand into mine and led me through the apartment.

Jamere stood in front of me as I leaned against the driver's side door of my car. "Be careful baby." I smiled as he rested his hands on my hips, my body throbbing with desire. "I will. When are you leaving?" He glanced at his watch and placed his hand back where it had once been. "In about an hour. They moved my start time back an hour. So, I'll be off at three instead of four." I put my arms around his waist and held him tightly to me. "Okay, well just get Ryan to give you my key so you can come in when you get here." Jamere kissed my forehead and shook his head no. "No, I'll just meet you at the club and follow you home. Anyway, I wouldn't have needed it because Chey will be there right?" I shrugged my shoulders and spoke while looking up at him. "Suit yourself. No, she's not coming until tomorrow. I have to go though baby. I'll see you tonight." Jamere let me go and lowered his head to kiss me. I clenched his shirt in my fists and let his lips massage mine. I hesitantly separated our lips and looked up into his gorgeous eyes. "I really have to go baby. As much as I would love to stay here and make out with you, I need my job." Jamere smiled at me and nodded his head. "Okay baby. Be careful. Let me know when you get there." I nodded and he opened my door to help me into my seat. "I will. See you later." I nodded and he pecked my lips once more, before closing the door. When the car was started, I pulled away from my parking spot, honking my horn at Jamere as I drove away. I watched him raise his hand and smile as he vanished from sight.

I pulled into a parking spot and sent a text to Jamere, letting him know that I had made it before getting out. As I walked toward the entrance, the tiny hairs on the back of my neck stood on end and fear crept into my belly. I looked around, but I didn't see anything, so I shrugged my shoulders and continued my trek. I sped up, looking back and forth constantly until I was safe in the confines of the hotel. I released a breath I didn't know I was holding and went to clock in for my shift. The uneasy feeling dissipated, so I slowed my walk while going to my place behind the front desk.

My workday was boring as usual but wasn't as fast paced as most days were. I tapped at my computer, entering information the customer in front of me gave. Once everything was entered, I looked up at the woman in front of me and handed her room key to her. "Checkout is at eleven a.m. on Saturday. Enjoy your stay." The lady smiled at me and stuck the keycard in her pocket. "Thank you, ma'am. I'm sure I will. Have a nice day." I nodded my head at her and smiled as she reached for the hand of the child standing beside her. "You're welcome. Thank you." She nodded and turned to walk away, an older child pushing a cart that held their luggage behind her.

I flinched when I looked up and Ryan was standing in front of me. "Hey Trina. Just wanted to drop your key off." I nodded and then glanced to my right when I saw something move from the corner of my eye. I smiled and watched Ryan turn his head in the direction I had looked and smiled when Chey launched herself into his arms. "Ryan laughed and squeezed her tightly. "Hey little sis." He put on her on the ground and kissed her cheek. "Hey R.J. I missed you." He smiled as I clocked out and picked up my phone from the desk. "I missed you too. But I gotta bounce. I got called into work. I love yall. See you both this weekend." I walked from behind the desk and Ryan hugged me. He then kissed my cheek as Cheyenne went behind the desk to clock out for lunch. "Love you too. Be careful and see you then." He nodded and walked back the way he came as Cheyenne walked back to where I was standing. "Ready to go?" I nodded and the two of us walked out of the hotel, side by side and headed to my car.

"So?" I suppressed my grin and waited for Cheyenne to tell me what she wanted to know. "So what?" I asked her, trying hard not to laugh at the expression on her face. "Stop playing with me Lil Bit. Tell me how it went." I laughed as I drove away from the hotel to a restaurant a few minutes away. "It went fine. Ryan seemed to like Jamere as well as Justus. They talked constantly and even exchanged numbers, so I think he's good. If Ryan likes him, I know Dylan and Tayler will too." I parked my car and we got out before Chey replied. "That's good. Jamere is a good guy, and I'm glad R.J. likes him. He's getting you back to the you we've missed for so long. And you're right, if Ry likes him, D.J. and Tay definitely will. I can't wait to meet Justus. If he's anything like Jamere, I know I'll love him." I smiled as we entered the restaurant and sat down. "He's a good guy too. He told me he would let me meet his daughter Angela. I can't wait. You know I love children." Chey smiled and we placed our orders. The waiter put our drinks in front of us and walked away. "Yeah, when you and Jamere have children, you're going to be a great mother." I raised my eyebrows in shock and looked at Chey after she spoke. "Where did that come from? What makes you think Jamere, and I are going to have children?" My heart pounded in my chest as the thought filled me with love. I would want nothing more than to have children with Jamere, but that was far off. And what made Chey voice her opinion on the matter, I didn't know. "I can just see it. Lord knows you love him, even though you try to hide it. And it's obvious he feels the same. It's only a matter of time. And having Jamere be the father of my future niece or nephew, I know he would love him or her with his whole heart. I can see it in his love for Amelia and L.J." I took in what Cheyenne said and smiled to myself. She was right on more than one account. I did love Jamere. He would make an excellent father. And one day, I hope that his child would be mine too. "Yeah, Jamere is going to be an awesome father one day." That was all I said, and I didn't elaborate. We prayed over our food, and I shifted the conversation to a safer topic.

Cheyenne and I walked back into the hotel to finish our shifts. I went to my place behind the desk and clocked back in. Once I had done that, I started helping the other concierge with the line of customers that was starting to form in front of the desk. I tapped away on the computer, looking up to help the next person. "Hi. How may I help you....?" My words stopped in my throat as Stephan stood in front of me, a sadistic grin spread across his face.

"Hello Trina." I looked him directly in the eyes, not letting him have any more power over me than he had already taken. He would never put fear in me again, and I had to make sure he knew that. "Leave Stephan. The restraining order I filed against you forbids you from coming to my home, or job." I picked up the phone as my manager walked up behind me. "I'm calling the police now." I started to press the nine, and my manager spoke. "Miss Hart, what is going on?" I turned to look at him and put the phone down. "This is my ex. I have a restraining order against him that states he is not supposed to be within five hundred yards of me." I watched security walk up behind Stephan and each one stood on one side of him. "Sir, I'm going to have to ask you leave, or you will have to be escorted out." Stephan stepped closer to the desk and the security guards each grabbed an arm. "Sir, you are no longer welcome in this hotel. You have disrupted the lives of my customers as well as my employees, so you are banned from here on out." Stephan got one of his arms free and went under his shirt, coming out with a .357 Magnum clenched in his hand and aimed it at my forehead. Before I had a chance to blink, Security had him on the ground and the gun kicked away from him. My heart pounded in my chest, as I stood to see him on the ground with his hands zip tied behind his back. My manager spoke into the phone, but I couldn't hear anything other than the sound of blood pumping in my ears. I had never had a gun aimed at me before, and I don't think I would sleep tonight, for fear that I would never wake up.

  After the police had taken the statements from myself and people that witnessed what happened, my manager called me back to his office. "Miss Hart, how are you feeling? Are you okay? Do you want me to call anyone?" I shook my head no as I clasped my hands in my lap. "I'm fine sir. No, I don't need you to call anyone." He gave a slight nod of his head and glanced at his computer before looking at me once again. "Why don't you take the rest of the day off? You deserve it." I shook my head no once again and answered his question. "If it's all the same to you sir, I would rather stay. If I go home, I'll make myself go crazy with fear. I'd rather stay here until it's time for me to go to my second job." Mr. Jefferies released a sigh but nodded his head. "Okay if you're sure. But let me know before you leave, and I will get security and we'll all walk you out. Okay?" My hands trembled, so I fisted them to stop it. "Yes sir." He stood, so I did the same. "You can get back to work now. If you change your mind about going home, just let me know. And don't forget to let me know when you're ready to leave." I stepped away from the desk and nodded my head at him. "I won't. Thank you sir." He nodded and sat back in his seat as I walked out of his office.

When I returned to the front desk, Cheyenne was standing there with a mix of anger and fear written on her face. "I just heard about what happened. Are you okay? Do I need to call Jamere for you?" I looked at her and shook my head slowly. She put her arms around me and held on tightly for a few seconds before letting go. "No. I'll tell him about it after work. I just want to get through the rest of this day and be with him." I sat in my chair and tapped at my computer while Chey rested her hand on my shoulder. "I know you do sis. I'm here for whatever you need. Text me before you leave. If I don't get back to work, my manager is going to pitch a fit." She leaned down to hug me again and then rested her hand on my head before moving it. "I will. Get back to work before Debra goes on the warpath." She nodded and backed away from me slowly, and then went back to where she was supposed to be.

 I sat in my car and waited for Jamere to pull up. My manager told me I could leave at 3:30, which was about the time Jamere would have been pulling up anyway. A horn sounded, and I jumped before looking in my rearview mirror. When I saw Jamere, I calmed myself down, started my car, and pulled away from the club with Jamere following behind me.

 I waited for Jamere to open my door, and then stepped onto the ground and out of the way. Once the door was closed, I locked it and led the way to my apartment. Jamere followed me quietly but stayed close enough that his hand would hit me as it swung. I sighed internally and unlocked the door and the two of us walked inside.

Once the door was locked, I wrapped my arms around Jamere's body and held on tight. The tears I had been holding in all day flooded from my eyes, and worry filled Jamere's tone. "Baby what's the matter? What happened?" I buried my face into his chest and tried to stop the tears from falling. But the harder I tried, the more that fell. I felt Jamere lift me into his arms, so I wrapped my legs around his waist as he carried me through the apartment.

Jamere laid me on the bed and removed my shoes while I covered my face with my hands and continued to sob. I felt the bed dip, and then Jamere's arms wrapped around me protectively. He whispered to me softly, letting me know that it would be okay. "It's going to be okay baby. Cry. Let it out. Whatever it is, we'll get through it. I promise. I'm here for you. I'll hold you all night if I have to. I want you to know that I'm here and that you're safe with me. I won't let anything, or anyone hurt you. I put that on everything." Jamere pressed his lips to my forehead as the tears subsided and the sobbing ceased. I felt my eyes closing and sleep encompassed me while Jamere held me to his chest.

I shifted and opened my eyes, looking up at Jamere's handsome face. My head was pounding, but as I looked at Jamere's sleeping face, I knew why. The memories of the day before flooded my brain and replaying Jamere's final words before I fell asleep put a smile on my face. We were both still fully clothed, but the sun streamed through the blinds in my room. I kissed Jamere's chin, smiling when I felt his lips touch my forehead. "Feeling better?" I nodded my head as he turned so that he was laying on his back. I rested my head on his chest and clenched his shirt in my fists. "Thanks for being there for me. I haven't had that in a long time." He rubbed his hand up and down my arm and then rested it on my hip. "Always and forever baby. I promise." I smiled while looking up at him and the gorgeous brown depths of his eyes. "Ready to tell me what happened?" I sat up and pulled my phone from my pocket to check the time. 8:10 a.m. flashed across the screen, so I plugged it up and sat it on the nightstand. "Let me brush my teeth and wash my face, then I will." I slid to the floor, and he followed me into the bathroom so we could freshen up a little.

    I sat on the edge of my bed as Jamere pulled my desk chair to the side of the bed I was on and sat in front of me. My eyes closed and I felt Jamere put one hand on the side of my neck. He used his thumb to rub my cheek gently and waited patiently for me to speak.

    I went through the story, starting from coming back from lunch and ending with talking to Chey. Jamere pulled my hands, and sat me on his lap, anger playing on his features but compassion in his voice. "I'm sorry you had to go through that. It should have never gotten to that point. Knowing he pulled a gun on you, with the intention to end your life, makes my heart ache more than you know. I don't know what I would have done if you had been hurt, or worse, killed. I'm glad you're okay now though. And as long as you're with me, I'll do whatever it takes to make sure you're safe." I rested my head on his shoulder and took in everything he had just told me. Three words threatened to spill from my mouth, but the knock on the door saved me from saying them before I was ready. I stood to go answer the door, but Jamere grabbed my hand and gently pulled me back toward him. "Let me get it. We don't know if he's out on bond or anything." I inhaled deeply but nodded my head as he walked toward the front door. I walked into the living room but stayed out of sight until Jamere let me know it was okay to come out.

"Baby, it's okay. You can come out." I moved away from the wall, watching as Quincy walked into the room in front of Jamere. "Q? What are you doing here?" Quincy closed the space between us and pulled me into his arms securely. "I just heard about what happened. He called me to pay his bond, but when I spoke to the cops and they let me know what happened, I refused. I told them to keep him there as long as they could. I am so sorry he did that to you. You, of all people didn't deserve to have him pull a gun on you. I'm just glad he didn't get a chance to fire it." I smiled at Quincy as he let me go, watching Jamere make his way to stand beside me. "Thanks, but you didn't have to come all the way over here for that. I do appreciate the concern though." Quincy smiled at me and then at Jamere, taking the shoulder bag he wore off of his shoulders. "I know, but I wanted to see for myself that you were okay. I've already told the police that I would testify against him when it was time for his trial. He needs to be straightened out, and at least if he's locked up, he won't be able to hurt you or any other woman." I nodded my head at him and took the bag he handed me from his hand. "Thank you. I appreciate that. The time I've known you, you've always treated me as a little sister. So even though all this has gone down between your brother and

I, I will always consider you my brother. That's my word." A smile spread across Quincy's face, and he hugged me close again. "Thank you. The same goes for you." The two of us let each other go and I looked down at the bag in my hand.

"What's this?" I raised my eyebrows when I looked at him, a wide grin flashing over his features. "It's yours. But don't open it until I leave. I see you're moving. That's good. Get as far away from this place as you can. And don't tell me where you're moving to. When I want to see you, we'll meet somewhere. I don't want anything I know to be used against you in court. Okay?" I nodded and he shook Jamere's hand. "Take care of her for me please." Jamere smiled at him, his face displaying the honesty in the words he spoke. "I will. I promise." The two of them released hands and Quincy spoke again. "I have to get to work. You two take care of each other. I'll be in touch, and we can get together soon." Jamere and I nodded and followed him to the front door. "Be careful out there man." Quincy pulled the door open and looked back at the two of us. "I will man. I'm legit now. I refuse to go back to prison. I'm going to make it and I'm going to do it the honest way. That I promise you." My heart swelled and I knew that he had grown up. The entire time I had known him, he was in the streets heavy. Seeing him now, showed me that over this last year, he had grown into a man. For that, I was happy and proud. "That's great Q! I'm so proud of you." Quincy smiled at me and then winked. "Thanks. I'll see you both later though. Love you." A smile appeared on my lips and I spoke as he started to walk down the breezeway. "Love you too." Once he was in his car, Jamere and I walked back in the house and locked the door.

    I looked down at the bag in my hand as I walked into my bedroom and opened the bag. I pulled the envelope that was inside out and started to read the letter that was inside.

Dear Trina,

After finding out about the things my brother has done to you over the years, I was determined to try to make up for it. And last night, after he called me, I knew that was the final straw. There is no excuse for any of the things he did to you. He should have never put his hands on you the way he did. The malice that is in his heart, lets me know that he really needs help, and hopefully, somehow, he'll get it. What is in the bag is the money from an account I found that had your name on it. Although your name was on it, after doing some digging, I was able to find out, that you never opened it. So, I got an attorney friend to go with me and have the account closed and all the money within the account is technically yours. What's in the bag, is half of the money. The other half is in a safe deposit box at your bank. I didn't touch any of it, other than to put it in the bag and the safe deposit box. The key to it, is inside the envelope this letter was in. Once you have retrieved the money, you can get rid of the safe deposit box. I love you Trina. You have always been the sister I never had, and that will never change. Get with Jamere. He makes you happy and I know he would never hurt you like my brother did. Get back to you. The you everyone knew you to be before my brother broke you the way he did. I'm sorry for what he did. Live your life. Be great. Be the woman I know you are meant to be.

I'll Be In Touch,

Quincy

I looked inside of the dark bag, glancing back at Jamere as a tear slid down my cheek. He used his finger to wipe it away and I looked at the dark bag once again. I dumped the contents on my bed, my eyes widening at the stacks of money that now lay on top of it.

Each stack had a band around it, showing how much it was, so I added it up in my head and looked at Jamere. "This is $500,000." Jamere's eyes widened, and he looked at the bed to count the money himself. "Why would he open an account in your name?" I shrugged and deep down, I know we both knew the answer to that question. I put the money back in the bag and hid it in my closet before walking out. "Baby let's see how much we can get packed before we have to shower and stuff for work. Lord knows, this has been a day already." Jamere smiled and nodded, pressing his lips to mine before going to retrieve some boxes from the living room. I sighed and pulled items from the closet to put in the boxes Jamere had gone to get.

Chapter 13:

Jamere

The morning of the move, I woke up before Trina and went to get us some breakfast before everyone started to arrive. Her keys were on the dresser, so I took them so that I could let myself out of the apartment, hoping I would be back before she woke up. As I walked through the living room, my eyes widened when I saw Chey asleep on the sofa. If I had known she was there, I would have let her get in the bed with Trina and I would have slept on the sofa. I walked around it and shook her gently until she opened her eyes. Once she was looking at me, I spoke softly.

"Go get in the bed with Trina. I'm going to get us some breakfast. I'll be back soon." Cheyenne nodded and sat up, turning toward the bedroom, and walking away from the sofa with her cover in her arms. I exited the apartment and walked to my car, taking in my surroundings once I was inside. The sun had just started to rise, so it was no longer dark outside. The smell of the damp air clouded my nostrils as I drove with the windows down to IHOP. Drake's newest album played from my speakers, and I nodded along to the beat, saying the words to each song that played.

When I got back to the apartment, I let myself in and put breakfast on the table. I ordered us all the same thing, so I didn't have to sort through anything. Once everything was out of the bags, I placed them in front of three chairs and went to get Trina and Chey. When I walked into the room, Trina was still sleeping as she had been when I I left an hour before. I walked to the side of the bed she was on and kissed her forehead before shaking her body gently.

"Trina wake up." Her eyes fluttered open, and she looked at me kneeling in front of her. "Good morning beautiful. Did you sleep okay?" I watched her head move up and down before she sat up. "I went and got us some breakfast. Let's go eat so we can be ready before everyone gets here." Trina yawned and got off of the mattress we slept on the night before. I broke down her bed the previous night, so all we would have to do was haul it out. "Okay. Let me go to the bathroom. I'll meet you in the kitchen." She yawned and turned toward the bathroom, so I walked around the bed to wake Cheyenne. Once she was awake, I told her breakfast was here and the two of us walked out of the room and went to the kitchen.

I smiled when I felt Trina's arms go around my neck, turning my head as her lips went for my cheek but landed on my lips. "Thanks for getting breakfast." I winked at her and watched as she sat in the chair beside me. I grabbed her hand as well as Cheyenne's and blessed the food before we all started to eat.

    A knock sounded at the door, so I pulled my gray T-Shirt over my head and went to answer it. Trina and Chey were in the bathroom getting dressed, so I told them I was going to answer the door before walking out of the room. I pulled open the door and looked at my dad and Lloyd standing in front of me. "Hey dad. What's up Bro?" I stepped back so that they could come in and pushed the door closed behind them. "Where's Trina?" I looked at my dad and motioned for them to have a seat. "She's in the bathroom getting dressed. We just finished eating, so she'll be out in a few." I smiled when I heard Trina and turned so that I could see her.

    "No, I'm out now. Hey Mr. Dennison. Hey Lloyd. How are you both doing?" They both stood and walked to where she stood, taking turns putting their arms around her. She put her arms around them and didn't flinch or stiffen up. I knew then, she was making progress and I was beyond happy for her. "We're doing good. How about you?" Trina gave them the thumbs up sign and walked toward the door as someone knocked on it. "Babe, let me get it." Trina nodded and stepped to the side, so I walked to the door and pulled it open. Two tall guys stood there, looking me up and down. One was about my height, which was six foot three, while the other was maybe an inch or two taller. The taller of the two spoke, causing Trina to step out from where she was standing out of sight.

"Jamere?" I nodded and watched them walk past me, the shorter one lifting Trina into his arms. He spun her around and the taller one put his arms around the two of them as tears fell from her eyes. "We missed you so much." I watched the two of them let her go and she spoke quietly while looking around. Cheyenne rushed out of the bedroom and launched herself at the two guys at the door. "I missed you both too. So much." Trina told them as the other guy caught Chey. When she spotted me standing behind the sofa, she walked to me and buried her face in my chest. I put my arms around her body and pressed my lips to the top of her head.

"It's okay baby. They're here now. Nothing will keep you from them again. I promise." I whispered those words to her and watched her head lift so that her eyes met mine. She pressed her lips to mine in a quick kiss, and then turned to the men in the room.

"Tay and D.J., this is my boyfriend Jamere, his dad Mr. Lawrence Dennison, and his best friend Lloyd. Jamere, Mr. Dennison, and Lloyd, these are my brothers Tayler and Dylan and my best friend Cheyenne." I separated the two of us and walked to where they stood, shaking their hands before allowing my dad and Lloyd to do the same.

"It's nice to meet you both. Trina has told me nothing but great things." I walked back to where Trina stood and put my arm around her shoulders. "Nice to meet you too. We haven't heard much about you yet, but I'm sure that is going to change." Tayler winked at Trina causing her to turn her head into my arm. My dad spoke, he and Lloyd looking at me with humor on their faces. "So, when were you two going to tell us you were a couple? Wait until I tell your mom. Who will be here after she drops Amy and L.J. off at your aunt's house. You are going to get it. You know she loves Trina." The two of them laughed at my expense as another knock sounded at the door. "I got it." Dylan said while walking to the door. "I was going to tell you as soon as I knew Trina was ready for people to know. And you know why. So, I'm ready for mom. And I'm not letting Trina go, so I'm glad she loves her." Trina smiled up at me, turning her head when a male voice spoke. "What's up Jamere? Hey

Lil Bit." R.J. walked to me and shook my hand before bending to hug Trina. "Hey R.J. This is my dad Lawrence Dennison and my brother Lloyd. Dad, Lloyd, this is Trina's other brother Ryan." They shook hands and Ryan spoke. "Nice to meet you both. I have the moving truck, so we can start loading the furniture now." I moved my arm from Trina's shoulder and stepped back. "Cool. The bedroom set is going to my parent's house, so that needs to go on my dad's truck. Let me put my shoes on and we can get the living room set on the truck." They nodded, so Trina and I walked into her bedroom to put on our shoes. We both put on some all-black Nike Roshe's and then walked out of the bedroom to get started.

When we walked back into the living room, my mom and Juss were coming in the door. "Hi Mrs. Dennison and Juss. These are my brothers Dylan, Ryan, and Tayler and my best friend Cheyenne. Chey, D.J., R.J., and Tay, this is Mrs. Aubrey Dennison, Jamere's mom. And his brother Justus." They shook hands after Trina made the introductions and all the men started hauling the furniture out of the apartment.

We loaded the dinette set and the sofa on the truck and returned to the apartment. My mom and Trina were carrying the TV's out to the car, so Tay and I lifted the love seat and maneuvered it out the door. The boxes would fit in the truck easily, so if we could get the furniture in, hopefully we could get everything moved in one trip.

    I watched my dad stop my mom, the grin that was on his face letting me know what he was about to do. "Baby. Jamere has been keeping secrets. He and Trina are a couple." My mom glanced at me and then looked at my dad with a straight face. "Baby, that is not a secret. It's obvious to anyone with eyes." The smile dropped from my dad's face and Juss started to laugh. "Dad, even I knew that. Even if I hadn't figured it out when I talked to Jamere last week, I would have when I met her the other day." My dad's mouth dropped open and he stopped Trina as she walked by him with a box in her arms. He grabbed the box and nodded his head for her to follow him towards the truck. My mom walked back to the apartment, D.J. and I lifting the mattresses onto my dad's truck and then closed the gate. People started to exit their apartments, glancing at us before going back to whatever it was that they had to get done. By the time they returned, hopefully we would be gone for good. Trina never had relationships with her neighbors, so there was no one she needed to say goodbye to. Hopefully, now that she was away from Stephan, she would be able to make friends without fear of what he may do to her for having them.

	Everyone piled into the vehicles while Trina drove us around to turn in her keys. Once they were handed to the apartment manager, she drove back to where everyone else was waiting in the cars. Justus was in the driver's seat of my car, while everyone else was in the car they came in. Trina pulled away from the apartment building, leading the way to her new place. She was getting a fresh start, and hopefully she would be able to continue to heal. Her heart was what I cared about. As long as she was happy, her heart healed, her mind free of those horrible memories, I would be happy. Happy for her and more in love with her than I am now.

	After getting everything unloaded and into Trina's new apartment, R.J. went to return the moving truck. Trina told everyone she would go get some pizza's as her way of thanking everyone for their help. Although we all told her it wasn't necessary, she wouldn't not do it. So, she, along with my mom and Chey went to get them while the men started to put her bed up in her room and the dinette set in the kitchen.

	Dylan followed me into the bedroom to put up Trina's new bedroom suit that had been delivered shortly after we arrived at the apartment. As we started our task, Dylan looked at me. He spoke, causing me to stop what I was doing and listen to what he had to say. "Jamere. I want to use this time that we have alone to talk to you. Now, I'm not going to bash you or anything, but I want you to know how serious I am." I nodded at him, keeping my eyes on his to let him know I was listening.

"My sister has tried to hide things from us for years. And although she thinks we didn't know, we're men and we could see the signs. Someone was abusing her, and she was afraid to come to us. Afraid that we would be upset with her for one reason or another. That couldn't be further from the truth. If she would have come to us, we would have helped her, no matter what. We wouldn't have judged her, and we won't judge her now. We love her, and we just want her happy and safe. So, I'm saying this to you. You don't seem to be the type of person that would hurt her in any way. But I don't know you. Now, I'm not accusing you of anything, or saying you will do it in the future. I just want you to know that we will be watching her a lot closer now. I know you love her; I can see it in your eyes. So, all I want is for you to love her. Keep her happy. Don't look back on her in the future and decide she isn't what you want. If you have any doubts, I would hope you would end it now. She's been hurt too much, and I don't want her to hurt anymore. Now, I know that's highly unlikely, but whatever we as her brothers can prevent, we will. I respect you Jamere. You make my sister happy and its obvious she feels the same for you. Just protect her. Love her. Be there for her when it seems to her that no one else can. She deserves that."

I looked at him, respecting him for wanting to still be the protector for his sister, even though she was an adult now. That I couldn't be mad at, because I will be the same way with my sister no matter how old she gets. I thought about his words for a minute or so before I opened my mouth to reply.

"Dylan, from the bottom of my heart and with everything I have in me, I will never not want Trina. She makes my heart smile. She makes my life better. She makes me a better man. She showed me what I've been missing for so long, without me realizing until it was too late. She saved me. In more ways than one. I want to be with her. I want to love her. I want to protect her. I want to be the one she can depend on and love. I can't let her go. I'll tell you what I told her a few weeks ago. I can't pull myself away from her. I'm in too deep. I've fallen too hard. So, there is nothing she could say or do, to make me let her go. She has my heart in the palm of her hand and I don't think she even realizes it. If I could take every bit of pain from her and put it in me, I would do it with no hesitation. I refuse to hurt her, intentionally anyway. I don't plan on doing anything to her other than love her and one day make her my wife. She completes me. She doesn't deserve the hand she's been dealt, but I'll be there to bring her back to the person everyone once knew her to be. As long as her heart heals, I'll be happy. Her heart is what is most important to me. I'm going to protect her, and I want you and your brothers to watch her. Add me in the mix, and I know she'll be good. She is my happiest moment. And I promise you, I will keep her protected and safe just as you would. I put that on everything."

Dylan released a sigh and held his hand out for mine. Once it was in his, he shook it and let go. "You've earned my respect Jamere. You're good with me. Make my sister happy. And let's exchange numbers before I leave. I think we could chill sometimes. Oh, and you can call me D.J." I smiled and nodded, and we started our task once again. "Okay cool. I'll do that." The two of us made small talk while we got the bed up, finishing as the women walked back in with the food.

Trina walked to where D.J. and I were walking out of her bedroom. She grabbed my hand and led me back into the room, pushing the door closed behind us. "I missed you." I grinned at her as she put her arms around my neck and stared into my eyes. I winked at her and pressed our lips together for a few seconds. I missed you too. Your brother and I had a nice conversation while you were gone though. He's a good dude." Trina raised her eyebrows, tilting her head at me as she spoke. "Oh really? Anything interesting?" I felt my grin widen and nodded my head. "Yes ma'am. But it was man stuff. You wouldn't understand." Trina rolled her eyes at me and eased back off of her tip toes and removed her arms from around my neck. I laughed as she walked to the door and spoke over her shoulder. "Come on. Let's go eat." I twisted the handle and pulled the door open to allow Trina to walk out. Once the two of us had stepped out, we were face to face with our families staring and grinning at the two of us.

"We were waiting for you two so we could eat. But if you need more time, we'll eat without you." Trina's cheeks reddened and she buried her face in my chest. "It's all good baby. Everybody has jokes. Let's wash up so we can eat." She slowly moved her head and walked into the half bathroom that was right off of the kitchen. When we were both finished, we walked into the kitchen where my dad blessed the food and we started to eat.

Trina's brothers talked to my parents as we all sat in various places around the apartment to finish our food. Everyone seemed to get along well and that was good, considering it was the first time everyone met. That was one of my reasons for being so happy after a tiring day. Trina was going to be my wife one day, and knowing that everyone got along, would make leading up to the day I got down on one knee and asked her, that much smoother. I stared at the woman I loved with all my heart, smiling as she and Cheyenne spoke to my parents. The smile on her face let me know, just how far she had come since the day I met her all those months ago. My head turned when I heard a voice next to me. I watched the smile form on Lloyd's face and waited to hear what he had to say. "Bro, Trina is really an amazing woman. And she loves you with all her heart. You found a good one man. I just want you to know, that I wouldn't mind having her as a sister for me and as an aunt for L.J. I mean that." I smiled at him and nodded to myself casually. "Thanks man. That's good to know."

Lloyd clapped my shoulder and nodded; the ever-present smile plastered on his face. "You know how I do it." I laughed and shook my head at him before standing to get rid of my trash.

"Well, we're going to head out. Trina, have a good night at work before your vacation starts. It was nice meeting all of you and we look forward to seeing everyone again soon." My mom started hugging everyone as my dad finished speaking. He pulled Trina into his arms as D.J. spoke. "We're going to head out too. Be good Lil Bit. Jamere, take care of our little sister." I nodded as he reached for my hand and shook it. "I will. That's a promise." D.J. nodded his head and everyone else said their goodbyes to us. We walked everyone out, waving as they each pulled away from their parking spots.

Once Trina had left for work, I started unpacking boxes and putting things where they were supposed to go. I knew she would most likely change some things around, but I was determined to help where I could.

Music filtered through Trina's bedroom from the Beats pill I had sitting on her dresser. I mouthed the words to Heaven by Jamie Foxx while I unpacked some of the boxes in her bedroom. When I had tired myself out, I stopped for the night and went in the bathroom to shower. There was still a while left until Trina got home, so I would relax until that time came. We managed to get a lot accomplished over the course of the day, and we could finish up the following day. With both of our vacations falling at the same time, I didn't have to worry about her trying to do it all herself.

My eyes stared at the TV, watching replays of a game that had aired earlier in the week. Tiredness began to wash over me, the events of the day finally starting to take its toll. I felt my eyes start to drift closed, the sound of yelling from the TV the only sound I heard as sleep pulled me under.

I felt a set of lips press against mine, the scent of smoke and perfume clouding my nostrils. I opened my eyes, blinking a few times until Trina's beautiful face came into focus. "Sorry baby. I wasn't trying to wake you." I smiled, watching her pull her black baby tee over her head. She stood in a black cami and dark jeans, looking around for boxes that should have had her clothes inside. "It's okay. I wasn't in a deep sleep anyway. I was waiting to make sure you got home safely. I started unpacking your clothes. You have some pajamas and stuff in your drawers. She looked at me and smiled, pulling out something to sleep in before returning her attention to me. "You are an amazing man. You make it so easy to be with you. That's why I love you so much."

My heart pounded in my chest as she made her way to the bathroom as if she hadn't just declared her love for me. "Trina, what did you just say?" She turned around, looking at me while she spoke. "You are an amazing man. It's true. Don't you see that?" I smiled and closed the space between us in two long strides. "Not that. But thank you for thinking so." She nodded and waited for me to continue. "You said you love me. You've never told me that before." Trina's eyes widened and she dropped the pajamas that she was holding. "I said that out loud? I was supposed to say it in my head. I'm sorry if I've scared you away. I wasn't supposed to just blurt it out like that. I." I cut her off and smiled, gripping her chin in between my thumb and index finger. "Shhh baby. You have nothing to be sorry for. I love you too. With all my heart. I was just holding back from saying it until I knew you were ready to hear it. So don't stop saying it to me, because I'm not holding those words back now that they're out. I Love You Trina!" A wide grin spread across Trina's face, and I felt my heart swell looking into the beautiful smile that graced her lips.

"I Love You Too! I realized a while ago that what I thought was love before, was the furthest thing from it. I guess I have you to thank for that. You opened my heart to love after it had been shattered in the worst way possible. So, know that when I tell you that I love you, I mean it. I'm not just saying it because I think you need to hear it. I'm not saying it to make conversation. I'm not even saying it because you said it to me. I'm saying it because I mean it with everything I have in me. I'm saying it because I want you to know. And most importantly, I'm saying it because I don't want you to ever forget it. I fell in love with you weeks ago. And even if I tried to, even if I wanted to, there is no way I could stop." Trina's eyes stared into mine, my heart beating a rapid thud as I listened to her words. I pressed my mouth to hers, my hands trailing over the contours of her amazing body. Heat filled me and I felt my erection start to stand at attention. I stepped back, breaking our kiss, and putting some space between the two of us. "You better go shower. I'm trying to be patient with you, but I'm losing control. I need to be separated from you for a while." I watched Trina's chest rise and fall rapidly, her eyes looking me up and down as I backed away. She bent to pick up her pajamas, never once taking her eyes off of mine. "I think you're right. I'll be out in a few." She turned and walked towards the bathroom, keeping her eyes straight ahead. Each step she took leaked seductiveness and my body throbbed with a need I had never before experienced. Looking at her body sway, it would take everything in me not to follow behind her. "You might want to lock the door. Otherwise, I can't promise I won't follow you." I watched her head turn so that she was looking over her shoulder at me. She nodded subtly and walked into the bathroom, pushing the door closed behind her softly.

    I exhaled loudly and walked out of the bedroom, pacing the length of the living room repeatedly, trying to get my body under control. I laid across the sofa with one foot on the arm of it and the other on the ground. With my eyes closed tightly, I let my breathing slow to its normal rhythm. "Babe?" I kept my eyes closed while speaking to Trina in a soft tone. "Baby, I'm going to sleep out here tonight. I think it would be for the best." The silence that followed made me nervous, but the nervousness was short lived when I felt Trina's body land on mine. Trina's lips pressed to mine, and I automatically put my hands on her hips, opening my eyes when I felt the terry cloth material on my hands. I separated our lips and opened my mouth to speak. Trina pressed her index finger to my lips and spoke in a husky tone.

"No, you're not. You're going to sleep in my bed with me. I'm ready for whatever happens. I want whatever happens, in whatever way it happens. If you lose control it will be okay because I'm losing control too. I know you won't hurt me, and I believe that whatever happens, won't cause me any pain." I sat up, holding on to Trina's waist, my fingers on fire even through the terry cloth material. "Trina, I don't think." She pressed her lips to mine once more, easing herself to the floor again. She pulled my hand until I was standing, and then led me into her bedroom.

"Get in the bed." I stared at her debating over what I should say. But before I could voice anything she extended her arm, using her finger to point at the bed. I smiled and walked to my side watching her walk back into the bathroom.

Trina emerged from the bathroom wearing one of my t-shirts that stopped at her thigh. I licked my lips as she stood in front of the mirror tying her hair up. She lifted her arms, causing the shirt to rise and allowing me to see the tiny shorts she was wearing underneath it. The smooth skin of her thighs taunted me as she wrapped her scarf around her head and turned to look at me. She smiled playfully and turned off the lights, the TV Casting a seductive glow over her as she made her way to her side of the bed. Trina slid under the covers, and as hard as I tried, I couldn't keep my hands off of her smooth thighs. The tips of my fingers danced across her inner thigh inching closer to her love garden. I released a sigh and moved my hand, wrapping my arms around her waist and pulling her close to me. I buried my face in her neck speaking softly as I felt my erection getting harder with each breath I took.

"Do you see what you do to me?" I mumbled into her ear, listening to her gasp as she wrapped her legs around my waist. "Not tonight. But the way you feel in my arms right now, our time is coming soon. Go to sleep baby. If you don't, I am going to have you up all night." Trina's lips pressed to my shoulder, her nails pinching my back until she was able to calm herself down. I rolled over onto my back, holding her as close as I could until she fell asleep in my arms.

Chapter 14:

Trina

My body filled with heat as I watched Jamere's chest rise and fall in his sleep. My legs were wrapped tightly around his waist, something that I had somehow managed to do over the course of the night. With each move he made; I felt his manhood rub against my middle. Heat rushed through my body each time and I had to force myself not to lose control. After he had shifted once again, I slid my legs from around his body and sat up slowly. I released a sigh and slid to the floor, walking to the bathroom in hopes of cooling my overheated body off.

I brushed my teeth while in the bathroom, knowing there was no way I would be able to sleep with Jamere next to me. My body would be cocooned in heat, and I knew there would be nothing to make it ease. Even though I knew that I exited the bathroom and returned to my place in bed. I exhaled and closed my eyes, praying that sleep would come. Hoping that the sunlight wouldn't catch me before it did.

Fingers trailed over my stomach, causing my eyes to flutter open. Jamere's eyes were closed, his fingers roaming my stomach as if he weren't lighting my body on fire. I moved my hand to show him how he was torturing me, dragging my fingers across his abs slowly. I watched his eyes open, the semi dark room making him look as if he was in the shadows. "You are driving me crazy. I don't know how much more of this I can take." Jamere smiled at me and then pressed his lips to mine, the faint taste of mint clinging to his tongue. I sucked his tongue slowly, my body throbbing at the sound of the moan that escaped him. His hand lowered until it was between my legs, playing with the fleshy folds of wet skin. I clenched my thighs around his hand, throwing my head back in pleasure. His fingers toyed with my moist inferno, sending me into a climax like I had never before experienced.

"That's right. Come for me baby." My body trembled as Jamere moved his hand and licked his fingers. "So sweet." He said softly while throwing the covers from our overheated bodies. "Are you sure you're ready for this baby? I don't want to do anything that you are not ready for." I smiled at him, biting his bottom lip, and speaking in a husky voice. "Baby, as long as it's with you, I am ready. I will go wherever you lead, and I know you won't hurt me. I love you baby. I ache for you. I crave you. I am ready for this. I am ready for you." The look in Jamere's eyes let me know he was still worried, still nervous. But when I pressed my lips to his, desire replaced the look that had once been there.

Jamere trailed kisses down my body, lighting fire to every part of me his lips touched. His hands caressed my breasts and his mouth covered one and then the other causing a flood between my legs. I screamed his name as he continued his downward trek, using his hands to slide my shorts down my legs. He looked up at me when he saw that I wasn't wearing any panties. I watched him lick his lips before his mouth covered the hot spot between my legs. He used his hands to spread my legs, his tongue doing things to me that I had never experienced. I grabbed a pillow and put it over my face, trying to muffle my screams.

Jamere moved his mouth and then I felt the pillow being moved from my face. I opened my eyes, trying to figure out why Jamere had stopped. I watched him fling the pillow across the room before he spoke. "Don't muffle your screams. I want to hear you. As loud as you need to be, I want to hear it. Understand?" I tried to focus as he used his fingers to rub my wet heat slowly. "I understand." I threw my head back as he returned his mouth and started his amazing torment once again. "Jamere!" I yelled, clamping my thighs around his head as I came again. My chest rose and fell rapidly as Jamere walked away causing me to sit up as much as my body would allow.

"Where are you going?" Jamere turned to me, a seductive smile on his face. I tried not to stare at his abs, but that was easier said than done. "Believe me. I'm not finished with you. But we have to protect ourselves." I watched him wink at me and bend down to dig through his suitcase. I released a breath and let my body flop back on the bed.

The mattress shifted as Jamere climbed back on the bed with me. He crawled over so that he was hovering over me, his eyes like fire as he stared into mine. "Baby, we don't have to do this. There is no pressure for you to do anything. I'm willing to wait as long as it takes." I slid my hand into his boxers, gripping his erection and stroking it slowly. "There is pressure. So much that I feel like I am going to combust. So yes, we do have to do this. Not because I feel like we have to, but because I don't think I can go another day without having you inside me." I pushed him off of me gently until he was on his back. I straddled his waist and slid my hands up his arms that were extended above his head. I gasped when his teeth grabbed my tight nipple. I exhaled slowly, grabbing the condom from his hand. I eased his boxers down his legs and dropped them on the floor. I used my teeth to open the condom and rolled it onto his thick shaft. I looked at Jamere as I pinched the tip of the condom and spoke. "Just go slow. I've never been with anyone as big as you before." I looked down before slowly positioning myself over him. He put his hands on my hips, his grip tightening as I eased lower and lower. When he was finally completely inside me, I let myself adjust to his size before starting a slow rhythm.

    The pleasure took over and I sped up, watching Jamere's eyes roll back. He grabbed me and shifted his body so that I was up under him, and he was nestled between my legs. He used his hand to put my legs behind his back and drove into me with a passion I never knew existed. I clenched myself around him and he screamed my name, reaching his climax seconds after I had reached my own.

    Jamere's body collapsed on top of mine, the two of us breathing heavily in the otherwise quiet room. After a few minutes had passed, Jamere rolled over onto his back, pulling me into his side. I threw my leg over his body and used my finger to trace a bead of sweat down his chest. "That was...." A smile appeared on my face, and I couldn't seem to wipe it away. "Well worth the wait." Jamere finished for me with a sexy smile on his lips. I lifted my head to look at Jamere, nodding my head in agreement with his statement. "Definitely. I never thought I would feel the way you made me feel. But you made me feel as if I were the only woman in the world. You made me feel loved. Special. I've never had that before you. I'm glad I didn't though. Now I know how it feels to be loved and made love to all at once." Jamere smiled at me, kissing my lips sweetly and with so much passion. "Good baby. That's what I was aiming for. I wanted you to feel the love I have for you. Because I don't ever want you to forget it. You showed me how difficult love could be because you never know what is attached to the other person. But even through all we've gone through together, I wouldn't want it any other way. I'm glad you are the one my love seeps out of me for. I will love you for the rest of my life. That I promise you." I felt my eyes droop as tiredness started to pull me under. "That's nice to hear. I will love you for the rest of my life as well. I promise." Jamere's lips pressed to my forehead as he held me closer. I inhaled his scent that was now covered in the scent of our love making. I kissed his chest and closed my eyes, ignoring the soreness and relishing in the way my body was unbelievably sated.

I woke up from my slumber, the smile returning to my face. Jamere still slept peacefully, his arm draped around my shoulders. I got ready to lay on top of him, sitting up when I heard a knock on the door. I raised my eyes in confusion before slipping to the floor. I slid Jamere's shirt over my head and then stepped into his basketball shorts before walking towards the front door.

My mouth dropped open in shock when my eyes landed on the two people in front of me. "Dad. Mom. What are you doing here?" My dad grabbed me and lifted me into his arms, holding on to me as if he thought I would vanish. "That is some way to greet your parents. We haven't seen you in three years." My dad put me down and my mom wrapped her arms around me. "Sorry. I didn't mean it like that. I'm just shocked. I wasn't expecting you." My mom let me go and I stepped back to allow them to walk inside. I locked the door securely behind them before ushering them to the living room to sit down.

Just as I was about to speak, Jamere's voice sounded in the room. I lifted my head and smiled at him, all while my face heated up. "Baby, why did you leave me alone?" Jamere chuckled as he turned so that he was looking at me. "Oh, I'm sorry. I didn't know you had company." I walked to where Jamere stood, thankful that he had put on his Golden State pajama bottoms. He was still shirtless, but I would take what I could get. "Yeah. Baby, these are my parents Bradley and Constance Hart. Mom, dad, this is my boyfriend Jamere Hayes." My parents stood as I linked our hands together. Jamere walked around to where they stood, holding my hand securely in the process. "Hi. It's nice to finally meet you. After meeting Trina's brothers, I couldn't wait to meet the people who raised them." Jamere shook both of their hands, motioning for the two of them to have a seat once the introductions where made. I put my arms around his middle, smiling as he kissed my forehead before helping me into my seat. "It's nice to meet you as well. The boys have had nothing but good things to say." Jamere smiled at them and then at me before speaking again.

"I'm glad. I don't want to be rude, but I was going to go get us some breakfast. Since we haven't been able to get everything unpacked yet, we don't have any dishes to cook with out. Do you both want to stay? I know Trina would love to catch up with the two of you and I would love to get to know you." Wide grins spread across their faces as my dad spoke. "We would love that. I'll even ride with you to give you a hand." Jamere nodded and looked at my mom as she spoke. "When did the two of you move in? This is a very nice apartment." My cheeks flamed in embarrassment as Jamere sat beside me and put his arms around my shoulders. "We don't live together. I'm just helping her move and get unpacked. My mom would kill me if I moved in with a woman I wasn't married to. No matter how much I love Trina, I wouldn't do that to her. There will be no playing house around here. We won't move in together until I become her husband and she becomes my wife." My parents grinned again, and Jamere looked at me.

"Baby, I'm going to take a quick shower and get dressed. Think about what you want to eat okay?" I nodded my head and he pecked me on the lips before standing to his feet. "If you will excuse me Mr. and Mrs. Hart, I'm going to get ready. I'll be back in a few minutes." Jamere walked past them as they nodded their heads, closing the bedroom door once he was inside.

"He seems like a nice young man. And you seem to be very happy with him. Where did the two of you meet? How long have you two been together?" I forced myself not to smile as I thought of Jamere and the amazing night we shared together. I shook my head and answered my mom's question as they both stared at me as if they had never seen me. "We met at school. We have a class together. It's been a little over two months, but we've known each other for about four months." My mom nodded her head, using her hand to touch my cheek gently.

"We have really missed you. Please don't stay away like that again." I turned my head when I heard Jamere's voice, the smile I had been holding in spreading across my face. "She won't. I promise. I refuse to let you both lose contact with the only daughter you have." My dad looked at him with respect beaming from his eyes as Jamere walked to where I was sitting. My mom dropped her hand from my face, watching Jamere hold his hand out for mine. Once it was in his, he pulled gently until I was standing in front of him. "Did you decide on what you wanted?" I shook my head no, leaning my face into his hand as he cupped my cheek. "No. Whatever you decide is fine. Nothing too heavy though. I'm not that hungry." Jamere kissed my cheek and then my forehead before letting his hand drop. "We'll be back shortly okay?" I nodded my head and he turned, looking at my dad as he spoke.

"Are you ready Mr. Hart." My dad stood and walked toward the front door as I watched Jamere follow him. "Ladies, we will be back in a little bit. You two have fun." I stared at Jamere, loving the way his Khaki cargo shorts and black V-Neck t-shirt fit his body. I wanted to rip the shirt from his body and lick his chest, but I shook the thought from my head. I looked at the black number 6 Jordan's that were on his feet, inhaled deeply, and spoke right as Jamere was about to walk out the door. "Be careful baby." Jamere turned and smiled at me, nodding his head as he spoke. "I will. I love you." My cheeks burned as I smiled and replied to him. "I love you too." I watched him wink before he walked out and pulled the door closed behind him.

"I'm glad to see that you're happy baby girl. I can see that when you and Jamere tell each other that you love the other, you truly mean it. I'm glad he makes you so happy." My mom watched me, a smile on her face as she waited for me to reply. I had missed her more than I thought I had over the past few years. She was always there for me when I was growing up, and I knew she would continue to be. "Thanks mom. He is a great guy. He believes in me, he supports me, and he protects me. I'm glad I have had him in my life these past few months." My phone started to ring from my bedroom, so I stood and rushed to go answer it. Once it was in my hand, I pressed talk and walked back into the living room with my mom.

"What's up Chey?" I stood in the living room, waiting for her to speak. "Hey girl. I'm on the way to help you and Jamere. Do yall need anything?" I grinned at the smile on my mom's face and put my finger to my lips. "Nope I think we're good. But if you haven't eaten, you may want to stop and get something. Jamere just left to get us some food." Cheyenne yelled at someone who blew a stop sign, yelling a few words I'm glad my mom couldn't hear. "Sorry Lil Bit. But okay. I'll get some Chick Fil A or something. I'll see you in a few." We ended the call and I looked at my mom who still had a grin on her face. "Cheyenne will be here shortly. I'm going to shower and get dressed. Will you answer the door when she gets here?" My mom nodded, so I handed her the remote for the TV. Thankfully, I was able to have my cable and internet set up the day I moved in, and she didn't have to sit in the quiet. "Thanks ma. I'll be out in a few." I walked out of the living room and into my bedroom, closing the door behind me. The scent of our love making hung in the air and that only made me crave Jamere that much more. He had already made the bed and put our dirty clothes in the hamper. But all I wanted to do was mess up those covers all over again. I walked over to get some clothes out and made my way into the bathroom. As hard as I tried, I couldn't shake the image of water dripping off of Jamere's naked body.

I dressed in a pair of black Adidas training pants with white stripes and a white Adidas crop top with white emblem. I finished my outfit with a pair of white and black shell toe Adidas. I sprayed my body with some BLV Notte and walked out of my bedroom.

Cheyenne walked into my line of sight and then closed the space between us before punching me playfully on my arm. "Why didn't you tell me that Ma was here when we were on the phone?" I grinned at her and shrugged my shoulders casually. "It didn't come up." Cheyenne rolled her eyes at me and looked at my mom. "You see what I have to deal with Ma." My mom chuckled and shook her head at the two of us. "You two haven't changed a bit." Cheyenne and I shared a look before smiling at my mom.

We heard a knock on the door, so my mom walked away from where she stood to answer it. She pulled the door open and Jamere and my dad walked in. "Daddy!" Chey yelled as she rushed to where he stood. My dad sat the drinks on the table and caught

Chey as she launched herself into his arms. He kissed her cheek and put her down, letting her know how much he missed her. Jamere smiled at the two of them, putting down the bags of food as Chey wrapped her arms around his body. "What's up Jam?" Jamere chuckled and hugged Cheyenne before they let each other go. "Hey little sis. I've missed you so much since yesterday." Cheyenne glared at him and punched him in the chest, shaking her hand in pain after she had done it. "Yeah, if you had asked me I would have let you know that wasn't smart. His chest is like a brick wall." Cheyenne rolled her eyes at me and shook her head. "Now she tells me." I laughed as Jamere called us into the kitchen to eat. "Chey, do you want some breakfast? We bought extra." Cheyenne shook her head no and retrieved her bag from the microwave. "No thanks. I stopped and got something on the way here. Lil Bit told me you had gone to get food, so I got my own. Thanks anyway." Jamere nodded his head and started pulling the food out of the bag. "Baby, I got you some grape juice since orange juice has been making your stomach hurt lately. Is that okay with you." I nodded my head and put my arms around his waist. There was something about the way he felt in my arms. I just couldn't not touch him. He turned and kissed the top of my head, motioning for everyone to have a seat.

"Mr. Hart, will you bless the food?" My dad nodded his head and did just as Jamere had asked before we all started to eat.

"Trina, we are going to LA on Thursday, and we want you to come. We already paid for your ticket, and we have a rental property that we have already paid for as well. We will be back on Monday. We got a ticket for you as well Cheyenne. Do you both think you could take off work and come with us? The boys will be there too." I looked at Jamere but nodded my head. I knew I wouldn't enjoy myself as much as I would like because Jamere wouldn't be there. But, we still had the following weekend when we were going to go to New Orleans together. "I can go because I'm on vacation and I'm done with school for the summer." My parents smiled widely as I leaned my body into Jamere's. "Great. What about you Chey?" Sadness crept onto Cheyenne's face as she shook her head no. "I can't. I've used all my vacation time until October when it resets. Thanks for thinking of me though." My parents nodded, but I could tell that they wished she could go. "Who else could we invite? The tickets are nonrefundable." My parents looked at each other and then at Jamere. "Jamere, would you like to go?"

Jamere's eyes widened, and he shook his head. "I couldn't impose on you like that. You both just met me." My dad stopped him from speaking and responded with honesty in his words. "Son, it is not an imposition. You are making our daughter happy. That's all we need to know. So, if you can get some time off, we would love to have you come with us." Jamere smiled at them, nodding his head as he listened to my dad speak. "Okay. I would love to come. My vacation just started too so I can go. I insist on paying for my ticket though." My parents shook their heads as they ate their breakfast, dismissing Jamere's statement. "Not going to happen. We invited you on a trip you knew nothing about. You will not pay for anything that we have already paid for." "But?" My mom reached over and tapped his hand as though she were reprimanding him. "But nothing. You just meet us at the airport on Thursday at five a.m. with our daughter in tow. Understood?" Jamere smiled and nodded his head, looking at me before returning his attention to my mom. "Yes ma'am." My mom gave a brief nod and returned to her food, the five of us making small talk while we finished our meals.

Cheyenne and I got all of my clothes put up while Jamere worked in the kitchen with Lloyd. My parents had left an hour earlier, after getting the bathroom decorations put up. After they were finished with the bathrooms, they put up the pictures that went on the walls in the living room. I enjoyed the time we were able to spend together, and I was really looking forward to our vacation in a few days.

Cheyenne walked out of the closet and pushed the door closed before sitting at the foot of my bed. "I can't believe we were able to get everything finished today. Lord knows, if Jamere and I weren't here you would have tried to do it all by yourself." I pushed one of the drawers on my dresser closed and turned so that I was facing her. "That's true. But you both were here. And for that, I thank you." I watched her slide to the floor and smile at me. "You're welcome Lil Bit. I was glad to help." She started walking toward the bathroom and spoke again. "Well, I'm going to go to the bathroom and then head home." I nodded and watched her walk inside and push the door closed behind her.

Jamere walked into my bedroom, smiling as he walked to where I was sitting on the bed. He leaned me back and hovered over me, pressing his lips to my neck before speaking. "All I have wanted to do all day is yank this shirt off of you." I moaned breathlessly as he slid his hand under my shirt and cupped my right breast in his hand. I arched off of the bed as he kissed my neck again, a puddle forming in my panties. "Ahem." Jamere removed his hand from under my shirt and I slowed my breathing down as I sat up on the bed. "Well, I think I'll leave you two alone." Cheyenne grinned at us as she stepped into her black Air Force Ones. She hugged Jamere and then me before picking up her purse from the dresser. "Trina, I'll call you later. We should all do dinner tomorrow after I get off. If you two can tear yourselves away from each other. My cheeks heated up and Jamere chuckled. "We'll see what we can do sis. Be careful going home. Let us know when you've made it in." Jamere and I followed her out of the apartment and to her car. Jamere held her door open for her and waited for her to sit down. "See you both later." Jamere pushed her door closed and walked to me, draping his arm around my shoulders. We waved as she backed out of her space and listened to her honk her horn as she sped off.

"Tell Lloyd I'm going to kick his butt for not telling me bye." Jamere pushed the door closed and locked it as he laughed. "I tried to tell him, but he told me to tell you he'd see you later. He had a date to get ready for." I rolled my eyes while walking back into my room. Jamere grabbed me from behind, resting one hand flat on my stomach while wrapping the opposite arm around my waist. "Are you going to stay again tonight?" I asked in a moan as he pressed his lips to my neck. "If you want me to. Lord knows I'd rather be with you than alone in my apartment tonight." Jamere trailed his fingers over my stomach before turning me around in his arms. He kissed my chest and then put his mouth over my breast through my shirt. I inhaled sharply and spoke in the loudest voice I could manage.

"Of course, I want you to stay." He pulled the shirt over my head and used his fingers to massage my nipples. I threw my head back, trying to finish my statement through his foreplay. "After last night, I never want you to leave." I felt myself being lifted from the ground and then being laid on the bed. "Well, I guess I need to see if I can do better." The seductive grin that spread across his face had my body trembling in anticipation. He pressed his lips to my stomach, using his tongue to lick slow circles around my belly button. I wiggled as he eased my pants off using his skilled tongue to kiss my thighs. My body was on fire and with each second that passed, more heat consumed me. Jamere spread my legs across the bed and then his mouth covered my moist inferno. I had no idea when he had gotten my panties off, but at that point, I really didn't care. I squirmed as his tongue assaulted me, screaming his name as my orgasm ripped through me.

    I panted rapidly as I sat up on the edge of the bed, looking at Jamere as he stood to his feet. I pulled his shirt over his head and kissed his chest softly, unbuckling his belt and freeing the button. His shorts fell to his feet, and he stepped out of them and kicked them away. I trailed my tongue through the creases in his abs before sticking my hand into his boxer briefs. I gripped his thick shaft, stroking it slowly and feeling it harden in my hand. "Baby, those hands work magic." I grinned at him, listening to him moan as I continued to stroke. As soon as I had him where I wanted him, he moved my hand and pushed me gently so that I was laying on the bed. I watched him bend down, my body quivering in anticipation. I heard the sound of the foil wrapper being ripped open and tried to wait patiently for the penetration I knew was coming. I gasped when Jamere entered me, gripping his arms tightly as we rode out each wave of pleasure.

    Jamere rubbed his hand down the length of my body as we laid sprawled across the bed. In the aftermath of our love making, it was all I could do not to fall asleep. His light touch had the fire starting up again, and I had no idea as to whether or not he knew. "I didn't think it could get any better than our first time, but clearly, I was wrong." I turned over so that I was on my stomach, looking at Jamere who was to the left of me. "I aim to please. I've never been one to get so turned on by something as simple as being stroked. But every time you touch me, my body comes alive underneath your touch. It's so hard to keep control when you are doing what you do so well. As simple as it is." I pressed my lip to his shoulder, smiling as I looked at him. "Oh, I can do so much more. You just take me to the moon and back before I can show you. But trust, you will see. That's a promise." Jamere slid closer to me, pulling the covers over us before he wrapped me in his arms. "I'm going to hold you to that." I felt him press his lips to my forehead and squeeze me tightly. I nodded my head as my eyes drifted closed and succumbed to the happiness that pulled me under.

 I shifted in Jamere's arms when my phone rang early the next morning. "What?" I moaned in a sleep clouded tone. "Well good morning to you too. But is that anyway to talk to your mother?" I pulled the phone away from my ear to check the time, putting it back to my ear to reply. "I'm sorry ma. But on vacation, there is nothing good about a nine a.m. wake up call. What's up?" I listened to my mom chuckle, but she went on with the purpose of the call. "I needed to get Jamere's information to put on the insurance for the rental car, as well as his plane ticket." I shook Jamere until he woke up, putting a finger to my lips so that he wouldn't speak. "Ma, I'll text him to see if he's awake. If so, I'll get him on three way. If not, I'll have him call you when he wakes up. Hold on for a second." My mom told me okay and I muted the phone, shaking Jamere to wake him back up. "Baby, my mom needs to get your information for the plane ticket and the rental car insurance." Jamere sat up and I slid to the floor, sliding Jamere's black V-neck over my head. "I'm going to go in the living room and call your phone. The last thing I feel like hearing early in the morning is my mom's opinions about our sex life." Jamere laughed but nodded his head as he took his phone off of the charger. I walked out of the room and closed the door, taking my phone off of mute to talk to my mom.

"Ma. He's awake, so I'm going to call him. Hold on okay?" My mom said okay again, so I dialed the number and added my mom back into the call. Jamere spoke into the phone, no trace of sleep in his voice. "Hey baby. Good morning Mrs. Hart. How are you doing?" I listened to Jamere's smooth tone, wanting this conversation to be over so I could be in his arms again. "Good morning baby. I'm good and you. We didn't wake you did we?" I heard the smile in his voice as he spoke, a smile appearing on my face. "No ma'am. Trina told me you needed my info. Are you ready for me to give it to you?" I felt myself yawn, knowing that I was going right back to sleep as soon as we got my mom off of the phone. "Yes baby. Thank you." I listened to my mom spout of questions, and then to Jamere as he answered them. When they finished, my mom spoke to the two of us. "Okay you two. That's all I need. Have a good day, and we'll see you on Thursday." I smiled and nodded as I stood and made my way to my room. "You too. See you then." Jamere and I said at the same time. My mom told us bye and we repeated her statement before the three of us hung up.

    I opened my door and walked into my room, yawning again as I crawled into bed. I sat my phone on the nightstand and slid my body next to Jamere's body. I relished in his warmth and smiled as he pressed his lips to my forehead. "Sleep, round two." I smiled at his statement, wrapping my arms around his waist as I let sleep claim me once again.

Chapter 15:

Jamere

I picked Trina up from home and the two of us made our way to my parents' house. Being that I lived closest to the airport, I figured leaving from there would be easier when we left the following morning. So, we were going to go drop L.J. off with my parents and then make our way there. I smiled to myself as I heard L.J.'s small voice as he talked to Trina from the back seat. "Auntie Trina, when are you and uncle Jamere going to be back from vacation?" Trina grinned widely, loving the fact that L.J. had started calling her auntie. She had been worried that Lloyd would have a problem with it the first time L.J had said it. But when Lloyd told her that L.J. had already asked him if it was okay, the worry left her mind. "We'll be back Monday sweetie. I promise." I glanced in the rearview mirror and watched the smile that spread across his face.

"Will you and uncle Jamere come see me when you get back?" I smiled at him and spoke before Trina could reply. "Yes we will little man. But you have to be good for Nanny and Poppy okay?" L.J. nodded his head up and down rapidly, a wide smile spreading across his face. "I will." I chuckled at his innocence, knowing that my parents were going to enjoy having him over for the weekend.

I got L.J. out of the car and watched him walk over to Trina's side and pull the door open. I smiled as he held his hand out and once her hand was in his, he guided her out of the car. Trina smiled at him, stepping out of the way as he pushed the door closed. "Good job little man." Trina told him as she bent down and kissed his cheek. I pulled his suitcase out of the car and set it on the ground before grabbing his booster seat. He walked to me and grabbed both, rolling the suitcase behind him as we walked to the front door.

We walked into the house behind L.J., watching as Amy jumped to her feet when she saw us. "Trina!" Amy ran and jumped into Trina's arms, Trina smiling and hugging her tightly before putting her down. "Hey Amy. How are you?" Amy continued to smile as she hugged my legs and answered Trina's question. "I'm good." Amy picked up L.J.'s suitcase and looked down at him. "Come on L.J. Let's put your stuff upstairs." L.J. nodded and turned to me, putting the booster seat in my hand before the two of them rushed off.

My mom walked into the living room where we still stood, grinning as she walked over to us. Trina and I shared a look, trying to figure out the reason behind her grin. My mom wrapped her arms around Trina, rocking from side to side before letting her go. "Hey future daughter. Has my son proposed yet?" My eyes widened as I looked at my mom, watching Trina chuckle as she responded. "No ma'am. Not yet." I shook my head while my mom hugged me, knowing that I was eventually going to do just that. "Really ma. You think I would propose and not let you know." My mom glanced at me and then Trina before squeezing my cheek gently. "Good boy. But just so you know, I do want some more grandchildren at some point." Trina's cheeks flamed as I yelled in embarrassment. "Ma!" My mom laughed, draping her arm around Trina's shoulders, and pulling her closer. "I'm just saying. I love Honey and L.J. with all my heart, but I need a fresh baby." I shook my head and looked down, watching as Trina grinned in embarrassment before speaking. "We'll keep that in mind." My mom released Trina, her eyes lighting up when my dad walked in from the garage.

"Hey yall. What did I just walk in on? Trina's face is as red as a tomato." I held my hand out for Trina and she walked to me and buried her face in my chest. "I just let them know that we wanted some more grandchildren." My dad smiled, pulling Trina from my arms, and wrapping his own around her. "Well, she's right. We need a fresh baby." "And on that note, we're going to leave. I haven't packed and we have to meet Mr. and Mrs. Hart at the airport at five a.m." I listened as Amy and L.J. bounded down the stairs, L.J. rushing to my mom when he saw her. "Nanny!" My mom lifted him off the ground and pressed her lips to his cheek.

    "Hey baby." He reached for my dad, so my dad grabbed him and hugged him tightly. "Poppy!" My dad smiled and held onto him as I spoke. "We're getting ready to leave you two. We'll see you when we get back." L.J. reached for Trina as Amy wrapped her arms around Trina's legs. She grabbed L.J. and kissed the top of his head before doing the same to Amy. Trina handed L.J. to me, pinching Amy's cheek before she walked to me. "I love you both. Be good." The two of them spoke at the same time, smiling at me as they did. "Love you too Jam." "Love you too uncle Jamere." I sat L.J. on the ground and we hugged my parents before walking to the front of the house. They all followed behind us, L.J. rushing outside when I opened the door. He walked to the passenger's side and waited for Trina, opening the door when she was next to him. He held her hand until she was seated and then hugged her, speaking loud enough for us to hear. "Love you auntie Trina. Have fun." Trina smiled and kissed his cheek before she replied. "I love you too L.J. I will. Have fun with Nanny and Poppy." L.J. nodded his small head and pushed the door closed, returning to the front of the car where we all stood. My dad rubbed the top of L.J.'s head, speaking as I walked to the driver's side of my car. "Yall be careful and have fun. Let us know when you land." I nodded and waved at them, sitting in my seat, and then pulling the door closed.

  Trina and I walked into the airport and went through all the proper procedures after checking our bags and going to our gate. I was carrying my carry on, on my back, Trina's carry on in my hand, and my other hand held Trina's. Trina bobbed her head to the music playing from her Beats headphones, but she had one side pushed back so she could still hear. My own Beats headphones rested on my neck as we scanned the small crowd of people for my parents. I quickly turned when I heard Trina squeal, calming down when I saw R.J. lifting her from the ground. I hesitantly let her hand go, laughing when she punched her brother on the back awkwardly. R.J. laughed as he put her down and then turned to shake my hand.

"What's up Jamere?" I nodded my head at him, watching as the others made their way to us. "Nothing much man. What about you?" D.J. grabbed me in a bear hug as R.J. spoke and everyone said their hellos. "Same man. Just working." Once we had all spoken to one another, I draped my arm around Trina's shoulders, and we all sat down to wait for our flight to be called.

Trina slid into the middle seat and lifted the earphones off of her ears. I stored our carry-ons above our seats and eased past her to sit in the window seat. D.J. sat next to Trina, the three of us pulling out books to read while waiting for our flight take off. I yawned from tiredness because Trina and I had yet to go to sleep. When I finally finished packing it was after two and we knew going to sleep was pointless. We would have had to be awake in under two hours anyway. So, the two of us watched Netflix until it was time for us to get ready. Trina turned her head to look at me, planting her lips on my cheek before going back to her book. I smiled and looked back at my own book until I heard the flight attendant start to speak.

Once the plane was in the air, I felt Trina grab my hand and interlock our fingers. I looked over at her, the book she was once reading closed and stuck beside her. She shifted her body and rested her head on my shoulder before her eyes drifted shut. I smiled to myself and kissed the top of her head tenderly as I closed my book. I rested my head on top of hers, letting my eyes close for the duration of our flight.

I felt someone nudge me, so I opened my eyes and tried to remember where I was. "Jamere. Wake Lil Bit up. We're about to land." I watched D.J.'s face come into focus before I nodded and released a yawn. "Trina baby, wake up." Trina shifted, burying her face into my chest while exhaling deeply. "Come on baby. We can take a nap when we get to the house. I promise." She moved her head and looked at me, so I pecked her lips before we buckled our seat belts. "That's my girl." Trina smiled at me, holding my hand once again as we started our descent.

The seven of us walked to the car rental area to pick up the two rental cars the Harts had rented. D.J. rented one car, while their parents rented the other. Trina and I were both on the insurance for both cars, so there shouldn't have been any issues with getting around. Both vehicles were 2015 Dodge Durango's with three rows of seats. So, on that note, we would all be comfortable.

While we waited for the cars to be brought to us, Mr. Hart spoke. "Do you all want to get something to eat before going to the house, or go to the house first?" Trina yawned, resting her head on my shoulder as we stood waiting. "I want to go to the house. I didn't get any sleep last night. But if everyone wants to eat first, we can do that." Trina's parents smiled at her after she spoke and then looked at me. "What about you Jamere? We can check in and get everything unloaded so you two can get some sleep. We'll get some food and bring you both something back." I stifled a yawn, answering his question while nodding my head. "Yes sir. I think that's a good idea. Trina and I had my god son yesterday, so we're worn out. If we could get a few hours of sleep, we'll be worth something then." Mrs. Hart laughed at me as the cars were stopped in front of us. "Okay that's what we'll do." I nodded and the men loaded the cars while Trina and her mom got in the car. When we finished, I slid into the car with Trina and her parents as they led the way to our vacation house.

We unloaded the cars and walked into the house, taking in our surroundings in awe. The house had a pool, outdoor bar, grill, and even a pool table. The decor in each room was different but coordinated with the rest of the house in an amazing way. There were six bedrooms as well as six bathrooms, which meant everyone would have their privacy.

"Trina, originally we thought Chey was going to come so the room we chose for you has two beds. Jamere, we know you and Trina are both adults, so we don't have a problem with the two of you sharing a room. If that's what you choose to do, please be respectful. Leave bedroom things in the bedroom please. Thank you. So, if you want to stay with Trina, then the room is right there." Mr. Hart pointed with his finger to a room that sat to the left of us. Trina's cheeks reddened as her dad continued to speak. "Trina, if you want to stay with Jamere, the room is at the end of the hall and to the right." I looked at Trina and waited to see what she wanted to do. She nodded her head towards me, so I grabbed both of our suitcases and wheeled them behind me towards the room.

Trina walked into the room minutes after I did, holding both of our carry-ons. "They're leaving. They said they'll be back in a few hours." I nodded my head and watched as Trina helped me unpack. When we finished, she went to take a shower in our bathroom, so I walked to one of the others to take mine.

I yawned while stepping into my boxers and a pair of basketball shorts. I picked up my dirty clothes and exited the bathroom and returned to the bedroom. Trina was sitting on the bed, pulling some socks on her feet when I walked into the room. I watched her crawl under the covers, so I walked into the closet and put my dirty clothes on top of hers in a corner. When I walked out, Trina was laying on her side. "Come on over here so I can go to sleep." I smiled and did just that, sliding under the covers and pulling her to me. "Sleep well baby. I love you." Trina linked the fingers of one hand with mine, shifting and causing her hair to brush my chin. "You do the same. I love you too." I closed my eyes and kissed the back of her head before letting sleep overtake me.

Trina shifted her body, so I opened my eyes to see what she was doing. My eyes bounced around the room, stopping at the doorway before looking at the tv mounted on the wall. Trina gently moved my arms from around her waist, probably thinking that I was still asleep. She sat up and looked at me, smiling when she saw that I was awake.

"Did you sleep okay?" I nodded my head, smiling as she kissed me on the forehead. "What about you?" She winked at me and nodded as she slid to the floor.

"Whenever I'm in your arms, I always sleep well. It's when we're apart that the problems start." I sat up and slid to her side of the bed, grabbing her hand, and pulling her back toward me. "I know baby. It will get easier though. It just may take a while." I wrapped my arms around her in a tight hug, letting her know that she would always be safe with me. And by the smile that was on her face when we pulled away, I could tell that she knew.

"Hey guys." I turned to the doorway, Trina looking in the same direction as I let her go. We looked at her parents, who I hadn't realized were standing there before right then. "Hey." They both walked further into the room, stopping on the opposite side of the bed that we were on. "We got you both some In And Out Burgers. We didn't get fries because we knew they would have been stale. Stale fries don't reheat well. Mrs. Hart stuck her tongue out of her mouth in disgust, easing a laugh from Trina and I. "Thanks." We told her as my phone rang loudly. "Excuse me." I told them as I slid across the bed and picked up my phone from the nightstand.

"Hey ma. Sorry I forgot to call when we landed. Trina and I were so tired, we came straight to the house and went to sleep. We haven't even been awake for ten minutes." I watched Trina walk around the bed and look at me. I muted the phone, waiting to see what she had to say. "I'm going downstairs. Tell your parents, Amy, and L.J. I said hello." I smiled when I heard L.J.'s voice come on the line and told Trina to hold on. I put my phone on speaker and then spoke into it.

"Okay L.J. Trina can hear you now." I watched the smile spread across her face as she stepped closer to me and grabbed the phone from my hand. "Auntie Trina! I miss you. Do you miss me?" Trina's smile widened as she listened to L.J.'s small voice. "Yes baby, I miss you too. Are you being good for Nanny and Poppy?" The Harts smiled at us, listening to Trina talk happily. "Yes ma'am." "That's good sweetie. I have to go though, okay? I'll talk to you later. Tell Amy, Nanny, and Poppy I said hello." L.J.'s excitement died down and he spoke again. "Okay auntie, I will. I love you." A wide smile spread across Trina's face as she put my phone back in my hand. "I love you too sweetie. See you on Monday." I took the phone off of speaker and watched as they all walked out of the bedroom while I finished my phone call.

I walked into the kitchen smiling as Trina stood and went to the microwave. She pulled the burger out and sat it at the table next to the one that was already there. "Sit down baby. I'm going to get you something to drink."

I did as she instructed, waiting for her to return to the table.

I turned my head when her arm reached over me, watching her sit the drink in front of me. I stood and slid her chair back, waiting until she was seated before sitting back down. I glanced at Trina's untouched burger and grabbed her hand, blessing the food in front of us before letting it go. The two of us finished our burgers but stayed where we were while we sipped our drinks. I glanced at Trina, moving her hair before pressing my lips to her neck. She looked at me and smiled, scooting her chair closer to mine and resting her head on my shoulder. I put my free arm around her waist, holding my cup in my hand as I finished my soda.

Trina's head lifted and we both turned when we heard our names being called. "Jamere, Trina, we're going to the Hollywood Wax museum, so you both need to get dressed." I stood and held my hand out for Trina's and helped her to her feet. "Okay Tay. We've already showered so it won't take us long. When are we leaving?" I picked up our trash as Trina took our glasses to the sink. "In about an hour and a half. Just go to the living room when you're done." The two of us nodded and Tay walked out of the kitchen.

Trina put the now clean glasses in the dish rack, and we both made our way upstairs.

I looked at Trina as she checked herself in the mirror, making sure she looked okay. She wore a pair of black Levi's and a dark gray tank top with the words 'Pain Is Temporary, Victory is Forever' printed on the front in white letters. On her feet, were a pair of black and gray socks, the bottom of one saying 'Later' and the other saying 'Hater'. There was a pair of dark gray number 9 Jordan's still in the box on the floor where she stood fixing her hair in front of the mirror. Once she was satisfied, she bent down and picked up the box and carried it to a chair that was in the corner of the room. She pulled both shoes from the box and put them on before carrying the empty box into the closet and leaving it there. When she came out, she looked over at me. "You look beautiful." I told her as she walked over and sat on my lap as I sat on the bench at the bottom of the bed. A smile spread across her face as she looked over my outfit. "Thank you. You're looking pretty gorgeous yourself." I looked over my outfit, standing with her in my arms.

I wore a pair of khaki Levi's and a white Polo logo shirt. Solid white number 13 Jordan's were on my feet, and a white G-

Shock was around my left wrist. I smiled as I put her down and thanked her before she grabbed her purse and we walked out of the room.

The two of us sat side by side, waiting for everyone else to meet us in the living room. I played with her fingers with one hand, using the other to trail over her thigh slowly. "Jamere, if you don't stop doing that we won't be going anywhere." She grabbed my hand and linked our fingers, stopping the connection my fingers had with her thigh. I looked at her, smiling when I saw that she had her eyes closed tightly. I covered her mouth with mine, kissing her slowly, and sighing as I felt her trembling in my arms. Just as I was about to get carried away, we heard a voice that caused us to separate.

"That's enough of that." Trina turned her head, so I did the same, our eyes locking on R.J. standing behind us. Trina balled up her fist and punched him in the stomach, his laughter stopping as he hunched over in pain. "Shit Trina, that hurt." I stifled a smile, but a laugh erupted when Mrs. Hart spoke. "Language Ryan." She hit him on the back of the head and his right hand flew to the place she hit. "Ow Ma!" Mrs. Hart looked back at him as Trina, and I stood. "Boy it didn't hurt that bad. You'll be alright." We all laughed while following Mrs. Hart out of the house and to the cars. Trina and I got in the car with her brothers, while her parents got in the other vehicle. Trina and I sat all the way in the back, R.J. in the middle, and D.J. and Tay were in the front. Dylan drove, pulling out of the driveway and letting his dad get in front of him before he followed him away from the house.

Trina and I sat in our seats, listening to her brothers argue about basketball. I kept my opinions to myself but listened to each of their arguments intently. They all had valid points, but they each showed favoritism to the team they loved the most. They refused to see the others point of view because to them, their team had no flaws whatsoever. I laughed to myself and looked down at Trina as her phone started to ring.

"Hello?" A smile appeared on her face, and she waited until whoever was on the line spoke. "Hey Chey. Yeah, we're good. We got here at about nine this morning. Jamere and I took a nap, but now we're all on our way to the Wax Museum." She laughed and looked at me, before speaking again. "Of course, I am. Hold on." Trina looked at me and handed her phone to me. "Chey wants to talk to you." I took her phone from her hand and put it to my ear. "Hey little sister. Do you miss me?" I listened to Cheyenne smack her teeth and then reply. "Whatever Jamere. I just wanted to say hey." I chuckled and shook my head while looking around outside. "Hey. Are you good though? You know I have to make sure you're straight." Chey spoke, a smile in her voice as she did. "Yeah, I'm good. You and my sister haven't been being grown have you? You know Dylan, Ryan, and Tayler will kick your ass if they find out you have been." I listened to her laugh, trying to wipe the grin off of my face. "No, we haven't. Not yet anyway. The vacation isn't over though." Cheyenne laughed loudly, causing Trina to turn her head in my direction. "You are crazy. I miss you big bro." I cut off her statement, a smile spreading across my face. "I knew you missed me." I told her with a laugh. "Whatever Jamere, bye. Put Lil Bit back on the phone." I chuckled, talking through it to reply to her. "I miss you too Chey. See you when we get back. Here's Trina." I gave Trina her phone, watching as R.J. turned to look at me.

"How long have you known Cheyenne?" I felt Trina hit me, so I turned my head to see why. Her cheeks were red, so I figured Chey had just told her what we talked about. I pecked her lips, and her face reddened even more. I looked back at R.J. and answered his earlier question. "About 4 months. I met her about a day or two after I met Trina." R.J.

nodded and looked at Trina, a smile spreading across his face. "What's with the red cheeks?" I smiled to myself but shrugged my shoulders as I spoke. "Who knows what those two are talking about?" R.J.'s eyes bounced back and forth before he shrugged and the two of us talked about our favorite cars.

Trina walked up to me and grabbed my hand, the two of us falling behind where everyone else walked around the Wax Museum. She pulled my arm gently, so I bent my head so that she could whisper in my ear. "Chey told me what you said. I'm going to have show you what it means to be grown tonight." I looked at her, my body heating up as I smiled at her. "Is that so? Well, I'm looking forward to that lesson." I winked at her and put my arm around her shoulders as we caught back up with the rest of her family.

We all walked around the Wax Museum, taking pictures, and having a good time. When we had seen everything, we left and went to the Ripley's Believe It Or Not Museum. Trina and I held hands and whispered back and forth with each other until her mom separated us. She grabbed Trina's hand and led her away from everyone, so I caught up with the men. Mr. Hart looked at me and smiled as he spoke to me.

"Thank you for making my daughter happy Jamere. I'm glad to know that I don't think I'll have to kill you. But I will if I have to." He smiled as he said it, but I knew by the look in his eyes that he was very serious. But I also knew that he didn't have to worry because I would never do anything to make him want to follow through with his promise. "Mr. Hart, I give you my word that I will never do anything to make you even think about killing me. I have a little sister and I know if any boy, let alone man hurt her, I would kill them with my bare hands. I can only imagine what it must be like from a father daughter viewpoint. I love Trina with all my heart, and one day, hopefully with your blessing, I am going to marry her. She is my heartbeat, and there is nothing in this world that would make me intentionally hurt her in any way. That's my word." Mr. Hart nodded and clapped his hand on my shoulder as he stopped to look at me. "Son, I believe that you mean that. As a man, I respect what you just said, and appreciate the fact that you want my blessing before you marry my baby girl. I want you to know, that when the time comes for you to propose to her, you have my blessing in every sense of the word. I would love to have you as another son in my family." I smiled at him and glanced at Trina before returning my attention to him. "Thank you. I would love that too. We should all have dinner so you can all meet my parents and my little sister and older brother before we go to New Orleans." Mr. Hart smiled as Tay put his arm around my shoulder. "We would love that. We can get some communication going and make that happen." I nodded as I watched Trina walk to where we stood. She walked around me and jumped on my back, causing her family to chuckle. I grabbed her thighs and adjusted her before we all continued our walk to the entrance of the museum.

"Trina baby. Wake up. We have to get ready for dinner." Trina shifted but didn't move to get out of the car. I listened to her brothers laugh as I tried a different tactic. I figured, maybe bribery would work, so I eased out of the car and called her name again. "Baby, if you get out of the car, I'll carry you inside." I watched Trina open her eyes and lift her head. I held my hand out for hers and helped her out of the car. Once the door was closed, she held her arms up for me to pick her up. I chuckled but picked her up carefully as she faced me. Once she was in my arms, I held on to her thighs as she rested her head on my shoulder gently. I turned and walked towards the house, holding her protectively while waiting for someone to unlock the door so that I could carry her in. "Jamere, we're leaving in an hour. So, if you are both showering again, make it quick." Mr. Hart touched Trina's head as I nodded and carried her up the stairs in my arms.

I laid Trina on the bed gently and started to let her go, but she clasped her legs behind me and pulled my body down on top of hers. I grinned and looked down at her, kissing the tip of her nose before I parted my lips to speak. "Baby you are going to get me in trouble. But at this point, I don't think I would mind." Trina smirked at me and put her hands on the back of my neck, pulling my lips to hers. My hand slid up her shirt as I used my other one to support my weight above her. Trina's body trembled under me, a moan escaping her as she shifted her body. I rolled over so that she was on top of me, using my fingers to undo the button on her jeans. I slipped my hand into her pants, only for someone to knock on the door. The two of us sighed in aggravation, so Trina eased her body off of mine. I walked into the bathroom as she made her way to the door and pulled it open.

"Trina, we had a change of plans, so now we have to leave in half an hour. So, we all have to speed up a little bit. Let Jamere know." I smiled as I listened to Tay talk and waited inside the bathroom for Trina to answer. "Okay Tay. Jamere was in the shower, so I'm going to run through really quick and I'll be set." I didn't hear Tay reply, but I heard the door close, so I walked into the room. "I guess that means we have to share the shower." A seductive grin spread across Trina's face as she grabbed a butterfly clip off of the dresser and put her hair on top of her head. "I guess so." She started pulling her clothes off and walked into the bathroom. My eyes widened before I stripped and followed her into the bathroom. Condom in hand, I entered the shower, knowing that we had to be quick. "No time for foreplay this time baby. But I'll make it up to you. I promise." I lifted her into the air after sheathing myself and entered her wet heat as the water splashed over our bodies.

We walked to the door as someone knocked and I pulled it open. Tay stood there, looking at Trina with a smile on his face. "I was just coming to see if yall were ready. Lil Bit, I thought you would never wear a dress, let alone heels. I don't think I've seen you wear one since you were like five." Trina glanced at me and winked before looking back at Tay. "Some guys are worth wearing dresses for." Tay looked at me and then Trina, before smiling at her again. "I guess so. You look beautiful though." Trina nodded and we walked out of the room, and we all made our way to the stairs. "Thanks Tayler." Tayler nodded as I took in what Trina was wearing for dinner.

Trina's casual dress was black and white striped at the top while the bottom of it was a deep purple color. The tank sleeves left her arms exposed, while the back was open. Black accessories graced her ears and fingers, the only thing that wasn't black was the silver guitar necklace that hung from her neck. Black peep toe stilettoes graced her feet and she held a purple Prada clutch in her right hand. I licked my lips as I drank in her appearance, counting down the hours until we were back home and in bed. I slid my hand into Trina's, her head turning to glance at me before she looked in front of her once again.

"Look Brad. Jamere and Trina are dressed alike. How cute is that?" I wore a pair of black slacks, purple button down, and a black tie. Black leather slip-ons were on my feet and a black Michael Kors watch was on my wrist. I was aware of what I wore, but I didn't even think about the fact that Trina and I were dressed alike. "Both of you stand together. I need a picture of this." I looked at Trina and she stood next to me, the two of us looking at her mom's phone. Trina leaned into me, and I put my arm around her, smiling as her mom took the picture. "Ma, send that to me. I don't think we have taken a picture together since we've known each other." Her mom winked at me and pressed a few buttons on her phone. After she finished, we all exited the house once again.

    Trina opened the message her mom sent her, forwarding the picture to Chey and me before saving it to her phone. Once her phone was back in her purse, she rested her head on my shoulder. I put my warm hand on her thigh and her body came alive under my touch. She shifted her head so that her lips touched my neck in the gentlest way possible. I felt her tongue leave a slow lick on my neck before her teeth grazed my skin. I felt my body heat up as I slid my hand further up her thigh. She inhaled sharply, clenching her thighs around my hand as my fingers reached their destination. The car was dark, and for that I was grateful. Lord knows, neither of us wanted her brothers to see what we were doing. Trina loosened her grip around my hand, so I slid it from under her dress and licked my fingers. "To be continued." I whispered seductively in her ear." I winked at her and smiled, but it was immediately wiped away by her lips covering mine. I felt her hand stroke me through my pants and my engorged length stiffened. "Looking forward to it." She moved her hand, and winked at me, starting a conversation I didn't hear a word of as Tay drove to the restaurant.

Chapter 16:

Trina

I stretched out across my bed, aching for Jamere's touch. But since he was at home, I would have to do without for a few days. In the two days it had been since we had been apart, I felt as if I had never been more alone in my life. And bored. If I didn't know that Jamere was having a men's day with his dad, Justus, and Lloyd, I would have had him over in a minute. But I knew I needed something to do, and I had to figure out what it would be, quick.

Just as the thought left my mind, my phone rang on the bed beside my head. "What's up Chey? Please tell me you're as bored as I am." Cheyenne chuckled, and I could picture her shaking her head in my mind. "Girl you've been without Jamere for two days and you act like it's the end of the world. He must have you wrapped around his finger in addition to the kryptonite in his- Well, you get the picture." My cheeks flamed as Cheyenne laughed, but I knew that she had spoken true words. He had me whipped, in more ways than one.

"Cheyenne, I love him from the very bottom of my heart. I never thought that would be possible after Stephan. But Jamere wiggled his way into my heart when I didn't think anyone would be able to. He is the one I'm going to hold on to for the rest of my life, because I don't think anyone else could protect my heart like he does. He doesn't just say he loves me; he shows me. And that is why if I could, I would spend every minute of every hour of every day with him. That is a realization I'm not ashamed or afraid of admitting." Cheyenne said nothing for a few minutes, but then her voice filled the line.

"Trina, I don't think I have ever heard you talk about anyone the way you've just talked about Jamere. You are a good woman, and he is an amazing man. I'm glad he was placed in your life to heal your heart and then capture it. He is a brother to me, just as you are my sister. I love both of you so much, and one day, I know I'll be watching you walk down the aisle to him." I felt a smile spread across my face as I listened to her words, hoping, and praying that they would come true. "Thanks, Chey. I'm glad you feel that way because the feeling is mutual, and I'm sure it is for Jam too." Chey spoke again, her voice back to its normal playful tone. "Thanks. Anyway, I was calling to see if you wanted to get together. I'm off and I figured we could do something before you leave on Friday."

I hopped off of my bed and immediately walked into my closet to find something to change into. Sweats and one of Jamere's t-shirts was not going to fly for hanging with my sister. "Yes. I'm changing right now. Where do you want me to meet you?" Cheyenne laughed at me but answered my question over it. "What would you do without me? I'm on my way to get you. I'll be there in twenty." I grabbed a hanger with an outfit on it and walked out of the closet. "Okay. I'll be ready." We ended the call and I quickly changed into a blue chambray dress and silver thong sandals. I stuck a pair of silver hoops in my ears, put on my guitar necklace, and my white Apple Watch before changing purses. Once everything was in my silver Alexander McQueen purse, I sprayed my body with some Vera Wang Princess perfume, and I was ready to go. Just as I put the bottle down, my phone rang Cheyenne's signature tone, so I picked it up along with my purse and walked out of the room. "I'm coming out right now." Once Chey said okay, I ended the call and exited my apartment.

When I was in my seat, I glanced at Cheyenne to see her staring at me with her mouth open. I raised my eyebrows and spoke while buckling my seatbelt. "What? Why are you staring at me like that?" She closed her mouth, only to open it again to speak. "You're wearing a dress. With the exception of your work suits, I haven't seen you in a dress since we were like five." I tried to suppress the grin I felt forming, speaking around it as I did. "Well, Jamere likes for me to wear them occasionally so...." I let my sentence trail off as Chey smiled and backed out of her parking space. "That's so sweet. You look nice though." I nodded my thanks and answered my phone that was ringing in my hand.

"Hey baby." My cheeks ached from smiling so hard, but I didn't care. I was talking to my baby and that was a price I was willing to pay to hear his voice. "Hey sweetheart. What are you doing? I hope you're not cooped up in the house." I rolled my eyes, looking out of the window as Cheyenne drove. "No, I'm not cooped up in the house. Chey came and got me, and we are going to hang out since she has the day off. Tell everyone I said hey." Jamere spoke to whoever was in the background and then replied to my statement. "That's good. They all said hey. What was your outfit of the day?" I looked down at myself and told him what I was wearing, anxious to hear what his response would be. "Blue chambray dress, silver thong sandals, silver earrings, silver guitar necklace, and my white Apple Watch." I heard Jamere's soft growl, and my body started to tremble. "What about underneath?" I felt my cheeks redden, but I kept my voice as steady as I could. I lowered my tone, but I knew Cheyenne would still be able to hear whatever I said. "That is not something I should say out loud. I'm not exactly alone as you know." I felt Cheyenne's eyes land on me before I heard a quiet chuckle escape her lips. "Well, maybe I'll just have to come over later and see for myself." I felt the moisture pooling in my panties as the anticipation of his promise filled me with desire. "Maybe you will. I'm pretty sure you'd like it though." The low rumble of his voice awakened my body, so I shifted my thighs to ease the lack of pressure there. "Oh, I know I would. But I still intend to find out myself. Let me know when you get home. I don't care what I'm doing or who I'm with. I'm coming to you, and later will have you coming for me. I promise. And now, we won't have to worry about anyone disturbing us." I bit my lip, trying to get the image of the Jamere's head between my legs out of my mind. "Baby, I have to get off of the phone. If I don't then Chey...." I paused, glancing at Chey before I spoke again. "I just don't think this is a conversation we should be having over the phone. I'll talk to you later baby. I love you." I could hear the smile in his voice, so I let it caress me as he spoke. "You're right. I'll see you later. Remind Chey about dinner tomorrow with the fam. I love you too baby. Have fun." I told him okay and we ended the call. I dropped my phone in my lap and exhaled slowly, willing my body to cool down.

"Jamere said to tell you hey and to remind you about dinner tomorrow." Chey laughed as she pulled into a parking spot at the mall. "I won't. I think you two are going to have a good night. Even though I couldn't hear most of what you said, your body language right now is speaking volumes." I didn't deny it, and I didn't hide the flush that crept up my neck. "That's the plan. I swear, I don't know if it's me that's insatiable or him, either way, I'm not mad." Cheyenne laughed again as the two of us exited the car. "So, I see." We closed our doors and locked them before walking side by side into the mall.

Cheyenne tapped my shoulder as we stood in a lingerie store looking at bras. I lifted my head to look at her, watching the smile that was spread across her face. "What?" She nodded her head in the direction of the entrance, so I turned to see what was there. When I saw Jamere standing there with his dad and brothers, I shoved my items into Cheyenne's arms and rushed out of the store. He had his back to me as they stood, talking to one another about something I couldn't hear. I knew when Justus spotted me, but he didn't do anything to alert Jamere that I was behind him. When I was inches away from him, I wrapped my arms around his body, resting my head on his back.

Jamere turned in my arms, so I looked up, watching the smile on his face form as he saw me. He put his arms around my waist, so I let go of him as he lifted me into the air. We pressed our lips together for a few seconds, only separating because we were in public. "I've missed you." I murmured against lips as he started to put me on the ground. "I've missed you too." I felt someone grab my hand before pulling me gently until I crashed into their chest. I smiled when I smelled the familiar scent, looking up into the eyes of Mr. Hart. "Hey Mr. Hart." I put my arms around him and squeezed before I was pulled away from him and wrapped in Justus' arms. "Hey Juss." He smiled and kissed the top of my head before Lloyd grabbed me. "Hey little sister. Where is Chey?" I hugged him and smiled as Jamere pulled me back into his arms. "Stop passing my girl around please. Thank you." Just as Jamere stopped talking, Chey's voice rang out. "I'm right here. Lil Bit, I paid for your stuff for you." I nodded my thanks, reminding myself to check the receipt so I could pay her back. "Okay Chey, thank you." Cheyenne went around hugging everyone and saying hi while Jamere held me to him as if he never wanted to let go. "Okay, we need to go back to our appropriate parties. We are supposed to be having a men's day, and the last time I checked, neither of you fit the bill." Cheyenne and I sent a glare at Lloyd, even though smiles formed on our faces. I turned my head to Jamere and looked at him with a playful frown on my face. He lowered his head and whispered in my ear, his warm breath sending shivers through me.

"I'll see you tonight. Don't forget what I said earlier. As soon as you get home." I slowly nodded my head, and he moved his mouth away from my ear and pressed it to my lips. "Love you baby. See you later." I smiled, hoping the heat I felt throughout my body didn't show on my face. "I love you too. Have fun. Call me tonight?" Jamere nodded and let me go, backing away from me and then hugging Chey. "See you later sis. Love you." Cheyenne nodded against his chest, putting her arms around him in a tight squeeze before letting go. "Okay brother. Love you too. Later." We all walked away from each other and went back to our plans for the rest of the day.

"What was Jamere whispering in your ear about." I felt my cheeks flame, so I looked away from Chey and focused my attention on the pictures that were hanging on the wall in front of me. "Oh, nothing really. Just reminding me of some promises he made me." I fought to suppress my grin, hoping that Chey wouldn't ask me anymore questions about that particular subject.

Cheyenne sat in the car, watching me walk towards my apartment. I held my phone to my ear as I unlocked my door. Once inside, I dropped my bags and stepped back outside to wave at Cheyenne. She honked her horn and pulled off just as Jamere answered his phone. "Hey baby. I just walked in the house." I locked up and picked my bags up once again and carried them to my bedroom. "Okay baby. Hold on." I listened to Jamere's whisper, before he spoke in a louder tone.

"Okay yall, I'm out. I'll see yall tomorrow evening. Be careful going home." Justus' voice sounded through the line, and I smiled as he spoke. "Jamere, its men's day. You are supposed to be spending time with us tonight. What do you have to do?" I could hear the implication in his voice, but Jamere's tone stayed neutral as he spoke to his big brother. "Juss, it is almost midnight. Men's day is over. I've been up since seven this morning and with yall since eight. I'm tired." I chuckled quietly as Lloyd spoke next. "Not too tired to go see Trina. I know that's where you're going." Justus and Lloyd laughed, but Jamere didn't. "Leave Jamere alone. He's found someone that makes him happy. So, if he wants to go see her, then let him. It's nice to see." I smiled at Mr. Dennison's response, knowing that he understood. "Thanks dad. Later yall." Lloyd spoke again, the laughter in his tone replaced with honesty. "Jamere, you know we were just joking right? We both love Trina." A brief chuckle came from Jamere as he answered Lloyd's question. "I know bro. It's all love. Love yall. See you tomorrow." Mr. Dennison spoke again, the sound of Jamere's voice becoming clearer as he put the phone back to his ear. "Love you too son. Tell Trina we said good night and we'll see her tomorrow." "Tell him I said for him to do the same and okay." Jamere relayed the message as I started unloading my purchases from the bags. Seconds later, Jamere's voice rang in my ear. "Baby, I'm right around the corner from your apartment. I should be there in under ten minutes." I checked the time on my watch and nodded to myself. "Okay baby. See you then." After saying okay, we disconnected the call and I continued putting my purchases away.

    I opened the door after hearing Jamere's knock, squealing as he lifted me and stepped into my apartment. He kicked the door closed and turned to lock it, pressing his lips to mine as he carried me to my bedroom. My back hit the mattress and then Jamere separated our lips. "Baby, I've been thinking about what's under this dress ever since I saw you at the mall." I smiled as he put his hand on my thigh and started to slowly slide it upwards. Little did he know, I took off the black lace thong I had on earlier in the day as soon as he told me he was on the way. I freshened up a little, thankful that I was able to finish before he arrived. His hand continued its upward trek, my smile widening when he reached his destination. "You weren't commando all day, were you?" I smiled seductively at him, putting my arms around his neck, and then responded. "Wouldn't you like to know?" Jamere's eyes darkened with desire as he lifted my left leg and placed soft kisses from my ankle all the way up. He repeated the process with my right leg, looking up and winking at me before burying his face into my moist inferno.

    The sound of Jamere's phone ringing caused the both of us to pop up out of our sleep. We were both still naked, and when I glanced at the time on my own phone, I knew we hadn't been asleep for more than two hours. Jamere read the name on his phone and answered it, worry in his voice as he spoke. "Hello?" He was silent for a few seconds before he spoke again. "Oh my God, what happened?" He turned so that his legs were hanging off of the bed, so I did the same. "I'm on the way. I was asleep, so as soon as I get dressed, I'm coming. I love you too." Jamere hung up and stepped into his boxers. "Baby, what happened?" I put on my bra and walked to my dresser for a pair of panties. "Amy, she had an asthma attack, and her inhaler wasn't helping. They had to rush her to the hospital. I'm sorry to leave like this, but I'll call you as soon as I hear anything."

 I raised my eyebrows at his back as I stepped into my panties and pulled my dress back over my head. I desperately wanted to shower, but we didn't have time. "No, you won't because I'm coming with you. And don't try to talk me out of it because it's not going to happen. Just let me brush my teeth. We may smell like sex, but my breath won't stink." That eased a smile out of him, but it was brief. He followed me into the bathroom where we brushed our teeth and then walked out. We stepped into our shoes, grabbed our things, and rushed out of the apartment.

 "I'm driving. No arguments." Jamere sighed, opening the driver's side door of my car, and then helped me into my seat. With the door closed, he rushed around and got in while I started the car. "What hospital?" Jamere's voice was full of worry, but I knew Amy would be okay. She was strong and she was a fighter. Jamere had to know that. I grabbed his hand as he answered my question and squeezed it in support. "Seattle Children's Hospital." I nodded and maneuvered the streets, rubbing the back of Jamere's hand as I sped to the hospital.

  Jamere and I rushed into the hospital ER, where he walked to the receptionist's area. "Hi, my parents brought my little sister in about an hour ago. Can you tell me where they are?" The receptionist looked up at Jamere and then at me before speaking. "Patient's name?" I entwined my fingers with Jamere's, stepping closer to him as he spoke. "Amelia Dennison. She's six." The nurse nodded and pressed some buttons on her computer. "Okay she is being seen by doctor's now, I can take you back to be with your parents and brother now but only immediately family is allowed." "But she's my wife. Why can't she come?" My stomach did a series of flips as I tried to force away the smile that wanted to appear. Hearing Jamere refer to me as his wife made me happier than I could have ever imagined, even if it were only to get me into the ER. "Okay then, she can come.

Follow me." Jamere squeezed my hand gently and the two of us followed her until we were where his parents were.

Jamere thanked the nurse as we stood a few feet away from where his parent's stood. She nodded her head and turned before walking away. I continued to hold his hand as we walked to where his parents were standing. "Ma, how is she?" Mrs. Dennison walked over to hug us, worry etched on her face. "We're waiting on the doctor to come back and let us know. She was having trouble breathing when we got here, but by God's grace, she never lost consciousness." Jamere exhaled as Mrs. Dennison pulled me into her arms and hugged me close. "Thank you for coming with him. We all appreciate it." I smiled as she let me go and wrapped my arms around Jamere's waist. "There is no reason to thank me. I love Jamere and I love you all as well. I would do whatever you needed, to make sure you were all good." I felt Jamere's lips press to my forehead, easing a smile out of me. "We love you too baby girl." Mr. Dennison kissed the top of my head as Justus walked into our line of sight.

"Any news?" He asked as we took seats in the waiting room. "Not yet. Soon hopefully." Justus nodded and sat on the opposite side of me as we all nervously waited for any news on Amy's condition.

"Dennison?" Jamere's parents stood and walked to the doctor, me, Jamere, and Juss following the path they took. "Hello Mr. And Mrs. Dennison. Amelia is doing better. She's breathing on her own, and after we gave her a new medication with the same dosage, she came around fairly quickly. She stayed alert and calm, but she fell asleep a few minutes ago. We are going to monitor her for a few hours, and if all goes as we hope, she can go home. Jamere exhaled in a soundless 'whoosh', and I put my arms around him and squeezed tightly. He held on to me, listening as his dad spoke to the doctor. "Thank you so much. Can we go see her?" The doctor looked at each of us before nodding his head up and down. "Yes, but only two at a time. Like I said before, she is resting now so please try not to disturb her." We each agreed, and watched the Dennison's follow the doctor to where they had Amy. The four of us walked toward the waiting room in silence, sitting close to one another while we waited for their parents to return.

Lloyd looked down at his phone, standing up right after he had done it. "I have to bounce. I have to go get LJ and get him dressed for school and then drop him off before work. Keep me updated. Tell Amy I love her, and I hope she feels better." Jamere stood and hugged his best friend, thanking him for coming. I would have never expected anything else from him, but Jamere wanted him to know he appreciated him. Once they let go of each other, he hugged me. I pecked him on the cheek and returned to my seat. "We'll call you when we find out when she can go home." Lloyd gave us the thumbs up sign and exited the waiting room while looking at his phone once again.

    We watched Jamere's parents enter the waiting room and then sit across from us. "Where's Lloyd?" Jamere's mom asked as she rested her head on his dad's shoulder. "He had to go get LJ and take him to school, and then he had to go to work. He told us to keep him updated." She nodded, Mr. Dennison speaking as she did. "Someone else can go see her. We'll wait here." Jamere nodded toward Justus, and he stood to his feet. He walked out of the waiting room with a nurse who was waiting to show him where to go. Mrs. Dennison's eyes closed, and his dad rested his head on top of hers. I lifted my head and stood, walking around the waiting room quietly. Jamere didn't bother me because he knew I must have been dealing with something internally. So, he watched me walk the length of the waiting room a number of times, until I returned to my place beside him. He grabbed my hand and squeezed, sitting quietly while waiting for Justus to return.

"Babe, wake up. We can go back now." I lifted my head from where it was resting on my hand and stood to my feet. Jamere and I followed the nurse to where Amy was being held and walked into the room. The room was quiet except for the sound of the beeping heart monitor. Amy's chest rose and fell in a steady rhythm, looking so peaceful in her induced sleep. We walked to the opposite side of the bed and sat down, each of us sitting down and grabbing one of Amy's small limp hands. I prayed over Amy, thanking God for keeping her safe and making sure she was protected. Just as I finished, I felt her hand shift in mine.

Jamere's head lifted, and my eyes went to hers, watching the smile that spread across her face. "Hey Jam." Jamere put a hand on her head and leaned forward to kiss her on the cheek. "Hey Amy. How are you feeling?" Amy turned her head after he kissed her, her smile widening in happiness. "Hey Trina." I returned her smile, rubbing my thumb across her cheek. "Hey sweetie. Your brother asked you a question." Amy turned her head back in his direction, speaking in a slightly hoarse voice. "I'm okay Jam. I can breathe better now. But my throat is a little sore." Jamere leaned forward and kissed her on the forehead, smiling as he looked into to her eyes. The love he had for her was different than the love he had for me or even his parents. I knew that he would keep her safe as long as he had breath his body. No one would prevent him from doing so.

"The sore throat will probably get better before too long. I'm glad you're breathing okay now though. Trina and I were so worried about you." Amy smiled at me and then looked at Jamere rubbing his thumb over her cheek as she spoke. "There was no need to be worried. God had me covered the whole time. I was never afraid. I knew that I would be okay." I looked at Jamere and then at Amy, the smiles on our faces full of love. I spoke in a soft tone, keeping my eyes trained on Amy.

"You know what Amy? You are one hundred percent correct. There was no need to worry because God is always there to keep us safe. You have just reminded me of something that I will never again forget. God's love never fails. There is a reason for everything on every occasion. Even if we don't know what it is." Amy nodded her head slowly, her blinks getting slower as sleep started to pull her under once again. "I'm going to go back to sleep now. I'll see you when I wake up." I kissed Amy's cheek and smiled at her as her eyes drifted shut. "Okay sweetie. Get some rest. We'll see you later." Jamere stood and kissed the top of Amy's head, thankful that his little sister was going to be okay. Knowing that she still had so much to live for, God wouldn't take her from this world until she had done all He had planned for her to do.

 When Amy was asleep once again, Jamere and I kissed her cheeks and exited the room as quietly as we had come. We returned to the waiting room, watching his parents as they slept quietly. Seconds after we walked in, the doctor entered the room. Jamere tapped his parents and watched their eyes open and land on the doctor standing in front of them. They both stood, as the doctor spoke to them with a smile on his face. "Mr. and Mrs. Dennison, Amelia is being discharged. She will probably sleep for the next few hours and remain drowsy throughout the day, but she should be back to her normal self by tomorrow. So, take her home and let her rest, and by dinner time, she'll probably be more than ready for a meal. Her throat may be sore, but cough drops should ease that discomfort. It shouldn't last more than a day or so though, so if it does, take her to the doctor to make sure everything is okay." Jamere's parents nodded their heads, thanking the doctor as he looked around at all of us. "No thanks necessary. I'm glad we were able to help her. If you would sign the discharge papers, I'll have her brought out to you." Jamere's parents took the clipboard he held out to them and read over the words on the paper. Once they finished, they signed their names and gave it back to him. "Thank you once again Dr. Morgan. We appreciate all you did to help our daughter." Dr. Morgan shook Mr. Dennison's hand after he had spoken, a small smile on his face. "You are all more than welcome. Have a safe drive home and get some rest. All of you. Doctor's orders." He shook Mrs. Dennison's hand, followed by Jamere's, and then mine before turning and walking out of the waiting room.

When the nurse walked in with Amy in a wheelchair sleeping, we all stood and made our way to the exit. Once outside, Mr. Dennison and Jamere went to get the cars while we waited with the nurse.

Jamere pulled up to the E.R. entrance and got out of the car. He walked around to the passenger's side to open the door and waited for me to get in. He then pushed the door closed behind me, watching his dad put Amy in her seat. Jamere walked to his parent's car and opened the door for his mom, smiling when she kissed him on the cheek before sitting down. He closed the door behind her and spoke to his dad as he closed Amy's door.

"We're going to go shower and I'll be over in a little bit." Jamere's dad nodded, and they walked to their cars and got behind the wheel. He pulled away from the curb behind his parents and made the way back to my apartment. "I'm going to take a shower and go to my parent's house. If you don't want to come, I'll come pick you up if we go to dinner." I nodded as I typed in my phone. "No, I'll go. I heard you tell your dad that, that was the plan anyway. I told my parents and Chey what happened, so they said if we want to reschedule that's fine. Whatever your parents want to do is okay." He nodded his head and linked our fingers as he continued the drive to our destination.

Chapter: 17

Jamere

I woke up and lifted my head, looking at Trina who was laying on my chest. She was still sleeping, so I carefully moved her arm from around me and placed it beside her gently. When she didn't stir, I stood and walked toward the restroom that was on the opposite side of the kitchen. The yawn that escaped my mouth as I entered let me know how tired I still was. But, knowing that Amy was better was worth the drowsiness I felt. Just knowing that she was back home with her family, was a blessing in itself.

I exited the restroom and returned to my place in the living room. As I crossed the threshold, I saw Amy where I had once been sleeping. She sat up as I walked closer and patted the space between herself and the arm of the sofa. I sat down and rested my head on the arm of it as she stood up and sat on the other side of Trina. She rested her head on Trina's shoulder, and then lifted Trina's arm and draped it over her shoulder. Trina shifted but didn't wake, so Amy and I closed our eyes and went back to sleep.

I felt my body shift, so I opened my eyes to look at Trina who was trying to get up without moving too much. "Sorry baby. I was trying not to wake you." I shifted until I was in an upright position and shook my head, careful not to wake Amy. "It's cool. I need to be awake anyway so that I won't be asleep all day when we get to New Orleans." I glanced at my watch and saw that it was 3:58. "How long has Amy been down here?" I shrugged and looked down at her as she started to stir. "About two hours I guess. Not too long." Amy stood and walked away as our parents walked out of their bedroom. "We're going to head to dinner in about an hour. That's the same time we were going to go anyway, but Trina if you would contact your family and let them know the plans are the same." Trina sat up yawned and nodded, picking up her phone off of the coffee table. "No problem. Same location?" My dad nodded his head at her, so she stood and walked toward the front of the house to make her calls.

  My dad walked to where I sat and rubbed the top of my head playfully. The two of us said nothing to one another, but he reached for the remote and started flipping through the channels. I turned my head when I heard footsteps, smiling as Amy walked toward the sofa and sat next to our dad. She scooted her body close to his and pulled her legs up onto the sofa. He kissed the top of her head, looking at her with concern written on his features.

"I'm okay daddy. I promise." My dad smiled at her, turning his head when he heard his name. "Mr. Dennison, I was able to talk to everyone and they said they will see us then." Trina walked towards us, and I pulled her onto my lap when she was within arm's reach. Her smile lit up her face as she glanced at me after watching my dad. "Great. Do yall need to go get ready? I'm almost certain you both aren't going in track suits." Trina chuckled quietly and shook her head no at him. "No sir. We both took showers before we came over. Our outfits are in the car. So, all we have to do is change, and I'll put on a little makeup if I feel like it." My dad laughed at her response and stood to his feet. "Well. Its 4:15 now, so I'm going to go hop in the shower and get ready. Amy, go upstairs and get showered and dressed." Amy stood, yawning as she spoke. "Yes sir." My dad walked away and headed back toward his bedroom as I slid Trina on to the couch. "I'm going to go get our stuff out of the car. I'll be right back." Trina's head moved up and down, so I stood and made my way out of the house.

Trina and I made our way up the stairs to get dressed once I got back inside with our bags. I let Trina use the guest room closest to

Amy's and I used the one at the end of the hall. I pulled off the layers of my track suit, standing in just my navy-blue Hollister boxer briefs and black Polo socks. I stepped into a pair of black Levi's jeans and pulled a navy-blue Polo shirt over my head. I put on my black Prada belt to my waist and secured it before putting my black G-Shock on my left wrist. I kept the square black diamond earrings I was wearing in my ears and stepped into my black number 11 Space Jam Jordan's. Once my black Burberry wallet and iPhone 7+ were in my pockets, I put the clothes I had just taken off in my bag. I sprayed some Hei by Alfred Sung on my body and placed the bottle in my bag before walking out of the room with it in my hand. As I walked to the stairs, Amy walked out of the bathroom with her terry cloth robe covering her body. She walked across the hall into her bedroom, closing her door behind her as I made my trek down the stairs.

  I sat in the living room alone, looking up at the ceiling while waiting on everyone else to get ready. The room was peacefully silent, and I was basking in that for all of five minutes. "Jamere!" I rolled my eyes and watched Juss' head appear over mine before dropping my head so that I was looking at the tv. "What's up Juss? What's up Lloyd? Where is L.J.?" They both sat on opposite sides of me, smiling as Amy walked down the stairs. "Aunt Dinah is on her way to drop him off. She picked him up from daycare for me." I nodded as Juss scooped Amy up into his arms and kissed her cheek. He put her back on the ground, and she smiled at us briefly before sitting on my lap and resting her head on my shoulder. The two of them walked away, and I looked down at my little sister lovingly.

Amy looked like a picture of innocence dressed in a light blue Lacoste Polo dress. All white slip-on Vans were on her feet and a light blue Michael Kors Ginny medium messenger purse draped across her body. She had a pair of sterling silver studs in her ears with a greyish blue stone. The anklet on her right ankle spelled the word 'Love' and a Tiffany's heart necklace hung from her neck. Last but not least, the novel 'The Secret Garden' was clenched in her hand as she rested her head on my lap. "You look cute Amy." She didn't move, but I saw her lips form a smile. "Thanks Jam." I rubbed my hand on her head and started to take out the cornrows that my mom had put in her hair for her braid out.

Trina walked down the stairs after I had done two braids, smiling at me as she sat next to me and started to help with Amy's hair. I glanced at her outfit and smiled at her. Denim dress with three quarter sleeves and red threading and buttons with a red bodysuit underneath. She wore a pair of red peep toe pumps on her feet with a bow on the backs of them. A small red Gucci shoulder bag was beside her, small silver knot hoops in her ears, and a necklace with the letter 'J' draped on her chest. "You look beautiful baby." She winked and smiled at me, looking back at Amy's head as she spoke. "Thank you. You look amazing as well." I nodded my head, and the two of us finished taking Amy's hair down.

Trina sat Amy up and fluffed her hair, telling her to go upstairs and get two headbands to match her outfit. Amy walked away, coming back just as my parents walked out of their room. She handed a light blue and a white headband to Trina, and Trina put them over her head and slid them into place. Trina gave Amy's hair one final fluff, and she was all set. "Thanks Trina. I was going to do that." Trina nodded at my mom, speaking as Lloyd walked in with L.J. and Juss. "No problem. But Jamere started it, I was just helping." My mom looked at me with a smile and kissed my cheek. "Thanks baby. Amy, go upstairs and get your white denim Levi's jacket." Amy turned and walked away, rushing towards the stairs with her book still clenched in her hand.

We sat in the restaurant, waiting on Trina's family to arrive. We all arrived at the restaurant ahead of them, but after Trina called to check on their location, we knew that they should be coming in right behind us. As soon as the thought left my mind, Trina's parents walked in, followed by Cheyenne and her brothers. The two of us stood, and Mr. Hart pulled Trina into his arms and squeezed, before shaking my hand. The hostess appeared and told us to follow her to our tables. We all followed behind her to a banquet room, that would give us plenty of space. As we started to sit, the hostess spoke kindly. "Your waiter should be with you shortly. You all have a nice evening." We thanked her and she walked away, so Trina stood to make introductions. "Mom, dad. This is Mr. Lawrence and Mrs. Aubrey Dennison. Mr. and Mrs. Dennison, these are my parents Bradley and Constance Hart." She touched each of them as she said their names and stood behind her brothers. "And I know you've met my brothers and sister; Cheyenne, Dylan, Ryan, and Tayler." My parents shook their hands, exchanging pleasantries and smiling kindly as they stood. Mr. and Mrs. Hart, you've just met my parents. These are my brothers Justus and Lloyd, and my little sister Amelia, but everyone calls her Amy. And little man is my God son/nephew Lloyd Jr. But we call him

L.J." Once the introductions were made, we all sat back in our seats as the waitress came into the room.

"Hello. My name is Felicia and I'll be your server this evening. Can I start you off with something to drink?" Felicia went around the table, taking drink orders and double checking them before she walked away to get them. We looked over our menus and decided on what we were going to eat so that we could tell Felicia when she returned. We had casual conversation while we waited, the parents getting to know one another and seeming to get along. Felicia returned and as soon as she had everyone's orders, she walked away again.

L.J. and Amy stood at the same time, each walking away from their seats between me and Lloyd. They both walked towards Trina, and when she noticed she slid her chair back. Amy perched herself on Trina's knee and Trina lifted L.J. so that he was sitting on her left leg. He held Lloyd's phone in his hand and played with an app that helped him with reading and adding. Amy read from her book for a few minutes before sliding onto my lap, resting her head on my shoulder, and closing her eyes. Her breathing became steady and slowed down as sleep overtook her.

"Trina told us about your daughter being in the hospital. We're glad to see she's been released and able to come out. Has she been okay since her release?" My dad looked at Amy sleeping on me, nodding his head as he answered Mr. Hart's question. "Yes, she's good. She even assured me of that not long ago. She's just still fighting the tiredness from when she was struggling to get air into her lungs during the asthma attack. We thank God that even though it was hard for her to breathe, she never lost consciousness. That was a major blessing." Mrs. Hart nodded her head in agreement, saying as much to my dad. "Amen to that. God takes care of His children. That's for sure." A chorus of Amen's erupted around the table and we all continued talking amongst one another while waiting on our food to arrive.

As hard as I tried, I couldn't get Trina to let me hold a sleeping L.J. to take him to the car. Whenever I reached for him, she would roll her eyes and walk further away from me, causing laughter to erupt around us. "Jamere, if you want to hold someone so bad, hold Amy. She's practically asleep on her feet." I turned to look down at Amy walking beside me, picking her up so that her head rested on my shoulder. My forearm acted as a seat, for her, and I carried her carefully to my parent's car.

Trina's parent's hugged me, watching Trina put L.J. into his dad's car. She kissed his cheek and eased out of the car, pushing the door closed quietly. Lloyd put his arm around Trina's shoulders, whispering something to her that I couldn't make out. D.J., R.J., and Tay shook my hand as their goodbye's, walking to my parents to tell them goodbye before going to their cars. My attention focused on Lloyd and Trina, but the look on their faces gave nothing away as to what they were talking about. "Thanks sis. Love you." Trina smiled and shook her head, walking away as she responded to Lloyd. "You're welcome Lloyd. Love you too." Trina walked to where her parents stood and hugged them before returning to where I stood. Justus rubbed her head as Lloyd punched me in the arm, the two of them getting into their cars as they laughed. Trina shook her head to get her hair to fall in place, bending into my parent's car to say goodbye to a sleeping Amy. Trina kissed her head and pushed the door closed standing beside me as her parents watched her.

"It was so nice meeting you both. It's nice to meet the people who raised this amazing young man." My parents smiled at

Mrs. Hart, glancing at me before returning their attention to her. "Thank you so much for saying that. And Trina is just as amazing, but now we see where she gets it from. We love her as if she were our own." Trina smiled shyly and looked away at nothing in particular. "Thank you." My dad smiled at Trina and pulled her into his arms. "Well, we should get going. We'll see you all soon hopefully." Mr. Hart nodded his head, opening his mouth to speak. "Yes. We're having a cookout this weekend and we would love for you and the boys, to come. Jamere and Trina will miss out, but oh well." Trina rolled her eyes as Chey stuck her tongue out at her. "I think we can do that. Let's exchange numbers so we can get the details." My mom and Mrs. Hart spouted off their numbers to one another, as my dad and Mr. Hart did the same. "Great. Don't forget to tell the boys. We better get going and get Amy into bed. Hopefully, we'll see you all this weekend. Be careful going home." The Harts smiled and nodded, kissing my cheek and then Trina's before waving and getting in their car. The remainder of us followed their lead, and pulled out of the parking lot, one behind the other.

"Okay baby, I have to go home and pack. I'll meet you here at 5 a.m. to drop your car off at my parent's house." Trina nodded her head as she unlocked the door and stepped inside. She turned and pressed her lips to mine, forcing herself to break the kiss. "Okay baby. Be careful going home. Let me know when you've made it in safely." I nodded my head at her, pushing her gently into her apartment, and pulling the door closed. When I heard the lock turn, I walked away from her door and back to my car.

 I watched my surroundings as I exited my car and made my way to my apartment. I had a weird feeling, so I was on alert, as I listened to my surroundings. I unlocked the door to my apartment and walked inside, flipping on the lights as I re-locked the door. I pulled my phone from my back pocket and called Trina as I walked toward my bedroom. My room was neat and in order, the only thing I would have to do other than pack, was to change my linens. I listened to the ringing in my ear, until Trina's voice filled the line. "Are you home baby?" I rolled my suitcase out of the closet, answering her question as I opened it and put it on my bed. "Yes. I just walked in. I'm about to pack my bag and get ready for our 9 a.m. flight." Trina had music playing in the background, and I could picture her catching a vibe to it. "Ok cool. I'm doing the same. I'm going to do that, shower, and do my laundry, before I go to sleep." I turned my tv on ESPN and glanced at the highlights that played on the screen. "Okay baby. I'm going to hang up, so we aren't a distraction to one another. I'll be there by 5:30 at the latest. I love you sweetheart." I walked into to my closet and stared at possible outfit choices. "Okay babe. Love you too. See you in the morning." The two of us hung up, and I started pulling clothes out of the closet and taking them to my bed.

 I woke up the following morning and walked to the bathroom to brush my teeth and shower. Once I was finished, I wrapped my towel around my waist and exited the bathroom. I stepped into some Polo boxer briefs, then walked to my bed to strip it of its dirty linens. I carried them, along with my shorts that I slept in, and my towel to the laundry room and put them in the washer. My hope was that I could have them washed and dried before I left. It was a little past 3:30, so I figured that should be more than enough time.

 I returned to my room and made my bed with the fresh linens, putting the pillows on last before I started to dress. My outfit, shoes, lotion, and cologne were all on the dresser where I had left them the night before, so I didn't have to find anything to wear. Lotion was first, so I rubbed it into my skin and put some Adidas low cut black socks on my feet. I pulled my black Adidas track pants up my legs and situated them on my waist. I pulled a white wife beater over my head, followed by a white Adidas big logo originals T-Shirt with black logo on top of it. I slid an Adidas logo print jersey track jacket on my arms, then walked out of my room to check on my laundry.

When I walked into the laundry room, the washer had stopped, so I put everything in the dryer and walked out once again. Once I was back in my room, I went to work with putting my accessories on. Black Diesel Mr. Daddy 2.0 watch on my left wrist, and blackout hip hop stud earrings in my ears. I put my blue studio HD Beats by Dr. Dre around my neck and sat in the chair at my desk. Once I was seated, I put my feet into my black and white Yeezy Boost 350 V2. I stood up and checked myself in the mirror to make sure I looked okay. I brushed my hair and sprayed my body with some Gucci Guilty Black. I checked my watch, and when I saw that it was 4:50, I went to check on my laundry. The dryer had stopped, so I opened the door to test the dryness. When I didn't feel any wet spots, I folded everything and took them to their appropriate places.

I put my black Adidas originals Trefoil backpack on my shoulders, stuffed my iPhone in one pocket, wallet in the other, and grabbed the handle of my silver American Tourister hard side suitcase and walked out of my bedroom, turning the light off as I exited.

Once in my car, I called Trina to let her know I was on the way. We only lived 20 minutes away from one another, so I was still on schedule. And she lived closer than that to my parents, so we should have more than enough time to get to the airport and to our gate on time. I texted my parents that we would be there by six to drop off the car, and when my dad responded almost immediately, it was to offer us a ride to the airport. *Okay son. I'm going to take you both to the airport. No need in paying the ridiculous parking fee if you don't have to. We'll make sure someone is there to pick you up on Tuesday too."* I didn't respond immediately, choosing to wait until I wasn't driving to do so.

I replied to my dad's text when I arrived at Trina's apartment building, telling him that he didn't have to do that. As I was getting out of the car, Trina opened the driver's side door of her car and stepped out. I watched her open the rear driver's side door, so I grabbed her suitcase and Nike backpack and put it in my car. She wore a pair of black Nike dry logo training leggings and a Nike performance dry hoodie. Black and white number 9 Retro

Jordan's were on her feet and a black Nike featherlight cap was on her head. My eyes roamed over her body, noticing the heart shaped sterling silver earrings in her ears and Gucci GG web doctor's tote in her hand. White Solo 2 Beats rested around her neck and her iPhone was clutched in her hand. I had already put her black Nike Hayward Futura backpack in the car along with her black Tumi suitcase. "Morning baby. Let's get on the road. I told my parents we'd be there by six." I pecked her lips and opened her door and waited for her to sit down again. She nodded and sat down, so I closed the door and got into my own seat.

"Yall pull into the garage. We'll keep your cars there until you get back." I started to argue, but I knew there was no point. So, Trina and I did as instructed, my dad and I retrieving our luggage once both cars were in the garage. We placed the luggage in my dad's truck and went inside to say bye to my mom and sister. They both held onto us tightly, still in their pj's as they sat down and ate breakfast. I knew my parents had work and Amy had school, which was the only reason they were up that early. "We love yall. We'll see you when we get back. The two of them nodded as they repeated what Trina and I had just spoken. We followed my dad out of the house, got into the truck, and we were on our way to the airport.

Chapter 18:

Trina

Jamere and I walked off of the plane, making our way to baggage claim. It was a little after one o'clock, so we planned to get checked into the hotel and get a nap before hitting the streets. The Lord only knew how tired we were. So, we maneuvered around the throng of people in the airport until we arrived at baggage claim. We waited a few minutes for our bags, grabbed them, and then sent for an Uber.

We spotted our Uber as we walked out of the airport, rushing to get our bags in the trunk and inside, to avoid slowing up traffic any more than it already was. The Uber driver spoke as we slid into the car, smiling as he glanced at us in the rearview mirror. "How are you both doing this afternoon?" I smiled at him as I buckled my seatbelt, replying to his question. "We're good and yourself." The driver checked his surroundings and eased away from the curb to take us to our hotel. "I'm great. There is water in the cooler and candy in the middle console. Help yourself to whatever you want." Jamere nodded at the driver and thanked him as he pulled his phone from his pocket. I did the same, sending texts to my family to let them know that we had made it safely.

We spent our ride to the hotel in silence, looking out of the windows at our surroundings since this was our first time in New Orleans. It was really hot. A lot hotter than it was in Seattle at the moment, so we were looking forward to having some fun in the sun for the next few days. I looked in front of me as the car slowed and then stopped. The driver stepped out of the car and went to the trunk as Jamere, and I did the same.

"Thank you. Have a nice day." Jamere put a ten-dollar bill in our driver's hand as he placed my suitcase on the ground and closed the trunk. "No, thank you. Enjoy your trip." We nodded our heads and adjusted our book bags on our backs. Jamere grabbed both suitcases and rolled them behind him as we walked through the entrance of the hotel.

Jamere and I stepped onto the elevator with our room keys, and I pushed the number 4. A couple got on the elevator with us on the second floor but stayed inside when we got off on our floor. We scanned the doors, until we came up on room number 448. I slid the key card in, turned the knob, and pushed it open. I walked inside, holding the door open until Jamere was inside. I let the door close and followed Jamere into the room. He left the bags beside the bed, and we walked around the room. I walked out onto the balcony and looked at the scenery in the bright sunlight. Jamere walked up behind me and put his arms around my waist, resting his chin on my shoulder as we stared for a few minutes. "I'm going to get in the shower and take a nap. I am so sleepy." Jamere let go of me and the two of us walked back into the room. "Yeah, me too. By the time we wake up, we'll probably be ready to eat." I laid my suitcase on the floor and opened it, pulling things out of it, and putting it all in the drawers. Jamere did the same, the two of us leaving out the appropriate items for our showers. "You can go first baby. I'm going to find a vending machine or something and get us something to drink." I picked up my Nike leggings and sports bra from the bed, along with some panties and socks. I nodded my head at Jamere as I walked into the bathroom and closed the door behind me.

    I decided to wait until we went to get food to put on lotion, so I walked out of the bathroom with my dirty clothes in my hand. I put them on the floor in the corner of the closet and walked back out. Jamere put a cold grapefruit juice in my hand and then walked into the bathroom and closed the door. As I opened the juice, I walked to the thermostat and dropped the temperature to make the room colder. After doing so, I walked to the bed positioned in the center of the room and pulled back the covers. I put my juice on the nightstand as I plugged my phone into its charger and slid under the covers. The remote sat on the nightstand, so I picked it up and turned the tv on, flipping channels absently. I stopped the tv on The Preacher's Wife and picked up my juice once again. I sipped from it a few times, turning my head when the bathroom door opened. Jamere put his dirty clothes in the closet, coming out and sliding under the covers with me. I put my juice down once again and slid closer to Jamere's body. He draped one arm around my shoulder, and the two of us focused on the movie playing on the tv.

    I woke up before Jamere did, so I got off of the bed and went to find something to wear. Once I had it, I went into the bathroom to brush my teeth and do my hair. I stared at my reflection in the mirror, lost in thought as I went through the motions of doing my hair. My thoughts were all over the place, and not just on one specific thing. My life with Jamere, my past with Stephan, my reunion with my family. So much had happened in the last year, it was almost unreal. But the happiness I now felt, the happiness I hadn't felt in so long, was so overdue. The new woman I had become because of the challenges I had faced, while holding on to the best parts of myself before Stephan; I was so at peace, knowing that Jamere had helped bring that out of me. I loved him to the death of me, and I hoped and prayed that every day with him would be a day I would remember for the rest of my life.

Jamere walked into the bathroom and pressed his lips to my neck. I smiled at him in the mirror, before turning and walking out of the bathroom to get dressed. I picked up my bra from the dresser along with my lotion and sat on the bottom of the bed. I rubbed the lotion into my skin and changed bras, finishing just as Jamere walked out of the bathroom. He glanced at me and winked, causing a grin to form on my face as I stood. I stepped into a dark wash denim mini skirt, watching Jamere go through a drawer to find something to wear. I pulled a white tank top over my head, picked up my socks from the top of the dresser, and dropped the sports bra in the drawer. I sat on the edge of the bed once again to slide my socks on and waited for Jamere to get dressed. My stomach rumbled loudly, Jamere laughing at the sound.

"I know, I know. I'm getting dressed. I'm taking you to get something to eat." He knelt as he spoke and put a hand on my stomach. I laughed as he kissed my stomach, and when it no longer made the sound, he stood to step into his shorts. He pulled a pair of khaki cargo shorts up his legs and fastened a black belt around his waist. A black wife beater went over his head, followed by a black Polo t-shirt. "What shoes do you want baby?" Jamere straightened his shirt and put his watch on his wrist, glancing at his outfit before responding. "My black Air Force Ones with the gum bottoms." I stood up and walked to the closet, grabbing my white Air Force Ones along with his black ones, and walked back out. I gave him his shoes and stepped into my own. I pushed some hoops through my ears and put my Apple watch on my left wrist. Once that was done, I picked up my Louis Vuitton Speedy bag and my phone and I was ready to go. Jamere slid his phone and wallet into his pocket, changed his earrings, and the two of us walked out the door.

  The two of us walked out into the warm air, the setting sun turning the sky to a beautiful orange color. We walked down the sidewalk with our hands clasped, enjoying just being in the company of one another. We walked into a seafood restaurant, the bustling crowd letting us know that the food must have been pretty good. The two of us waited to be showed to our seats for a minute or two before the host showed us to where we would be sitting. "Can I get your drink orders?" His New Orleans drawl made me smile as I looked at the drink menu. When I looked back up, I read his name tag and saw that his name was Auguste. We told him what we wanted, he smiled and nodded as he wrote it down. The dimples in his young cheeks made him look so adorable and innocent, and I knew he was probably a heartbreaker. "Okay, I'll go get your drinks and be right back." Jamere told him okay, so he walked away while Jamere and I looked at the menu.

Auguste came back to our table and set our drinks down in front of us. "Okay. You two enjoy your meal. Your waiter will be with you shortly." I smiled at him once again, his accent so cute to me. "Thank you. Have a nice evening." He nodded his head at me and smiled before walking away from the table.

Jamere looked over his menu at me, speaking as he moved it below his lips. "Do you know what you're going to eat?" I put my menu down and watched him look back at his. "Yes. A cup of seafood gumbo and the Forrest's Seafood Feast. You?" As I asked, he put the menu down and answered my question. "A cup of New England clam chowder and Shrimp New Orleans." I pushed my menu to the edge of the table and Jamere put his on top of mine. He smiled at me, which made me think that he was up to something. "Did you have a nice nap?" I returned his smile, answering his question as I rested my hands in my lap. "Yes, I did. Did you? The bed feels like a cloud." Jamere chuckled, taking a sip from his sprite before replying. "Yes I did. And you're right. I wish I could pack it up and take it home with me." I nodded my head as I laughed, agreeing with him completely. "Yeah, but it probably wouldn't feel the same once we got home." Jamere looked at me as if he were thinking about it, and then looked as if he had come to a conclusion. "You're probably right. They probably had those mattresses custom made for guests so that they would come back." I laughed at his statement, knowing he probably thought that was truly accurate. But I knew that that particular hotel didn't have the finances to have custom mattresses made for each room. It was a beautiful hotel, but it was definitely not at the custom mattress level.

    The waiter walked over to our table, smiling as he spoke his practiced spiel. "Good Evening. My name is Marcel and I'll be your waiter this evening. Have you had enough time to look over the menu, or do you need a few more minutes?" Jamere and I looked at him, but Jamere replied. "Good evening to you too. We're ready to order. Baby, you go first." I nodded and waited for Marcel to get his notepad and ink pen ready and then told him what I wanted. Marcel looked at Jamere, and Jamere spouted off his order as well. Marcel repeated our orders, and when we told him they were correct, he dropped the pen in his apron pocket. "Okay, I'll go put your order in and your meal should be ready shortly." I nodded at him and then spoke with a smile on my face. "Okay thank you." He looked at me and smiled kindly before replying to my statement. "You're welcome." He then turned and walked away from our table.

    Jamere and I walked out of the restaurant an hour later, full of the delicious meal we had just shared. "That was really good." Jamere clasped my hand as I walked on the inside of the sidewalk. I glanced up at him briefly, nodding my head in agreement. "It really was. If we go back before we leave, I think I'm going to try the crab legs." We turned right on the sidewalk across from our hotel and took in our surroundings. We weren't going to do a whole lot tonight, but tomorrow we were going to get out bright and early. Early for us anyway. So, we looked at the shops along Canal Street, spotting a mall, and some other stores we may go in the following day. A yawn escaped my lips, my lack of sleep the previous night starting to catch up to me. My earlier nap was starting to wear off, and fatigue was beginning to wash over me. "Babe let's head back. We have an idea of where to start tomorrow, but sleep is calling my name. It is after midnight, and I got no sleep at all last night." I nodded my head, and we crossed the street, walking down the sidewalk to head back to our hotel.

    My steps got slower, and by the time we reached the hotel, I didn't want to walk any further, but I still had to make it to our room. "Baby, get on my back." I looked at Jamere as we stopped outside of the hotel and shook my head. "Baby, I can't. I'm wearing a skirt." Jamere raised his eyebrows as we started to walk again. He stopped as we stepped into the lobby, so I stopped too. He pulled his t-shirt over his head, leaving him standing there in his wife beater. "I'm going to pick you up. Use my shirt to lay across your lap." Before I could respond, Jamere had lifted me into his arms, my legs draped over is right arm and my back against is left arm. "Baby, you don't have to carry me." I spoke, noticing the people in the lobby looking in our direction, some with smiles and some with frowns on their lips. "Hush. Put the shirt over your legs. Unless you want these people to see what the Lord blessed you with." My cheeks flamed as I draped the shirt over my legs and buried my face in Jamere's chest. I could hear a soft chorus of "Ahh's" as Jamere spoke once again. "Baby, I need you to push the button for the elevator." I did as he said, and we waited for the doors to open. When they did, Jamere walked inside, and I pushed the number 4 to take us to our floor.

    I unlocked the door and Jamere walked into the room and placed me on the bed gently. He walked into the bathroom and closed the door, so I stood and went to the dresser to pull out my pajamas. I scrolled through my phone, checking my social media while waiting for Jamere to come out. Jamere walked out minutes later with a towel around his waist and his dirty clothes in his arms. I grabbed my pajamas and toiletries and went in the bathroom to shower.

    I exited the bathroom with my dirty clothes, placing them in the closet with our other dirty laundry. I walked out and made my way to the dresser, grinning at Jamere as he winked at me. I stood in front of the mirror and pulled my hair up into a messy bun on top of my head. I wrapped it up in my scarf and went to my side of the bed to lay down. The bed seemed to be just as comfortable as it had been before we left, and as I scooted my body close to Jamere's, he draped his arm around me. I threw my right leg across him, his free hand resting on my bare thigh. The shorts I was wearing weren't long, but my movement had caused them to bunch up higher than they had been. I lifted my head up and watched him angle his own, pressing our lips together in an endearing kiss. "I love you baby." My lips formed a smile, and I grabbed his chin, pulling him down to kiss me again. "I love you too baby. More than you will ever know." Jamere smiled, staring at me for a few more seconds before turning his attention to the tv and flipping channels.

    I woke up breathing heavily with my toes curling. I suppressed a moan, looking down at Jamere's head between my thighs. The covers had been thrown off of us, and I barely made out the pile sitting on the floor. I grabbed his head, watching his eyes find mine. The mischievousness in his eyes turned me on that much more and he returned his focus to what he was doing. My thighs clenched around his head as my orgasm ripped through me. As my body shook in its aftermath, I unclenched my thighs, freeing Jamere's head. He kissed his way up my stomach, his mouth covering one breast and then the other, respectively. I felt his lips on my neck, and before I could process he was entering me. I gasped as the length and width of him filled me, exhaling slowly as he began a slow sensual rhythm. After a few minutes of the slow rhythm, he picked up the pace and I could feel my orgasm building once again. I held back as long as I could, and when I felt Jamere nearing his release, I let go, both of us falling into our own shattering orgasm. Jamere collapsed on top of me, my body twitching as the aftershocks took over my body. Jamere rolled himself over, pulling me on top of him as we basked in the aftermath of our love making.

    Once my breathing slowed, I spoke, my voice not much more than a whisper. "That was quite the way to wake up." I heard the rumble in Jamere's chest as he laughed, which brought a smile to my face. "I'm glad." The two of us laid there in silence for a few more minutes before I eased myself off of him. I pulled my bunched-up T-shirt down, not sure where my panties and shorts were, but not really caring either. "I am so hungry." Jamere sat up, pulling his Hanes boxers up his legs. "Well, we should get ready to go eat then." I nodded as I found my shorts and panties, stepping into my shorts as I tossed the covers back on the bed. I was itching to make it up, but I knew housekeeping would just change it while we were gone, so I didn't. I checked the drawers for an outfit, settling on one I liked before going into the bathroom for a shower.

    I walked out of the bathroom with my towel around my body, sitting on the edge of the bed to put my lotion on. Once that was done, I put on a matching black bra and panty set from Victoria's Secret. Jamere walked by me, picking up his boxers before walking in the bathroom and closing the door behind him. I walked to the mirror and put on some mascara and a nude lipstick before working on my hair. I pulled the hair tie, releasing the bun that was sideways on my head. After combing my hair out, I parted it across the middle and put the top in a ponytail. I then pulled a gray Polo T-Shirt dress over my head. All I had left to do was put on my shoes and accessories, so I put on some silver hoops and a silver Tiffany's necklace. Once my Apple watch was on my wrist, I walked into the closet to get my silver sandals. I sprayed my body with some Kenneth Cole Black, and I was ready to go.

    Jamere exited the bathroom just as I finished making the bed. I tried my hardest not to, but I couldn't not do it. "Give me five minutes baby. I just need to dress and brush my hair." Jamere stepped into a pair of dark wash Levi's slim jeans and pulled a white wife beater over his head. He then put a white

Levi's shirt on and a pair of white no show socks. He glanced at me as he brushed his hair, so I looked up from my phone. He put the brush down and checked his reflection, sliding his phone and wallet into his pocket as he did. He held his hand out for mine, grabbing his Apple watch as I placed my hand in his. We stopped at the closet, and he walked inside, coming out with a pair of all white number 4 retro Jordan's his feet. He led the way to the door, holding it open for me to walk out.

    We ate breakfast at the hotel, seeing as we got going later than we had planned. But as soon as we exited the hotel and felt the warm air, we made our way to the mall we had seen the previous evening. The streets weren't really busy, but they weren't dead either. I knew that was going to change before too long. Jamere reached for my hand, so I placed my hand in his. We walked along the sidewalk, pointing out things we hadn't noticed the previous night. When the mall came into view, Jamere and I crossed the street and into the building.

    The cool air welcomed us as we walked past the first store on the inside. "We should get an Uber into the city tonight for dinner. We can eat lunch around here, but let's see more of the city while we're here." We turned and walked into J. Crew, looking around at the selections. The two of us browsed, but we didn't see anything that caught our eye, so we walked out. "Baby, I'm going to go look for something for Amy, Honey, and L.J. in Vineyard Vines. Are you coming?" Jamere let go of my hand and shook his head no. "I'll meet you in there. I'm going to go get us some Starbucks." I stood on my tiptoes and kissed his cheek, walking into the store and leaving him to go to Starbucks.

    I looked around the store, finding an adorable outfit for L.J. and moving to another part of the store to find something for Amy and Honey. I jumped when I felt a kiss on my neck, smiling when I saw Jamere's face. "Here you go baby. I got you an Iced Strawberry Lemonade." I grabbed the drink from his hand, thanking him before taking a sip. "What's in the bag?" Jamere glanced down at the bag in his hand and shrugged his shoulders. "I found something for our brothers. Let me tell you, they better be glad I love them because this stuff was not cheap." I laughed at him as I continued checking the racks. "Well since you got the brothers, I'll get the kiddos and Chey. And we can split the cost for the parents. Cool?" Jamere nodded his head and the two of us continued looking for the girls. "We should go to the movies after this. I saw a sign for one somewhere in the area." I was more than ready to accept that invitation, so I nodded my head excitedly.

After our movie, Jamere and I went back to the hotel to shower and change for dinner. We hadn't decided on where to go, but we would figure it out before we got our Uber. Just as we walked into our room, my phone vibrated in Jamere's pocket. He put the bags he held down and held my phone out to me. "Here baby. Your phone is vibrating." I dropped my own bags and my purse, grabbing my phone from Jamere's outstretched hand.

"Hello?" Jamere went to the closet with our purchases as I waited for a response on the other end of the phone. "Hey Trina. This is Mr. Jeffries from the hotel. How are you doing?" I raised my eyebrows, Jamere looking at me questioningly as he stopped at the dresser. I shrugged my shoulder and answered my Hotel Manager's question. "I'm doing okay and yourself?" Jamere went through the drawers quietly as I continued my conversation with Mr. Jeffries. "I'm okay. Look, I don't want to hold you up. I know you're on vacation." I paused and waited for him to continue. "I want to promote you to Front Office Manager. You have been our Head Concierge for a while now, and I have been watching you closely. You're doing an amazing job, and everyone seems to look up to you. Are you interested?" My eyes went wide as Jamere turned from the dresser, his eyes landing on mine in confusion. I put my phone on speaker, trying to contain my excitement. "Yes, I'm interested. Front Office Manager? Really?" Mr. Jeffries laughed as a wide smile spread across his face. "Okay great. Well, you'll have to go through some training when you get back, and you will receive a $6 an hour pay increase during training and a $20 an hour increase in addition to that after your training is completed. So, in total you should be making close to $40 an hour. We will allow you to set your schedule to go with your schooling. And when you graduate, we'll help you find work in your area of study." I bounced up and down on the bed, unable to hide my joy. "That's great! Thank you Mr. Jeffries." Jamere sat beside me and put his arms around me, kissing my cheek with the widest grin on his face. "You are more than welcome. You definitely deserve it. Sorry to call on your vacation, but I wanted you to be ready when you return." I slid onto Jamere's lap, hugging him tightly as I spoke into the phone. "That's okay. I'm glad you did. I'll see you next Wednesday when I come back." "See you then. Enjoy the rest of your vacation." "Will do." I hung up the phone and kissed Jamere on his gorgeous mouth.

"Congratulations baby. Looks like we have two things to celebrate tonight." I raised my eyebrows at him and watched a sneaky grin appear on his face. "About a week before we met, I had applied to be a Driver Manager. Right now, I am a Fleet Supervisor, but I have other tasks that I do on a day-to-day basis. They told me when I applied that it would be months before I heard anything. Well today while I was at Starbucks, I received the call that I had got the promotion. My training starts the Monday after we get back. I had planned to tell you at dinner." The grin that covered my mouth was full of love as I pressed my lips to his once again. "Congratulations baby. I am so happy for you." Jamere tightened his hold around me, kissing my neck while saying 'Thank you' in between each kiss. "You are welcome baby. Now, let's get ready to go eat, so we can come back and give each other a proper Congratulations." I winked at Jamere as I stood, walking to the closet to find something to wear. I heard Jamere rush into the bathroom and then the sound of running water, causing a chuckle to erupt from within me. But I knew how serious he was, and I was more than happy to take him up on his offer. So, I searched for something to wear to dinner, and redid my hair in its bun while waiting for Jamere to get out of the shower.

Chapter 19:

Jamere

Trina and I remained in our seats as our plane taxied on the runway. We were back to reality, and tomorrow we would both return to work. We planned to meet everyone for dinner later on in the evening, so as soon as we got our cars, we were going to head home. We waited patiently for the plane to stop before I stood to retrieve our carryon's. I let Trina exit in front of me and the two of us walked to baggage claim. I contacted my mother, and she let us know that she was circling pickup, waiting for us to come out. Trina and I watched the luggage appear on the belt from our plane and rushed to grab ours when we spotted them. I grabbed both suitcases, rolling them behind me as we made our way outside.

Trina spotted my mom first as she pulled up to the curb. She popped the trunk, and the two of us walked to her 2017 matte black BMW X5. I put our luggage inside, grabbing Trina's carryon and putting it inside as well. Once I had closed the trunk, I walked to the passenger's side and helped Trina into her seat and closed the door behind her. I got in the back, grinning as I watched my mom hug Trina tightly. When she let go, Trina had an adorable smile on her face.

"I missed you guys so much. Did you have fun?" My mom pulled away from the curb and made her way toward the interstate. "I bet you are both tired. There is what, a two-hour difference between Seattle and New Orleans?" I looked at my watch, listening to Trina respond. "Yes ma'am. I'm tired, but not overly tired. Since we're two hours behind, its only 8 a.m. here, whereas it would be 10 there. We have time to get unpacked and a nap before dinner this evening. So, we should be good by the time we get to work tomorrow." My mom merged onto the highway, nodding her head as she made her way to the far-left lane. "Well, that's good. Lawrence, Lloyd, and L.J. detailed your cars for you on yesterday. They gassed them both up too, so you should both be good for the next few days to a week. Depending on how well your cars are on gas." I stared at the back of my mom's head and then looked at Trina as she looked at me. "Okay mom. I know dad is at work now but ask him how much I owe him, and I'll pay him back." Trina opened her mouth to speak as I finished, but I cut her off. "No, you won't. I've got it. Ma, just tell dad to call and let me know." My mom laughed, making her way back to the far-right lane. "He already told me that if you asked to tell you that you don't owe him anything. They were already doing their own, so they did yours too. And as far as the gas, you were both just under three quarters of a tank, so I don't think he spent $30 total between both of your cars." I released a breath, knowing how my dad was about stuff like this. "Well tell him we said thank you. I'll tell him myself this evening, but you'll see him first, so just tell him that for us okay?" My mom exited the interstate, nodding her head as she made her way home. "Will do." We finished the ride in silence, listening to the gospel music that played from the radio.

    I opened the door for Trina and then walked around to open the door for my mother. Once I had closed the door, I went to the trunk to get our luggage out. Trina grabbed our carryon's and I shooed her away to follow my mom into the house. I closed the trunk and made my way in the house to get the keys to my car.

    When I walked inside, my mom was grabbing her briefcase. Trina held our keys in her hand, holding mine out to me. "Okay ya'll. I'm off to work. Try to get a nap. I'll see you both this evening." The three of us walked back to the garage, as my mom went through to get back in her car. "Be careful mom." I told her as I put our luggage in the appropriate vehicle. "I will. Ya'll do the same." I held Trina's door open for her, and pushed it closed once she was inside. I rushed to my car and got in, letting my mom and Trina back out of the driveway before I followed. Once I was clear, my mom let the garage down and we all made our way to our destinations.

    I woke from my nap and checked my phone for the time. 5 o'clock read on my screen, so I checked the 6 texts and 4 calls that I had missed. The calls were from my mom, dad, Lloyd, and Trina. My parent's and Lloyd all left voicemails just to let me know that we would meet at Red Lobster for dinner at seven. Trina didn't leave a voicemail, but she left two texts. One asking what time I was picking her up, and the second asking if I had her laptop charger. I responded to her texts, letting her know that I would pick her up at 6:15 and that I did have her charger. I had it on the dresser with my keys so that I would not forget to take it to her. I sat my phone back on my nightstand and went to go take a shower.

    I stood in my closet with my towel around my waist, searching for something to wear. I knew that Red Lobster was a casual restaurant, but I didn't want to go there looking any kind of way. So, I pulled a pair of khaki pants and a bright red patterned button-down shirt. I looked at my boxes of shoes on the floor and grabbed my red and white authentic Vans. I walked out of the closet and laid my stuff on the bed before going to put my clothes from my trip in the dryer. All I had left to do was dress and head out to pick up Trina.

    I stuffed everything I needed in my pockets, chap stick, gum, wallet, and phone. I sprayed some Lacoste Red on my body, picked up my keys, and Trina's charger, and walked out of my bedroom. As I locked the door to my apartment, I pressed Trina's speed dial. I listened to the ringing, sliding into my seat as Trina picked up. "Hey baby. I'm leaving home now to come and get you. I should be there in about 15 minutes." I checked my surroundings, backing out of my parking spot as I listened to Trina's reply. "Okay. I just got out of the shower, but I'm ready other than putting my clothes on. I'll be ready when you get here." I exhaled quietly; Trina's body covered in only a towel flashing across my mind. "Okay baby. I'll hang up so you can finish getting ready. Be there in a few." I stared at the light I was stopped at, waiting for it to turn green. "Okay. Be careful. See you when you get here." I let her know that I would be, and we hung up our phones. I continued my drive, listening to Drake play from my speakers the entire way.

Trina and I made our way to Red Lobster, making small talk the entire way. We turned into the parking lot and found a spot, which was surprisingly not hard. There were quite a few cars, but there were plenty of open spots. So, I pulled into a spot and turned the car off, stepping out and walking around to open Trina's door. When her door was closed, I locked the door and grabbed her hand, the two of us making our way to the entrance of the restaurant.

I watched Trina stand in front of me, even though there was a seat beside me that was unoccupied. She was wearing a white off the shoulder crop top and dark wash denim overalls. She had had one strap hanging down her back and a pair of all white slip-on Vans on her feet. I wanted to bite her she looked so good. But instead, I just grabbed the hand closest to me and pulled her gently until she landed on my lap. She looked back at me and smiled, continuing to scroll through Instagram on her phone. Her scent assaulted my nostrils, making it impossible for me not to bury my face in her neck. She squirmed and giggled, causing random people to grin at us. The two of us ignored them but cut out our PDA.

Trina's parents walked into the building, smiling when they saw us. "Hey guys. How was your trip?" Trina stood from my lap, smiling as her dad embraced her. "Good thanks." I shook his hand as she hugged her mom, moving out of the way so I could do the same. "That's good. I'm glad you enjoyed yourselves." Mr. Hart stopped speaking just as my parents walked in the door. Trina and I walked over to them, thanking my dad for detailing, and gassing up our cars. Trina tried to get him to tell her how much she owed him, but he wouldn't budge. He just kissed the top of her head and told her that he refused to let his future daughter pay him for that. Trina smiled at him, squealing as Lloyd hugged her from behind. She looked down, grinning at Amy and L.J. as they each hugged her. "Auntie Trina!" Trina smiled and kissed the top of their heads as Chey, and her brothers walked in. After we greeted them, we waited a few more minutes to be taken to our table.

 Minutes after we sat down, we had placed our orders and received our drinks. We all sat around the table, talking amongst one another about nothing in particular. I slid my hand into my pocket, gripping the small box tightly as nerves filled my body. I tried to keep my breathing steady, and when I was sure it was, I stood and got everyone's attention. My palms sweated as everyone looked over at me. "So, I just have something I want to say. It shouldn't take long, but it's something that has been on my heart for a while." Once everyone was focused on me, I started to speak.

"Months ago, when I met Trina, she was going through a very difficult situation. I saw the pain she was in, and I made it my personal mission to bring her out of it." I turned to look at Trina, watching her stare at me intently. "We didn't know each other outside of class, but we managed to become so close. Closer than you would think in such a short period of time. Nothing would make me want that to change. She opened her heart to me, and my life has been so much better since that day. She is a beautiful woman inside and out. She made it through that rough situation and allowed me to be the one she could lean on. And when she fell, I couldn't do anything but catch her. I know that she knows I will always be waiting with open arms to catch her. She has such a pure heart, even after everything she has gone through. What was meant to kill her, bring her down, only made her that much stronger. Each day I look at her, and I am blessed to be able to call her my girlfriend." Trina looked at her mom sitting next to her, keeping her attention in that direction long enough for me to get down on one knee and pull the box out of my pocket. "That's why, in front of everyone we love, I want to ask you Trina…" Trina turned, ready to look up at me, her hands covering her mouth as she saw me on my knee. "Will you please, Be My Wife?" Trina's eyes went wide, a single tear sliding down each cheek. Seconds later, she dropped her hands, and squealed "Yes!" excitedly. I smiled and grabbed her left hand, sliding the ring on her ring finger. She threw her arms around me, so I stood, holding her to me as everyone around us clapped.

The two of us broke our embrace, Trina's mom wrapping her arms around Trina's body. Her dad put his arms around the two of them as my own parent's embraced me. This went on for a minute or two, each family member embracing us happily with tears falling from our mother's and father's eyes. We all sat down, watching as a few waiters brought our food and sat it in front of the appropriate person. I watched Trina steal glances at her ring, a wide smile appearing on her face each time. She turned to look at me, her eyes brightening as if she was seeing me for the first time. "I love you so much baby." A smile of my own spread across my face as I stared into her eyes. I pressed my lips to her forehead and gripped her hand in mine briefly. "I love you too. So much." I released her hand as Mr. Hart got everyone's attention and blessed the food.

We all walked outside to our cars, getting ready to go home for the evening. I watched Cheyenne walk Trina off to the side, wrapping her arms around her body for a few seconds before speaking to her. Lloyd and Juss congratulated me once again, both grabbing their children before going to their cars. "Juss, let me know when you and Honey make it back home. Yall have a safe flight." Juss waved his hand in acknowledgement, gripping Honey's hand in his free one. I looked back towards Cheyenne and Trina, watching as the two of them walked back toward where I stood with the parents and her brothers. We all said our goodbyes and went to our cars. I walked Trina to the car and opened her door for her.

"Want to spend the night with me? Or are you tired of me after 2 back-to-back trips?" She smiled up at me, pressing her lips to mine with a soft kiss. "I thought you would never ask. And for the record, I would never get tired of spending time with you. Not this soon anyway." She chuckled and eased into her seat as I clutched at my heart playfully. I pushed her door closed and walked around to my side to get in. "So, we'll go get your car and let you pack a bag. And then head to my place." I started the car and pulled away from my parking spot. "Sounds good. Training for my new position starts tomorrow, and I have to do paperwork. So, I have to go in at 11 instead of 1. But at least I don't have to get up at 6:30 to get ready for class." She played with the radio, trying to find something to listen to. "We can both be happy about that. Yeah, I have to be there at 12. I'll get off earlier though." Trina got quiet, so I turned my head to look at her. "I'm thinking about letting my job at the club go. I enjoy working there, but it was really only just extra money in my pocket. With my promotion though, I won't need it. And I can be home at a decent time every night." I reached for her hand and squeezed it gently. "I support you in whatever you decide. But I definitely won't be mad if you let it go. And hopefully I can get a 2nd shift instead of third. That way I can be off by 10 at the latest." Trina linked our fingers, speaking as I made the turn into her complex. "After graduation next year, we should be doing good, and hopefully able to find something in our fields of study fairly quickly. This will definitely look good on our resume's." I stopped the car, agreeing with her as I turned off the engine before getting out of the car.

 The two of us walked into her apartment and locked up before walking to her bedroom.

I sat on the trunk at the foot of the bed, and watched her move around her room, getting the things that she would need. She moved from place to place, grabbing things from her drawers, then her closet, and finally from her bathroom. She placed everything in her bag, with the exception of her hotel uniform which she had in a garment bag. "Alright. I'm ready to go." I stood and grabbed her duffel and garment bags. Trina led the way out of the room, grabbing her key off of the bar as we walked back to the front door.

  We walked into my apartment, and I locked the door behind us. I carried her things to my bedroom and put it all in the closet. "Babe, are you going to shower tonight or in the morning?" I turned around, thinking Trina was still in the living room only to bump right into her. I grabbed her shoulders, trying to stop her from falling back. "Sorry baby. I didn't know you were behind me. Trina grabbed my arms, smiling as she went back a step. "You're fine. I shouldn't have been that close without letting you know. But to answer your question, in the morning." We let each other go, and Trina unbuckled her strap on her overalls and walked to my dresser. She pulled a T- shirt from inside and pushed the drawer closed. She then went to the closet and started going through her duffel bag. She pulled out a pair of shorts and stood inside to change her clothes. I stood and watched her fluid movements, walking away so that I could get something to sleep in. I opened my drawer and pulled out a pair of basketball shorts and started to get undressed.

After Trina and I finished brushing our teeth and washing our face we exited the bathroom. Trina put her hair on top of her head in something she told me once before was called a pineapple. She then tied a scarf around her head and walked over to her side of the bed. She climbed on the mattress and slid under the covers, scooting her body close to mine. I turned on the television, scanning channels until the two of us decided on what we wanted to watch. The happiness I felt, knowing I was marrying the woman of my dreams keeping my body warm. I kissed the top of her head and held on to her, thankful to God that moments like these would soon go on forever. And I couldn't wait until the day I that I never had to come home without her ever again.

www.ingramcontent.com/pod-product-compliance
Lightning Source LLC
Chambersburg PA
CBHW071949070526
44583CB00015B/1118